New Directions in C

'Who are the Celts?' is a question that has been asked time and again, and one which has recently been at the centre of a heated debate. But this volume asks a different question.

Recognising that 'Celtic' is an imprecise and contested term which covers a range of phenomena far exceeding language or material culture, this book looks again at the scope and nature of Celtic Studies. At this critical juncture in the field's history, the book initiates a reassessment, and examines who is practising, where, and with what methods. Written by international scholars and practitioners in fields such as folklore, ethnomusicology, art history, religious studies, tourism and education, the primary aim is to focus on contemporary issues and to promote interdisciplinary approaches within the subject.

Amy Hale is Research Fellow in Contemporary Celtic Studies at the Institute of Cornish Studies, University of Exeter. **Philip Payton** is Reader in Cornish Studies and Director of the Institute of Cornish Studies, University of Exeter.

Also published by University of Exeter Press and edited by Philip Payton is the continuing annual series, *Cornish Studies*, to date Volumes 1 to 8. Cornish Studies as a subject area has itself grown out of the wider field of Celtic Studies, and has sought to learn from and contribute to broader academic discourses and to encourage its own 'new directions'.

The title of the cover illustration is 'Remote Control' by Steve O'Loughlin, a Los Angeles artist of Irish ancestry who combines traditional Celtic design with elements of Latino and African influence. His work reflects contemporary urban issues and his narrative pieces have treated such themes as the Los Angeles riots, freeway culture, the Irish famine and alien abduction, all with a distinctively Celtic flavour.

New Directions in Celtic Studies

EDITED BY

AMY HALE AND PHILIP PAYTON

UNIVERSITY
of
EXETER
PRESS

First published in 2000 by
University of Exeter Press
Reed Hall, Streatham Drive
Exeter EX4 4QR
UK
www.ex.ac.uk/uep/

© UEP 2000

British Library Cataloguing in Publication Data
A catalogue record for this book is available
from the British Library.

Paperback ISBN 0 85989 587 4
Hardback ISBN 0 85989 622 6

Typeset in 11/13pt Goudy
by XL Publishing Services, Tiverton

Printed in Great Britain by Short Run Press Ltd, Exeter

Contents

Notes on Contributors	vii
Preface	ix
Introduction AMY HALE and PHILIP PAYTON	1

Part One: Popular Culture, Representation and Celtic 'Lifestyles' 17

1. Reading the Record Bins:
   The Commercial Construction of Celtic Music
   SHANNON THORNTON — 19

2. Stone Circles and Tables Round:
   Representing the Early Celts in Film and Television
   LESLIE JONES — 30

3. Pre-Packaged Breton Folk Narrative
   ANTONE MINARD — 52

4. Contemporary Celtic Spirituality
   MARION BOWMAN — 69

Part Two: The Celtic Diaspora 95

5. Pagans, Pipers and Politicos:
   Constructing 'Celtic' in a Festival Context
   AMY HALE and SHANNON THORNTON — 97

6. Re-inventing Celtic Australia
   PHILIP PAYTON — 108

7 Creative Ethnicity: One Man's Invention of Celtic Identity
   DEBORAH CURTIS   126

Part Three: Celtic Praxis   **139**

8 Provision of Manx Language Tuition in Schools in
   the Isle of Man
   BRIAN STOWELL   141

9 The Gaelic Economy
   ROY PEDERSEN   152

10 Rural Tourism and Identity:
   Stories of Change and Resistance from the West of Ireland
   and Brittany
   MOYA KNEAFSEY   167

   Conclusion: New Directions in Celtic Studies:
   An Essay in Social Criticism
   COLIN H. WILLIAMS   197

   Index   230

Notes on Contributors

Marion Bowman is Senior Lecturer with the Open University.

Deborah Curtis is English as a Second Language Specialist for the Writing Centre at the University of Western Ontario, Canada.

Amy Hale is Research Fellow in Contemporary Celtic Studies at the Institute of Cornish Studies, University of Exeter.

Leslie Jones is a Folklorist and Celticist working as an editor and writer in the Los Angeles area.

Moya Kneafsey is a Research Fellow in Geography at Coventry University.

Antone Minard is a Ph.D. candidate in the Folklore and Mythology Program at University of California Los Angeles with a specialization in Celtic Studies.

Philip Payton is Reader in Cornish Studies and Director of the Institute of Cornish Studies, University of Exeter.

Roy Pedersen is Head of Community Affairs and Transport for Highlands and Islands Enterprise.

Brian Stowell is the developer of the peripatetic Manx teaching programme and is a well-known writer and lecturer on Manx.

Shannon Thornton teaches part-time in Brookhaven Community College, Farmers Branch, Texas, while working full-time in the field of career management.

Colin H. Williams is Research Professor in the Department of Welsh at University of Wales, Cardiff and is Adjunct Professor in the Department of Geography, University of Western Ontario, Canada.

Preface

This book is one result of a major research project undertaken at the Institute of Cornish Studies, part of the University of Exeter and based in Truro, Cornwall. The project has been devised and led by Amy Hale, Research Fellow in Contemporary Celtic Studies at the Institute, and she is joined in this volume by her co-editor, Philip Payton, the Institute's Director. Dr Hale has constructed an international team of distinguished contributors, specialists in a number of disparate areas that comprise at least some of the 'new directions' that are now making themselves felt in the field of Celtic Studies, and it is their work that graces the pages of this book.

At a time when Celtic Studies is in a state of flux—on the one hand under pressure from critics who seek to expose the ideological foundations of the field as well as to question the whole notion of 'the Celts', and on the other faced with an explosion of contemporary (and often contrasting) 'Celtic identities' that demand scholarly attention—*New Directions in Celtic Studies* is designed to grasp the opportunities of the moment. That the book has been compiled under the aegis of the Institute of Cornish Studies is no accident, for although Cornish Studies as a subject area has itself grown out of the wider field of Celtic Studies, it has in recent years moved to accommodate and encourage its own 'new directions'. Anthropologists, sociologists, economists, environmentalists, political scientists, language planners, geographers, modern and contemporary historians, and cultural studies practitioners have all contributed to this intellectual movement, much of their work appearing in the series *Cornish Studies*, their activity creating what has been termed a 'new Cornish historiography' and 'a new Cornish social science'. Cornish Studies as a subject area has sought both to learn from and to contribute to broader academic discourses, and nowhere is this process more important than in the contribution it can make to the further development of Celtic Studies.

That the book should have been conceived and completed in Cornwall is also apposite, for Cornwall is a stage upon which various contemporary Celtic identities are performed. From Cornish-language enthusiasts, the cultural revivalists of the Cornish Gorseth, and the party-political nationalists of Mebyon Kernow, to New Age Pagans, Neo-Druids and latter-day Celtic Christians, self-ascribing Celts of various hues—some indigenous and some from outside—are making a major contribution to the dynamics of identity-formation in Cornwall at the Millennium. Their iconography is all around, from the St Piran's flags that fly proudly from public buildings across Cornwall to the renewed veneration of holy wells and other ancient sites, and the economic development possibilities of this phenomenon are evident in a 'Celtic tourism' which ranges across activities as disparate as the manufacture of Celtic jewellery and the production of Celtic music CDs. Indeed, this book is itself in one sense a product of Celtic Cornwall.

Amy Hale and Philip Payton
Truro, Cornwall
11 August 1999, Eclipse Day

Introduction

AMY HALE AND PHILIP PAYTON

What is Celtic Studies?

One might expect that the largest international academic Celtic Studies conference in the world would provide a significant overview of the current research and preoccupations in the field. Indeed, the programme for the 1995 Tenth International Celtic Congress (held in Edinburgh) revealed a great deal about the present state of Celtic Studies. The majority of the presented papers were about the Irish or Welsh languages and their literatures, normally with a strong historical emphasis, investigating such subjects as infixed pronouns in early Irish nature poetry and various aspects of medieval Welsh or Irish hagiographies (Black et al., 1999). Other themes presented at the Congress were medieval law, archaeology, comparative Indo-European linguistics, and prehistory. Moreover, the programme was overwhelmingly medieval in focus, with only the occasional foray into modern literature or sociolinguistics. Interestingly, in the over 200 papers that were presented during the course of the conference, there were few concerning politics, contemporary religion, popular culture, economics or anthropology. Why?

'Who are the Celts?' is a question that has been asked time and again and at the end of the 1990s it is an issue at the centre of a heated debate. Although there have been a variety of definitions, often situated in language or material culture, none seems to provide an adequate description of the variety of 'Celtic' phenomena that are flourishing at the close of the twentieth century. The programme of the International Celtic Congress of 1995 indicated that scholars within Celtic Studies are somewhat reticent to address these complex, varying and meaningful subjects.

Certainly, in choosing the best and most representative papers for publication as conference proceedings, Ronald Black, William Gillies and Roibeard Ó'Maolalaigh were careful to include contemporary as well as historical material, recognizing 'the extent to which the territory covered by Celtic Studies has expanded over recent decades generating debate and fresh thinking' (Black et al., 1999, xv). Similarly the Eleventh International Celtic Congress, held in Cork in 1999, indicated a degree of shift, with subjects such as 'Languages, Politics and Identities in Northern Ireland' and 'Features of Welsh-medium Education in Cardiff' appearing alongside the familiar 'traditional' material. However, for the most part the focus was as before, with its emphasis on early and medieval Celtic languages and literatures (Programme of the Eleventh International Congress of Celtic Studies 1999, 35, 52).

With one or two notable exceptions, the political scientists, anthropologists, geographers, economists and students of popular culture and contemporary religion were absent from Cork as they had been from Edinburgh, notwithstanding their often specialist preoccupations with subjects such as Scottish and Welsh nationalism, 'Celtic tourism' and 'Celtic religion'. Their absence raises important questions and leads us to inquire why scholars who do address these topics generally do not interact with 'traditional' Celtic Studies practitioners? With these complexities in mind, we ask not 'Who are the Celts?' but 'What is Celtic Studies?'

At this critical juncture in the field's history it is important to initiate a reassessment, to examine who is practising, where, and with what methods. Many academics are beginning to do just that. Nevertheless, although Celtic Studies scholars are quite diverse and motivated by a number of interests, there is no doubt that the traditional core of Celtic Studies remains dominated by the study of medieval literature and historical linguistics. There have been several excellent reviews of the central themes and history of Celtic Studies, but for those new to these debates it is necessary to stress a couple of salient points.

Patrick Sims-Williams claims that Celtic Studies is less a 'discrete branch of research than a moderately coherent and by now traditional area of interdisciplinary study' (1998, 8). Sims-Williams, like others, places the origins of Celtic Studies along with the development of the social sciences, archaeology and linguistics at the end of the nineteenth century. In Hildegard Tristram's assessment of Celtic Studies she has noted that of all the scholarly influences on the field, it is the Indo-European hypothesis with its attendant model of linguistic and cultural change that has provided the template for Celtic Studies as practised today (1996, 43).¹ The Indo-European model allowed vernacular languages to take their place beside the languages of Greek, Latin and Hebrew in this evolutionary model (Anderson 1983, 70). Tristram notes that the effect of the Indo-European model on the status of the Celtic languages was immense:

> The Celtic languages (and cultures) were now allowed to assume a venerable position in the ranking list; due to [the linguists] Bopp and Zeuss they were hoisted into the limelight of serious research and placed close to the Italic languages, whose paragon was, of course, Latin ... This prestige lifted the Celtic languages above some of the more widely used languages in Europe, because of the ancientness, archaicness and plentifulness of their oldest documents. (1996, 59)

Here we must also examine the interrelationship between the developing social scientific disciplines and the rise of nationalism—both of which greatly affected the Celtic peoples and how they have been studied.² The process of classifying and ordering families of languages was also linked to promoting individual and discrete cultures which were becoming defined primarily by language groupings. The project of delineating particular cultural groupings by identifying 'distinctive' traits gave way to the 'one culture, one nation' paradigm which has shaped much of modern cultural nationalism. That the analogies used in cultural description were organic (trees, families and so on) provided a vocabulary of 'natural' inheritance for these traits. Thus, the emerging scholarly discourses of linguistics, the social sciences and nationalism in the eighteenth and nineteenth centuries become inexorably intertwined.

However, the connections between Celtic Studies and the ideologies of nationalism are rarely critically discussed and for some this relationship is an uncomfortable one. Sims-Williams argues that Celtic Studies today is predominantly about 'national' traditions (1998, 8), and indeed it always has been. The concept of the Celtic nations and cultures as being discrete *and valuable* entities worthy of study has always been at the basis of the field, shaping both methodology and the sites of practice.

Perhaps the first effects of nationalism upon the institutionalization of Celtic Studies were seen in Napoleon's establishment of the Académie Celtique in 1805, which is possibly earlier than many would think. The Académie was designed to elevate the study of the Celtic antiquities of Europe to the status of Greek and Roman studies. Michael Dietler argues that the academic enterprise of the Académie Celtique justified the

French empirical project as a natural reclamation of ancient Celtic Gaul (1994, 588). Of course, throughout the latter part of the nineteenth century, as the 'Irish question' became a central issue in British politics and as Celtic Studies was being pursued by scholars in or of Celtic-speaking territories, the development of Celtic Studies departments in universities, most notably those in Brittany, helped to draw attention to the various nationalist and 'Home Rule' debates that were emerging.[3] Certainly, there is no doubt that Celtic Studies departments and individual scholars have continued to take a keen interest in promoting at the very least the contemporary recognition of Celtic cultures.

Although there is not the space here for a full examination of the relationship between nationalism and Celtic Studies, we must acknowledge the connection if we are to understand the origin and subsequent impact of the field. This is not a criticism of the relationship, for nationalism has impacted upon most area studies and several academic disciplines. Yet today Celtic Studies departments are found world-wide, inside and outside Celtic regions, in North America, Germany, Australia and Japan, often where immigration from Celtic areas has left its mark. However, we must ask whether or not Celtic Studies is practised differently in these areas, and if so how? Furthermore, will the same areas of inquiry have a different meaning when practised inside or outside a Celtic area? The answer is probably yes. The various struggles for determination and recognition in Celtic areas have lent an urgency and relevance to the discipline that is sometimes (but by no means always) not as recognized outside those areas. Put more simply, even though the focus on medieval language and literature is shared, there is a different political and social context for this type of research inside the Celtic regions. It is important that when we critique Celtic Studies we take into account the various sites at which it is practised, and allow for variations of influence and motivation.

Deconstructing the Celts

Within Britain and Ireland these very same debates about self-determination and devolution came into high relief in the late 1990s; the modern 'Celts' have come under closer scrutiny than ever at both popular and academic levels. Patrick Sims-Williams wrote in a 1996 essay:

> A number of us in or around the discipline of Celtic Studies have already been starting to question its historical basis, validity and identity. Uncomfortable problems relating to 'Celticity' include the

> following: ancient and medieval writers never used the term Celtic to describe the peoples and languages of Britain and Ireland; the medieval Irish and Welsh did not believe that they sprang from a common stock and showed no fraternal feelings for each other; the vernacular literatures of Wales and Ireland seem to have been less open to mutual influence than to influences from Latin, French and English; the Irish and Welsh seem hardly to have perceived the special affinities between their languages before Edward Lhuyd (1707); and the idea of 'Celtic literature' hardly existed before Ernst Renan (1854). Even today it is arguable whether many Celtic speakers regard themselves as having a 'Celtic' ethnic identity over and above their undoubted Welsh, Breton, Irish or Scottish identity ... (1996, 97–8).

Many of these concerns are not new. Since the 1980s the entire notion of 'the Celts' has undergone a number of critiques. Some of the earliest challenges to affect Celtic Studies as a field, albeit indirectly, were those which challenged the foundations of nationalism by examining the construct of the nation as an organic unit, and questioned the links between language, culture and ethnicity (particularly Anderson 1983; Hobsbawm and Ranger 1983; Hobsbawm 1992). These challenges shook the foundation upon which the Celts were constructed. As Hildegard Tristram observes:

> The idea of the genetic and organic unity of Celtic countries, cultures and lifestyles was created and widely propagated (pan-Celtic movement). People thought they belonged to the Celtic community because they spoke a language recognized by the philologists as Celtic; or one was Celtic because one lived in a country in which historically a Celtic language had been spoken or still was. The genetic argument was held to be valid because it was historically and therefore academically sanctioned. (1996, 57)

Malcolm Chapman also warned: 'It is unwarranted to continue treating the spread and survival of languages as being entirely congruent with the spread and survival of named biological populations' (1992, 22).

As nationalism was being critiqued as a modern phenomenon, the traditions and symbols of Celtic identity that were often associated with nationalist movements were also being closely examined. The 1983 volume *The Invention of Tradition* included an essay by Prys Morgan on the development of Welsh traditions during the eighteenth century (such as the Gorsedd and the Eisteddfod), and a chapter by Hugh Trevor-Roper about the nineteenth-century origins of Highland tradition (Morgan 1983, 43–100; Trevor-Roper 1983, 15–41). The central argument of *The Invention of Tradition*, which had significant ramifications for the overall study of Celtic cultures, is that those who are in the process of forging nations and legitimizing institutions will 'invent' practices that imply continuity with the ancient past although they are modern creations (Hobsbawm 1983, 9, 13). These 'invented traditions' serve to communicate a sense of antiquity and authority to the populace of the emerging nation (ibid., 13). Malcolm Chapman in 1992 then questioned assumptions about the cultural relationships between modern Celts based on linguistic affinity, and raised questions about whether or not there could be any direct continuity possible between the cultures of modern Celts and their medieval or classically attested counterparts. Essentially, he asked: if there can be no proven continuity between modern self-ascribed Celts and ancient Celts (Chapman 1992, 22–3), then can there be any 'authentic' modern Celtic traditions at all?

Chapman's *The Celts: The Construction of a Myth* (1992) was among the first well-known critiques of the idea of 'the Celts'. Chapman asserts that the Celts never actually existed as a recognizable group of people with unique traits (ibid., 251). He believes that the cultural meaning of 'Celtic' has been created, defined and refined from a distant viewpoint, that of a dominant culture, and that ultimately the cultural attributions were reified by the Celtic peoples themselves (ibid.). Greek and later Roman classificatory systems created an empty category that has been perpetually filled by the 'others' of Western culture.

Chapman concludes by stating that those today who identify themselves as 'Celts' are only unified by their opposition to the establishment, whether that is England, France, modernity, pollution or Christianity (ibid., 228). As the Celts are poised to play the moral other, many left-wing movements of the 1960s, 1970s and 1980s found sympathy and clarity within a Celtic metaphor (ibid.). Here Chapman addresses the phenomenon of people who identify with a Celtic culture, or with pan-Celticism, but are not from an area where a Celtic language is spoken. He interprets these elective affinities as evidence that 'Celtic' is more a category of opposition and resistance than an ethnographic or historical reality (ibid., 223).

Responses to Chapman's work have been varied. Archaeologists have tended to engage more directly with Chapman's critiques than linguists, as archaeology has been critically assessing the term 'Celtic' for a longer period. Barry Cunliffe (and others) have challenged Chapman's claims that the Celts have never existed as a recognizable people (or group of peoples) by reasserting the coherence of the archaeological, classical and linguistic evidence (Cunliffe 1997). Other archaeologists have responded more positively to Chapman's interpretations. Timothy Champion, for instance, calls Chapman's depiction of the Celts as 'Other' in the Greek world view 'persuasive' (1996, 65). Importantly, Champion also reflects upon the importance of the political and academic climate, particularly the influence of nationalism and Romanticism, in forming interpretations of the archaeological record which subsequently stand as 'fact' (ibid., 65–76).

Most recently, Simon James has reasserted an archaeological position in a more popular format with *The Atlantic Celts: Ancient People or Modern Invention?* (1999). James states that there is no evidence connecting insular peoples of Iron Age Britain and Ireland with the named Celtic populations of the Continent. James instead prefers the term 'Iron Age peoples of Britain and Ireland', arguing for diversity and indigenous cultural developments rather than populations being supplanted by Celtic invasions from the Continent. Like Chapman, James attempts to shatter the grand narrative of a widespread, self-naming Celtic civilization which has survived until the present day in the far western reaches of Europe, the notion of which has become so entrenched in the popular imagination.

These critiques of the Celts have threatened to undermine the integrity of Celtic Studies as a field. Certainly, in the United Kingdom, James's theories in particular have received a great deal of media attention at a time when devolutionary strategies are being implemented. James asks (like Chapman): if there were never any ancient Celts in Britain, are modern Celts (and by extension Celtic Studies) therefore 'bogus'? He concludes that modern Celts are, in fact, a legitimate grouping constructed not in the ancient past, but in early modern Europe (1999, 136–7). He places the legitimacy of modern Celts in a shared sense of difference, an agreed sense of history and a chosen ethnonym rather than inherited characteristics (ibid., 137–8). Although he has also claimed that 'The ancient Celts of the isles, especially in the simplistic way they have been traditionally conceived, have been discredited' (ibid., 143), the debate is far from over. In a masterful 1998 essay, Patrick Sims-Williams re-examines the evidence for the ancient Celts, and also looks at the current debate about the 'battleground' of the terms 'Celt' and

'Celtic' (1998, 1). What many scholars now agree is that 'Celtic', as used and understood today to refer to the peoples and languages of Cornwall, Ireland, Wales, Brittany, the Isle of Man and Scotland, is in many ways a construction dating from the early modern period and the development of certain academic disciplines. This is nothing new; many identities have been historically constructed in the same manner.[4] That there may be, as Sims-Williams suggests, different disciplinary criteria for describing Celtic phenomena (culture, language, the archaeological record, or even perhaps politics and contemporary identities) should not be perceived as a threat to Celtic Studies. In a sense, it could be the springboard for expansion.

Authenticity and the Study of Celticism

A number of scholars now realize that rather than emphasizing the lack of continuity between the ancient Celts and contemporary Celts and focusing on the 'inauthenticity' of contemporary Celtic traditions, the ambiguities and complexities surrounding the Celts and various expressions of Celtic identity are in themselves worthy of study (see essays by Hale 1997 and Leersen 1996, and volumes edited by Brown 1996 and Tristram 1997). In a response to Maryon McDonald's 1986 essay 'Celtic Ethnic Kinship and the Problem of Being English', Teresa San Román articulated several points that place the constructed nature of contemporary Celtic identities into perspective:

> The past is a source not only of material for the elaboration of symbols but frequently also of explanations for existing structures ... The question is not so much whether Breton is closer to French or to its hypothetical origin as, for example, what the social relations have been between those who speak it and the various central powers ... Nationalist political movements that appeal to ethnicity might be said to correspond to effective divisions of historical roots, and it is precisely their tradition of difference and their history of opposition that endures, whatever their cultural content or their interpretation at any moment of their origin or culture. (1986, 343)

Likewise, Anthony P. Cohen notes: 'But it is less important for anthropologists to cast academic aspersions on the authenticity of a group's putative lineage than to attempt to understand why a distinctive and oppositional identity should be so compelling to its members (some of whom are only voluntary affiliates)' (1986, 342).

INTRODUCTION

Chapman's 1992 book adds to the number of studies that have examined the stereotype of the Celt since the 1980s (see Saunders 1983, 255; McCormack 1985, 219–8). In his *The Gaelic Vision in Scottish Culture* (1978) Chapman first outlined the oppositional categories of the Celts with respect to Gaelic-speaking communities in Scotland. In 1986, Patrick Sims-Williams's essay 'The Visionary Celt: The Construction of an Ethnic Preconception' charted the development of the stereotype of the poetic, otherworldly Celt. In the 1990s several scholars such as Terrence Brown, Hildegard Tristram and Donald Meek (in Brown 1996) have done valuable work assessing the effects of 'Celticism', a term coined by W.J. McCormack (1985, 219–38) after Said's *Orientalism*. 'Celticism' refers to the ways in which the Celts and Celtic identities have been constructed and manipulated both by those who are associated with groups traditionally labelled as 'Celtic' (from Celtic-speaking areas), and by others (ibid.).

However, even within the important work being done on Celticism, there is still a suggestion that the Romantic and oppositional constructions of the Celts that have existed throughout the ages are somehow different or separate from 'the real thing', even when the constructions are designed and manipulated by Celts themselves. Often popular Celtic culture is left out of the equation. There is almost a tacit understanding and agreement among scholars that traditional *sean nós* singers from the west of Ireland are acceptably classified as 'Celtic' while U2 is not. Celtic saints' lore is perceived as a 'genuine' manifestation of Celticity, but Neo-Druidism is 'false' and should be avoided at all costs. African-American is a powerful and meaningful self-designation while Celtic-American seems somehow laughable and romantic.

Rethinking Celtic

We now realize that Celtic, like any other ethnonym, is an imprecise term which covers a range of phenomena far exceeding language or material culture. People who use it to describe themselves or their cultural products may interpret it in a number of different ways. Scholars who attempt to limit or define what is or is not Celtic, particularly when referring to contemporary culture, will have a difficult task, for popular culture and belief change rapidly and are not easily restricted by academics.

The essays in this book address 'Celticity' as being modern and multi-voiced. The term at once designates a group of languages, art styles, music, religion, politics, ethnicity or a marketing strategy—all of which deserve the attention of Celticists. We also acknowledge that there is diversity within Celtic cultures—the Irish have not had the same experiences as the Cornish, who again differ from the Galicians. There is no one right way to be 'Celtic'. Celts can be urban or rural, technologically advanced, wealthy or disadvantaged, and speak a variety of languages—just like anyone else.

We do not locate Celticity exclusively in the medieval or Iron Age past, but also in the present context of globalization and modernity. These conditions create many contradictions and ambiguities for Celticists to explore. For instance, juxtapose the annual Celtic Film and Television Festival which promotes cutting-edge media representations of and by Celtic peoples with the New Age travellers who simultaneously are attempting to recreate and reimagine the lifestyles and value systems of Iron Age Celts. What happens when people who are not generally considered to be 'ethnically Celtic' (such as many New Age travellers) adopt a Celtic identity, either through religion or politics? Again, this is a complex issue which should not be dismissed immediately as an appropriation or as inauthentic.

What are 'New Directions'?

Chapman and Tristram have commented that even at the end of the twentieth century, Celtic Studies still reflects nineteenth-century methods and concerns (Chapman 1992, 5; Tristram 1996, 39–40). Celticists are still primarily attempting to reconstruct early Celtic (and Indo-European) cultural motifs through linguistic analysis. These highly comparative methods have been critiqued in recent years. Malcolm Chapman comments on the dangers of using comparative historical linguistics to derive evidence about cultural practice:

> This apparent unity of argument concerning the evolution of species, race, society and language had the effect of collapsing and confusing very different timescales ... The Indo-European model is, strictly speaking about languages, and not about people at all; rarely, however, does one find an account which does not, so to speak, fill the language categories with mobile and expanding populations ... (1992, 18, 20)

The overriding critique of this method of cultural analysis is that it does not account for shifting ethnic and linguistic identities. Controversially, Hildegard Tristram calls philology 'snow of yesteryear, a dated method', noting that in most other disciplines methods such as structuralism, transformationalism, sociolinguistics, New Historicism, reader response and hermeneutics long ago replaced philology. She comments:

> For various reasons, not least among them the very limited number of researchers throughout the world in this vast study field, Celtic Studies are sadly lagging behind the critical discourse practised in the study of more widely used languages and literatures such as English, French and German, where the accumulation of knowledge and methodological progress in general is accelerating with breathtaking speed from year to year. Critical discourse has only just begun in Celtic Studies and research with more modern methodologies than philology is as yet rare. (1996, 39–40)

Celticists still tend to focus their studies on medieval or earlier Celtic peoples. This is partially due to the project of reconstructing earlier Celtic and Indo-European belief patterns and languages through medieval literature—Kenneth Jackson's famous 'window into the Iron Age'.

Within Celtic Studies there is also often a clear sense that the modern literatures and cultures of the Celtic peoples are somehow 'degenerate' and 'corrupt', too influenced by other languages and cultures. As Kenneth Jackson commented in the preface to his collection *A Celtic Miscellany*: 'In this book, however, recent literature is excluded, precisely because it is so largely a modern European one and no longer so characteristic of traditional Celtic thought' (1951, 19). Naturally, Celtic literature in languages other than Celtic ones poses even more of a classification problem; is it even to be considered as Celtic at all, and if so on what grounds? As our understanding of populations and cultures in both the present and past change, so will the ways in which we study them. Celtic Studies needs to respond to these developments.

We believe that Celtic Studies is an interdisciplinary 'area studies', like African Studies, American Studies or Cultural Studies, rather than an isolated and unconnected discipline on its own. The essays in this collection reflect this viewpoint and represent a wide variety of academic perspectives, from ethnomusicology to religious studies. As noted above, there is a significant body of academic work concerning Celtic peoples that has been advanced by political scientists, anthropologists, historians, economists and others which is rarely if ever included in Celtic Studies journals or conferences. However, such academics regularly publish in area studies journals such as the series *Cornish Studies* or the various Welsh, Scottish or Irish Studies publications, and this also raises the question of why Celtic area studies such as Irish Studies, Cornish Studies, Welsh Studies and Scottish Studies have emerged alongside Celtic Studies departments, and are generating the cultural, historical and social perspectives that Celtic Studies itself often lacks. These area studies have both engaged with critiques of Celticity and demonstrated at least some of the possible 'new directions' for Celtic Studies. Thus Celtic Studies remains somewhat fragmented, with valuable research being conducted in different, sometimes isolated, university departments, with very few opportunities to engage and share information. We hope that this volume begins to redress the balance.

The selections presented here confront directly the sometimes uncomfortable questions surrounding contemporary Celtic scholarship, questions of exploitation, appropriation, representation and authenticity. The first three chapters by Thornton, Jones and Minard explore popular interpretations of Celticity and address how Celts are represented (and invented) in the media and in the market-place. The chapter by Bowman explores the subcultural manifestations of Celticity in Celtic spirituality, which foregrounds the controversies over Celtic elective affinities and who has the 'right' to be a Celt. These chapters also highlight processes of cultural feedback, indicating how popular conceptualizations are often reified at some level by Celtic peoples themselves, regardless of the debates over appropriation that sometimes occur. Section Two examines a topic that has often been neglected in studies of Celtic emigration: how are Celtic identities performed in territories which are not Celtic? The chapters by Payton, Hale and Thornton, and Curtis explore the emergent phenomenon of New World Celts, who are increasingly engaging in a resurgence of pan-Celtic conceptualizations of identity. Deborah Curtis examines a particularly relevant theme: the relationship of the individual to identity-formation.

This collection also addresses the applied socio-cultural and economic functions of Celtic Studies. This facet is often excluded in Celtic Studies, particularly as it is taught in North America and other areas without significant Celtic communities. Language planning and tourism are global issues which have special relevance for Celtic peoples, which is why we have included chapters on them in this volume. Brian Stowell chronicles the trials and tribulations of developing a peripatetic language teaching programme in the Isle of Man, while Roy Pedersen and Moya Kneafsey describe the development of tourism in Celtic territories. Both

Pedersen and Kneafsey write from a practical perspective, and challenge stereotypes about how native populations respond to tourist initiatives, and how tourism can possibly enrich, rather than detract from, the host cultures.

These are exciting times for Celtic Studies. Although the responses to Chapman's critiques have ranged from praise to hostility, with many Celtic Studies practitioners preferring to ignore him altogether, his challenge has allowed us to confront difficult questions about both the ideological origins and the current practice of Celtic Studies. This, in turn, has encouraged us to look beyond the 'traditional' boundaries of the subject, to recognize aspects of human behaviour that, in our opinion, might also be considered within Celtic Studies, and indeed to acknowledge work that has already been undertaken. This collection draws attention to key elements of this work and, we believe, lays foundations for those new directions in Celtic Studies which will take our subject area forward into the twenty-first century.

Notes

1. The Indo-European hypothesis suggests that a number of languages from Sanskrit, Greek, Latin and so forth are genetically related to and evolved from a single 'parent' language. From this theory a dendritic 'language tree' emerged, with various language 'families' represented as branches developing from the hypothetical Proto-Indo-European.
2. For an assessment of the relationship between nationalism and the development of the social sciences see Handler (1988).
3. It is important to note that the interest in ethnology, taxonomy and linguistics in mid-nineteenth-century Germany contributed to the emergence there of several significant Celtic language scholars.
4. For a detailed history of the construction of 'Britishness' from the early modern period see Colley (1992).

References

Anderson, B. *Imagined Communities*. London, 1983.
Black, R., Gillies, W. and Ó Maolalaigh, R. *Celtic Connections: Proceedings of the Tenth International Congress of Celtic Studies, Volume One, Language, Literature, History, Culture*. East Lothian, 1999.
Brown, T. (ed.) *Celticism*. Amsterdam, 1996.
Champion, T. The Celts in Archaeology. In T. Brown (ed.) *Celticism*. Amsterdam, 1996.

Chapman, M. *The Celts: The Construction of a Myth*. London, 1992.
Cohen, A.P. Comments. *Current Anthropology*, 27 (4) pp. 341–2, 1986.
Colley, L. *Britons: Forging the Nation 1707–1837*. New Haven, 1992.
Cunliffe, B. *The Ancient Celts*. Oxford, 1997.
Dietler, M. 'Our Ancestors the Gauls': Archaeology, Ethnic Nationalism and the Manipulation of Celtic Identity in Modern Europe. *American Anthropologist*, 96 (3) pp. 584–605, 1994.
Hale, A. Rethinking Celtic Cornwall. In P. Payton (ed.) *Cornish Studies Five*, Exeter, 1997.
Handler, R. *Nationalism and the Politics of Culture in Quebec*. Madison, 1988.
Hobsbawm, E.J. *Nations and Nationalism Since 1780: Programme, Myth and Reality*. 2nd. edn, Cambridge, 1992.
Hobsbawm, E.J. and Ranger, T. (eds). *The Invention of Tradition*. Cambridge, 1983.
Jackson, K. *A Celtic Miscellany*. Harmondsworth, 1951.
James, S. *The Atlantic Celts: Ancient People or Modern Invention?* London, 1999.
Leersen, J. Celticism. In T. Brown (ed.) *Celticism*. Amsterdam, 1996.
McCormack, W.J. *Ascendancy and Tradition in Anglo-Irish Literary History from 1789–1939*. Oxford, 1985.
McDonald, M. Celtic Ethnic Kinship and the Problem of Being English. *Current Anthropology*, 27 (4), pp. 333–47, 1986.
Megaw, V. and Megaw R. The Prehistoric Celts: Identity and Contextuality. In M. Kuna and N. Venclová (eds) *Whither Archaeology*. Prague, 1995.
Morgan, P. From a Death to a View: the Hunt for the Welsh Past in the Romantic Period. In E.J. Hobsbawm and T. Ranger (eds) *The Invention of Tradition*. Cambridge, 1983.
Programme of the Eleventh International Congress of Celtic Studies, Cork, Ireland. 1999.
San Román, T. Comments. *Current Anthropology*, 27 (4) pp. 343–4, 1986.
Saunders, T. Cornish: Symbol and Substance. In C. Ó Luain (ed.) *For A Celtic Future*. Dublin, 1983.
Sims-Williams, P. The Visionary Celt: The Construction of an Ethnic Preconception. *Cambridge Medieval Celtic Studies*, 11, pp. 71–96, 1986.
Sims-Williams, P. The Invention of Celtic Nature Poetry. In T. Brown (ed.) *Celticism*. Amsterdam, 1996.
Sims-Williams, P. Celtomania or Celtoscepticism? *Cambrian Medieval Celtic Studies* 36, pp. 1–35, 1998.
Trevor-Roper, H. The Invention of Tradition: The Highland Tradition of Scotland. In E.J. Hobsbawm and T. Ranger (eds) *The Invention of Tradition*. Cambridge, 1983.
Tristram, H.L.C. Celtic in Linguistic Taxonomy in the Nineteenth Century. In T. Brown (ed.) *Celticism*. Amsterdam, 1996.
Tristram, H.L.C. (ed.) *The Celtic Englishes*. Heidelberg, 1997.

PART ONE

POPULAR CULTURE, REPRESENTATION AND CELTIC 'LIFESTYLES'

Portrayals of Celtic peoples have often relied on nineteenth-century constructions of 'folk' cultures, which it was believed existed in opposition to, or possibly even in resistance of, modernity with its conventions of depersonalization and mass production. Thus ethnographic depictions of Celtic peoples have often emphasized oral traditions such as storytelling, and localized face-to-face interactions, such as community music and dance events. However, the reality is that Celtic jewellery is now being stamped out in vast quantities at factories rather than being laboured over by individual artisans, Celtic music is manipulated at every stage by A&R (Artist and Repertoire) people and producers, and 'traditional' pub culture is now a finely tuned and sophisticated corporate enterprise.

What has happened to 'real' Celtic culture? Who controls it and who sells it? The answers are not always that simple. This section raises questions about self-representation and exploitation, and challenges discourses about 'pure' folk culture. Shannon Thornton shows us that much of what is marketed as 'Celtic' music in the United States relies upon the traditional popular categories of 'folk' that developed in the nineteenth century. Leslie Jones looks at how the portrayal of ancient Celts by modern film-makers relies on constructions of 'Celt-as-other' in the process of commenting on contemporary society. However, the chapter by Antone Minard addresses the ways in which Celts themselves use popular culture and new technology, in this case postcards and websites, as a way of telling their own stories.

This section also addresses the uncomfortable notion of elective Celtic affinities, meaning people who affiliate with Celtic cultures without actually having been raised in one. Malcolm Chapman has suggested that Celtic cultures have long held an attraction for the English middle classes, who have affiliated with the Celts as a part of a privileged critique of modernity. Yet, although Celts themselves have often protested at what is perceived as an appropriation of their culture, this other-driven construction of 'Celticity' has also shaped how Celts understand and represent themselves.

Nowhere is this debate more apparent than in the area of contemporary Celtic spirituality, a topic that many Celtic experts dismiss as inauthentic and a purely modern invention. Here, Marion Bowman examines the origins and complexities of Celtic spirituality, as well as looking at the tension between those who are Celts by elective affinity and those who are Celts by culture.

1

Reading the Record Bins
The Commercial Construction of Celtic Music

SHANNON THORNTON

The exclusive use of the term 'Celtic' as a linguistic category has perhaps served folklorists concerned with documenting the oral traditions of Celtic-language communities, but this limited focus has not always encouraged a more holistic approach to cultural activity within these areas. For instance, instrumental musical practice (other than song) in these same communities has often been a secondary consideration—an extension within the cultural practice of a linguistically bounded group. In this light, music, as well as other cultural extensions such as dance, dress or festival make a somewhat dubious claim to being as intrinsically 'Celtic' as something like language, which has had its lineage carefully and scientifically documented. In other words, we cannot do the same kind of 'science' with music, based on the paucity of archaeological evidence; and because music flows quite easily through linguistic boundaries, the task of a music taxonomy relative to language seems almost irrelevant. 'Celtic music' then, perhaps with the exception of Gaelic Mods, *sean-nós* singers, and male Welsh choirs, remains a popular notion with an increasingly popular usage.

As such it makes sense that for social scientists, especially those interested in popular phenomena, the currency of the category Celtic will also show an upward trend. This collection of essays attests to the value invested in the category in contemporary usage. My own contribution attempts to explore how notions of what is both commercially and academically constructed as 'Celtic music' are founded and how these constructions are evidenced by commercial labelling and buying practices in a global music industry. My focus for this chapter relies on research conducted in Los Angeles, and will thus necessarily reflect this particular urban American experience.

A popular notion of Celtic music has a parallel in the idea of a generalized ethnic 'sound' which is itself in part a product of digital sampling techniques in contemporary commercial music production. The rate at which digital technology has advanced over the past decade has made available to recording artists and production engineers an infinite number of digitally produced instrumental and vocal sounds (not to mention, ironically, a recent 'revival' of analogue technology). This new spectrum of sound choice has been aptly described as metaphoric of the 'postmodern condition', where living in a world dictated by technological innovation demands that technology provide us with unlimited choice and the opportunity to construct our visions of the world through an individual process of personal selection (Théberge 1993).

Much of what is marketed and sold as 'Celtic' music is either rooted in or draws its musical/conceptual inspiration from the traditional music of the individual countries that make up the Celtic periphery: Brittany, Cornwall, Ireland, the Isle of Man, Scotland, and occasionally Galicia in northern Spain. Although the countries share a common linguistic root, and certain features of their histories due to the forces of cultural oppression, the musical traditions of each country or region are viewed by most of their adherents and specialists as culturally discrete (Ireland and Scotland excepted in certain instances due to migration patterns which introduced and helped to integrate Scottish-Gaelic traditional music into areas of Northern Ireland). It is 'Celtic' in the second sense indicated above that I am concerned with in this essay: how a contemporary musical concept that conveys a collective, ethnic significance defined as Celtic has come about; what it means and for whom it is relevant.

It has become evident recently that 'Celtic music' conveys a spectrum of meanings—seemingly as many as there are people who have an opinion on the subject. In 1994 an on-line debate on an e-mail discussion group devoted entirely to Irish traditional music generated upwards of 35–40 responses from list subscribers writing about what Celtic music is and whether the term holds any value as a meaningful, musical category. Most respondents seem to subscribe to the opinion that its only value is in its use as a marketing tool. Even in this use, its meaning has become rather vague, the category having subsumed so many different kinds of music, so that those who might have warranted it legitimate as a title for different streams of traditional music have backed away as the connotations of the word 'Celtic' broaden to contain references to extra-musical, New Age, and other contemporary spiritual practices.

This broadening of the category's references and meanings can be seen in one instance as part of a process described by Malcolm Chapman (1994), who argues that Celtic is a category defined not from within, but almost exclusively from without—a projection onto a group of communities that maintains them as peripheral in a general hegemonic power relationship. Part of this process includes what Chapman terms 'romanticisation'—an imbuing of the subordinate, peripheral group with the features and characteristics the dominant group have left behind on the path to 'progress' and enlightenment via the industrial revolution (1994, 40–2).

Chapman's argument does makes sense in light of the fact that 'Celtic' as a term of self-identification seems to be used exclusively among those who, often born into and brought up in 'non-Celtic' (or sometimes Celtic-immigrant) environments, choose Celtic as part of the process of identity-formation later in life, usually after discovering some bit of information about the Celtic language(s), history(ies), and culture(s) by way of books, documentaries and other media. This kind of identity-formation is found among and around the communities of all ethnic groups, particularly those with some history of forced migration, such as the ethnic minorities of the United States. In an age of post-modernism we have at our disposal endless options and information for use in making decisions about how to fashion our respective identities. Identification with a minority or other ethnic group, their culture and politics is simply one of many paths we choose to follow in building our individual identities. Why we choose one group(s) over another has more to do with the nature and strength of the links we find or believe to be in existence between ourselves, our histories, and the people with whom we choose to identify. It might also go some way toward explaining our own professional fascination with things Celtic, when we stop and think back to what our first impressions and images were all about.

But I think Chapman's argument is unsatisfactory, particularly where music is concerned, and further limits itself to a romantic/modernist dichotomy. Even if Celtic was, is, and will forever be an outsider's term, it has some, if limited currency within increasingly professionalized traditional music circles, particularly among players and promoters with Irish-Scottish connections, as well as those playing tours and festivals across the Continent. As a modern idea imposed from without, Celtic music has been taken up by those with an interest in expanding the earning potential of traditional music. Celtic music festivals in Britain, Ireland and on the Continent, though perhaps not as representative of everyday musical life as music practised in the pub or the home, nevertheless still attract fans of traditional music, abound with after-hours session playing, and feature largely up-and-coming as well as more established talents.

The launching of Ireland's Celtic Heart label in the early 1990s was a significant event within the world music industry, indicating the inroads in sales markets made by contemporary Irish music. 'Celtic music' then would seem to have reclaimed some value among promoters of Irish popular music; or is it simply another instance of commodification? As these kinds of boundaries blur it is increasingly difficult to ascertain the divisions between insiders and outsiders. When the category 'Celtic music' shifts to encompass popular as well as traditional music, has it been 'appropriated'? Or can we really claim 'outside interference' when the categorical shifting is actually occurring within the industry of the 'insider?' The criteria we use to make judgements about cultural authenticity become increasingly irrelevant the more we turn our critical attention toward what Stokes has called 'music out of context', e.g. performers' experiences of musical tourism as 'world musical ambassadors' (Stokes 1994a, 99–100). If it is indeed the case that the powers that be in Ireland, in the case of Celtic Heart for instance, are co-opting what they have long regarded as a historical category, purely for economic gain, who is to say they haven't the right? Do they have more right than, say, the California-based Narada label, who sell New Age music under the title Celtic Odyssey? If the music resonates with some personal or emotional understanding for the people who buy it, who is to say Narada isn't fulfilling some kind of collective expectation? We (critics, historians, music specialists and authorities) can observe them, perhaps tell them politely that they have been misinformed about the whole Celtic/Irish music picture, but we can not deny or invalidate their experiences.

This essay addresses the phenomenon not from the basis or experience of any particular ascribed 'Celtic' locality. It is rather an attempt to locate discourses of music marketing and cultural assumption at the level of product, where most of us come into contact and interact with this conflation of corporate and cultural myth, and where Celtic is defined as much by what strikes the personal eye and mood as it is by more musical criteria.

Again as an identifier imposed from without, Celtic music is more about what *sounds* Celtic than what *is* Celtic.

Celtic music then, as marketed to the urban consumer, is located in a number of musical and ideological contexts which often combine and overlap to produce a range of product from what we might call conservative 'traditional' to innovative or transformational. These contexts include:

1. the instrumental: the use of a particular set of instruments defined as Celtic (or digitally reproduced facsimiles of these instruments);
2. the linguistic: the use of a Celtic language;
3. the cultural: the artist's claim that his/her music is 'Celtic', based on personal beliefs about what 'Celtic' means.

The factor of personal definition is important because much of what is commercially labelled 'Celtic' can be a hybrid of different musical styles which in academic endeavours typically tend to be separated by language, but grouped under the rubric of 'Celtic'. I would suggest that these individual arrangements are representative of what I. Sheldon Posen describes as the modern folk performer's 'references to all manner of past styles and sources … bound together by an overall sound' (1993, 129). By looking at what constitutes 'Celtic' in the market-place, we may come closer to understanding what 'Celtic culture' means in the modern experience of forming individual and personal identity.

Reading the Record Bins—Celtic Music in a World Music Market

As sources of recorded music for most consumers, retail outlets provide what is most readily available at any one time in industry terms of current, commercially viable product. In addition, they are fairly reliable barometers for measuring levels of corporate interest in and support of different categories of music. It is important to recognize corporate support as a major factor in shaping consumer tastes, since the range of what is offered to us directly affects and necessarily limits our choice. This sets in motion a kind of cycle: as consumers develop more specialized tastes, they tend to seek alternative sources of music outside the mainstream retail industry; this in turn leads to an increase in, for example, mail-order music catalogues and independent 'alternative' outlets.

As one of the largest stores on the west coast of the United States, the Tower Records store on Sunset Boulevard in Los Angeles is one example of the kind of range of musical product available at any given moment. The spectrum of choice, if one is unaccustomed to it, can be overwhelming: so much so that the selection has overwhelmed even the building's physical structure. Tower now operates separate stores for classical music and video, devoting its main venues to popular music. Virgin Records, down the street, has overcome this problem by housing all of its product under one roof, a 'Mega-Store' specifically designed to accommodate carefully selected and arranged categories of music. Classical music is still housed separately, next door. But Virgin Records has accorded all of its categories equal status in terms of presentational style. As regards physical space, no one genre seems to overshadow another, and every category is merchandised at an aesthetic level of sophistication that graces jazz, blues, world, and folk, with the same corporate respect we typically associate with the more commercially successful genres of pop or classical. There is a paid disc jockey on-site, playing the Top 100 from various industry lists. No doubt this presentational style and use of space has as much to do with what is selling well than with anything else, but it is certainly indicative of the inroads that have been made by categories of music formerly regarded within the industry as so marginal as to be relegated to dark corners or bargain bins.

Tower Records' world music compact disc section, for instance, occupies roughly 10 per cent of the total floor space and is categorized by country in alphabetical order. The bin card labelled, 'Ireland' also reads in smaller lettering the sub-labels 'Celtic', 'British', and 'Scottish'. This organization might raise a few eyebrows among scholars who use 'Celtic' as the umbrella term for locating language groups. Where we might expect to find Celtic as a heading for the subheadings of Irish, Scots, Manx, Welsh, Cornish and Breton, we find instead an organization based on sales logic: the sub-headings 'Celtic', 'British' and 'Scottish' fall under the heading of the country with the highest volume of product and the country whose music is perhaps most well known.

Under the heading 'Ireland', the product is then organized in order of artist name, mixing up Irish, Celtic, British and Scottish. So what we really get are all of the 'sounds' of Celtic countries (including England) from generic collections of pub songs, céilí bands, and all the recordings of the Chieftains and Clannad, to the pan-Celtic neo-traditional harp music of Breton artist Alan Stivell, and the Celtic Odyssey collection of New Age artists, all within the 'Ireland' bin in the world music section. The image of 'Celtic' constructed by this arrangement, although a mixture of instrumental and vocal, Gaelic and British, traditional and contemporary, is one dominated by the country with the highest sales: Celtic is synonymous with—or subordinate to—Irish. As one of the top retailers in the country and beyond, this is the image of Celtic music that a large percentage of music buyers first encounter.

If we turn to look at a smaller, more specialized venue, the independent Rhino Records for example, we detect a different agenda. As an outlet for alternative pop, world beat, and folk music, Rhino's approach to classification reflects these promotional priorities. World music still equals 'third world' and there are 'folk' bins devoted to contemporary American, Canadian and European singer/songwriters and 'traditional instrumental' groups. To me this scheme conforms closely to early classification practices of folk music scholars and ethnomusicologists who, following an evolutionary model, distinguished Euro- and Anglo-American 'folk' traditions from both non-Western (then termed 'primitive') music and Western European 'art' music. These distinctions have long been abandoned in the academic literature; but it is interesting to consider how culture research has informed the culture market.

Consider the demographic sector to which this alternative venue caters: slightly more informed, educated consumers; those not completely satisfied with the typical output of most mainstream popular music and seeking an alternative. These consumers, and the challenge they represent to the industry in meeting consumer preferences and needs, reveal different retail venues' categorization practices to be based on different marketing strategies within the profit-based system of commercial music. Marketing strategies of companies such as Rhino Records help to mask the profit motive by playing up their emphasis on 'other' music; 'alternative' music as a meaningful category works here. The small, independent venue offers an ideological (read: intellectual) alternative to the whole principle of the 'mega-store'. Classification practices which dictate what music or which artist gets put in what bin reflect the assumptions about musical genres, and the contemporary politics of shifting national boundaries as defined both by cultural analysts and chief executives of music companies.

There is no heading for Celtic or even Irish music in the World Music bins at Rhino. Celtic music here is conceived of in the traditionalist sense, and can be found in the folk section, alongside contemporary American and Canadian singer/songwriters and bluegrass artists. As much as availability, classification in part can determine buying practices (and vice versa): if our individual collections are dictated by a particular genre (i.e., jazz, opera, soul) we patronize the venue where we find more selection within that genre, assembling our own individual variations on particular modes of recorded expression. Likewise, the personal collection built around the music of a particular culture(s) is more readily accommodated by the venue which organizes music in the same way. The specialist music store is a response to increasingly specialized tastes and interests.

The world music phenomenon can also be seen as a response to this increase in specialized consumer interests. In the short time since this research was performed in 1994, 'Celtic' as a mainstream music marketing term continues in use, becoming increasingly established as part of the world music industry parlance. An early release (with a recent successful follow-up) on Peter Gabriel's Real World label is an experiment in combining traditional Irish and African musics and instruments, called *Afro-Celt Sound System, Volume One: Sound Magic*.

Collecting and listening to music as a hobby and following a particular recording artist or musical style can be deeply fulfilling. The more choices we are faced with as consumers in the expanding global music market, the more we seem to specialize our present interests and tastes. The specialist music store responds by catering to this intensification.

The Celtic Sound in New Age Music

In 1988 *Billboard* magazine added a New Age chart to its weekly ratings, indicating that this once-marginalized genre had reached a particular level of economic success that earned it a viable format in the industry. As a genre now acknowledged to be meeting the musical tastes of a particular demographic sector, New Age music established itself through the incorporation of recording companies and distributors, time slots on network radio, and the eventual defining of sub-categories such as New Age folk, Native American/Indigenous, New Age traditional, and New Age world musics (Birosik 1989). In 1989 the first International New Age Music Conference was held in Los Angeles, where attendants met to discuss issues ranging from marketing strategies to music therapy.

Although a topic ripe for investigation in terms of the selection and uses of musical traditions by various communities, almost no scholarly work has been produced which examines New Age music in this light. This reflects a general resistance among those who see New Age music not as a unified genre but as an odd amalgam of disparate stylistic reworkings or borrowings of the world's musical traditions, a 'transcultural' music along the lines of disco. One scholar has suggested that the coherence of New Age music can be found in the consistency of its visual representation: in its cover art—a strategy employed to market a music whose artists normally carry little name recognition (Zsravy 1990, 33–53).

But more importantly, as one discussant at the New Age Music Conference remarked, 'listeners are "asking for instruments, asking for feelings, they're asking for what the music does to them. They don't care who plays it"' (*Billboard,* 24 February 1990, 95). Consumers of New Age music want a 'sound', and with a range of stylistic sub-genres from which to select, consumers are met with yet another envisioning of Celtic music. A few uillean pipers, for instance, make the rounds as guest artists and studio musicians on the recordings of popular music stars such as Kate Bush, whose musical and lyrical interpretations of Celtic mythological texts are an expression of an emotional connection to particular ethnic sounds: '"Although there's a lot of ethnic music that I find really moving," she says, "there's something about Celtic music that really does touch me. The sound of Irish pipes—it's a sound of elation. It's like a big wave. I do get this very oceanic vision. Big waves rolling in"' (quoted in Toop 1996, 277). Known also for her renditions of the more contemporary literary works of Joyce, Kate Bush shares with Canadian artist Loreena McKennitt a penchant for casting the writers of the Celtic literary renaissance into modern musical molds; McKennitt has set W.B. Yeats to original music incorporating Irish as well as other traditional instruments.

Artists who seem to move easily among the categories of folk, Celtic and New Age seem to be those whose original compositions consciously fuse elements of different Celtic musical styles, particularly in terms of 'traditional' instrumentation. Two examples are Alan Stivell and Loreena McKennitt, artists whose primary instrument is the Celtic harp. Where the harp is not the showcase instrument, it is electronically enhanced vocal tracks that are forefronted, made lush to echo the singing in Celtic languages. To those unfamiliar with what spoken Celtic languages sound like, the sound is often mistaken for either Latin or simply as sung vocables. This ambiguity makes artists like the Irish group Clannad particularly appropriate for a variety of other commercial settings: from the accompaniment to a German car company advertisement to the score for a film about the plight of Native Americans, where Mohican and Cherokee languages are also used for effect in the soundtrack (Bond 1993, 50–5).

The New Age genre seems a fitting home for our notion of Celtic music broadly conceived of as a 'sound'. Celtic imagery, like much Native American imagery, is widely popular in New Age spiritual movements. For a community that wants a purposeful, perhaps ritual musical element,

Celtic music would seem to fit the bill: its popular associations with antiquity and a mythic, Pagan past make it preferable for groups seeking alternative belief systems.

'Celtic folk music' as scholars have come to understand it, music whose primary communicative importance and reason for revival and preservation has been its location within the cultural matrix of Celtic language communities, must now be considered alongside commercial 'Celtic' musics that have become tremendously popular beyond the Celtic language community. This may give us cause to consider what role language plays in shaping identity, apart from and as part of music.

Conclusion

The ability of Celtic musics to cross commercial stylistic boundaries is indicative of an adaptive strength on the part of musicians who see themselves as the progenitors of transformed traditions. In many ways Celtic music is marketed as a 'sound'. The sounds of Celtic musics represent a revival and transformation often by combining contemporary and 'traditional' elements of different music cultures (or different cultures' musics). The popular associations many people carry of 'Celtic' with mythology, Paganism and magic are associations drawn in part from such sources as turn-of-the-century popular collections of folklore and mythology, published by enthusiast-scholars. To talk about what constitutes the notion of a popular 'Celtic' identity is in part to acknowledge the impact of historical scholarship on public perceptions of culture. People believe in a conception of a Celtic past, and are aided in this belief by media and scholarly based production. As scholars we are obliged to look at how popular conceptions about music are constructed and by what sources they have been informed. Further investigation along these lines would encourage the analysis of the practices of artist and repertoire agents, to understand how the taste-makers' own tastes are informed and on what cultural authority they base their choice of 'traditional' artists. There is also, as has been suggested and barely outlined in this chapter, a need to do further reading of the corporate display. World music today is marketed with a very specific aesthetic designed to attract all kinds of potential consumers: an aesthetic which is different but not far removed from that promoted by national archivists not long ago. The concern with presenting the 'real' and 'true' folk people in their 'natural' environment has shifted to a concern with assuring folk music artists respect and equality in a highly competitive, global music industry.

References

Birosik, P.J. *The New Age Music Guide: Profiles and Recordings of 500 Top New Age Musicians*. New York, 1989.

Bond, L. Clannad: An Interview with Lead Singer Maire Brennan. *Dirty Linen* 47, pp. 50–5, 1993.

Chapman, M. Some Thoughts on Celtic Music. In M. Stokes (ed.) *Ethnicity, Identity and Music: The Musical Construction of Place*. Oxford, 1994.

Posen, I.S. On Folk Festivals and Kitchens: Questions of Authenticity in the Folksong Revival. In N.V. Rosenberg (ed.) *Transforming Tradition: Folk Music Revivals Examined*. Chicago, 1993.

Stokes, M. Place, Exchange and Meaning: Black Sea Musicians in the West of Ireland. In M. Stokes (ed.) *Ethnicity, Identity and Music: The Musical Construction of Place*. Oxford, 1994a.

Stokes, M. (ed.) *Ethnicity, Identity, and Music: The Musical Construction of Place*. Oxford, 1994b.

Théberge, Paul. Random Access: Music, Technology, Postmodernism. In S. Miller, (ed.) *The Last Post: Music after Modernism*. Manchester, 1993.

Toop, David. *Ocean of Sound: Aether Talk, Ambient Sound, and Imaginary Worlds*. London, 1996.

Zsravy, H.C. Issues of Incoherence and Cohesion in New Age Music. *Journal of Popular Culture*, 24 (2), pp. 33–53, 1990.

2

Stone Circles and Tables Round
Representing the Early Celts in Film and Television[1]

LESLIE JONES

The unreality and the externally constructed nature of the ethnic stereotypes of the 'visionary' or 'Otherworldly' Celt has been the topic of increasing academic discussion over the last fifteen years (Sims-Williams 1986; Chapman 1992; Morgan 1983, to name a few). Patrick Sims-Williams, discussing the repercussions of the ways in which 'Renan and Arnold set up the spiritual, impractical, rural, natural and poetic Celts as the antithesis to materialism, "Saxon" philistinism, utilitarianism, excessive rationalism, artificiality, industrial urbanism, and all the other failings of the modern European world' (1986, 72), concludes that:

> The easy opposition of Celt and Anglo-Saxon ... can be more of a hindrance than an aid to clear thought. If, as the structural anthropologists teach, thinking in polarities is a universal characteristic of the human mind, it seems inevitable that the *Kulturkampf* of Celt and Anglo-Saxon will continue to grip the scholarly and popular imagination; yet I should like to leave you with the question of whether it is a valid or even a helpful model through which to perceive the world. (1986, 96)

To the stereotypical vocalisms, then, of the Visionary Celt, the

Forthright Englishman and the Effeminate Frenchman, I would like to add the voice of the Boorish American. If thinking in polarities is universal and inescapable, then questioning its validity or helpfulness is rather beside the point. Furthermore, while ethnic Celts have every right and every capacity to be just as philistine as Englishmen, Belgians, and even Spaniards, while enlightenment may strike on city streets and poetry may derive more often from the memory of the glen than the actuality of slogging up the hillside in a downpour, we should also guard against throwing out the Breton with the bath water, and in our eagerness to dispel the illusion of the 'periphery', forget that the 'centre' is also an illusion, equally a construct. As Charles Fort said, 'One measures a circle beginning everywhere.'

There are real failings in the modern world, and many of these failings may be, if not remedied, at least counterbalanced by the characteristics stereotyped above as 'Celtic.' The persistence of this cluster of qualities in the popular imagination indicates and caters to a deep longing—known in Welsh as a *hiraeth*—for Someplace Else, for a limin (or a fence) to straddle, for escape, for freedom, for alternatives. Of course there was no ideologically unified, ethnically pure 'Celtic race' streaming through western Europe in the Iron Age; and oddly enough, you could lay pretty much the same charges against the Romans, if you were willing to give up the idea of them being somehow central (to what?). Basically, there are just people wandering around trying, with greater or lesser degrees of success, to communicate with each other, and that is all there ever is. In order to think clearly—in order to think at all—we have to devise categories, we have to compare and contrast them, bundle them together, play with them, and most importantly share them.

Perhaps it requires the view from the left periphery of America even to notice that the discovery of the inventedness of ethnic identity is somewhat old hat. While self-identification as a Celt, regardless of family history or physical upbringing, may be a new phenomenon in Britain (see Bowman 1995), choosing among several possible ethnicities for one's primary identity has long been a necessity for many Americans, as researchers in ethnic folklore are well aware (see, for instance, Kirschenblatt-Gimblett 1983, 43-4). Take it from a Jew named Jones. Indeed, the problematics of categorizing people from 'Celtic' Britain can be seen as a prominent thread in the hangman's rope of American racial politics (see Ignatiev 1995). Perhaps in America, the land of self-invention, we are too inclined to toss around ethnic identities like pairs of cheap but fashionable shoes, easily worn out and easily replaced. Perhaps this is why Hollywood (*Tír na nÓg* with a vengeance) makes such silly movies. But surely we are not the only ones who warrant such accusations ...

If we take it as a given that the Visionary Celt is a sliding signifier with greased wheels, if we accept that people construct stereotypes out of some deeper need than the satisfaction of sheer stupidity, if we operate from the assumption that 'myth' means more than simple lies, then we have to ask the question, why is it necessary for the popular image of the spiritual, romantic, passionate Celt to exist? If, as Sims-Williams argues (1986, 77, 94), both Celts and non-Celts are complicit in the perpetuation of this stereotype, what do they get out of it? If this construct has little or nothing to do with the real existence of historical or contemporary peoples or cultures, what is it here to say? To this end, then, I would like to look at the ways in which early Celts, in various guises, have been represented in American and British popular film and television, with particular reference to the long-standing, and seemingly ineradicable, association of Stonehenge with the Celts, and more specifically with those notorious Celtic priests, the druids.

Throughout the history of the literature on druids, there has been ambivalence and uncertainty about the moral value of druidism. Were the druids the practitioners of an austere but pacific faith, as implied when they are compared to Hindu *brahmans* and the followers of Pythagoras, or were they blood-thirsty human sacrificers and deceivers of the gullible masses? In part this uncertainty derives from the fact that everything written about druids was written by outsiders. But in a way, the persistent interest in the topic of druidism that has prevailed, to a greater or lesser degree of enthusiasm, for nearly two millennia derives precisely from the fact that with so little known about druids, one can write nearly anything without fear of contradiction. Thus, writings on druids often say more about their authors' agendas than those of the Pagan Celts.

One of the earliest, and incidentally most amusing writers on matters druidic in English was John Toland. Toland was notorious as one of the most hated men of his age—no mean feat in the late seventeenth century—and he seems to have been not awfully fond of everyone else, either. His main contribution to the druidic image was to manipulate the idea of druid-as-sorcerer into the idea of druid-as-stage-magician, replacing the supernatural with parlour-tricks. Where medieval hagiographers saw druids summoning demonic mists and lightning bolts, Toland saw them stage-managing smoke and mirrors. The purpose of their trickery was purely and simply to keep the gullible populace in a state of happy ignorance, so that the druidic Establishment could maintain power and prestige. Toland's representation of druidism was presented as an argument against the evils of an over-organized religion, where a true connection with God is stifled amidst bureaucracy and the pursuit of worldly wealth and position. However, his version of druidism still resonates in contemporary media representations of Celtic magic and druidry as mere fakery, as well as in the Frazerian paradigm of (traditional) religion and superstition as misunderstood (modern) science.

Parallel to this stereotype of Celtic religion, the association of Stonehenge (and stone circles in general) with the Celts and thus with the druids dates from the tail end of the seventeenth century. John Aubrey is generally credited with first making the connection in his unpublished *Monumenta Britannica*. The theory gained popular credence in the first half of the eighteenth century through the writings of William Stukeley, Henry Rowlands, William Borlase and numerous other writers (see Jones 1998). Although they often argued beyond the limits of the evidence, these writers did base their arguments on the findings of the nascent science of archaeology. Whatever his later excesses, Stukeley based his assumptions about the provenance of stone circles on actual fieldwork, observing, for instance, that Stonehenge must pre-date the Roman occupation of Britain, since a Roman road cut through part of it. As far as anyone knew at the time, the only people in Britain before the Romans were the Celts. Ergo, any remains of human activity prior to the Roman era must be Celtic, and as the writers of Classical Greece and Rome inform us that the priests of the Celts were the druids, any pre-Roman remains of a religious nature must be druidic.

What is frequently forgotten in twentieth-century efforts to combat this misconception is that it came at the conclusion of a long controversy over the age and provenance of what we now know to be the Neolithic archaeological remains of Britain (see Piggott 1975, 1989; Hutton 1991). During the early modern era, however, sites such as Stonehenge could be claimed to be Roman (as argued by Inigo Jones), Danish (as Walter Charleton asserted) or Welsh (following the medieval tradition of Geoffrey of Monmouth) (see Piggott 1989, 87–122). To assign it to the pre-Roman Celts was actually closest to the truth of all the available options. But more pertinent to current arguments about 'Celtic' nationalism and ethnicity, the assignment of these rough but impressive monuments to the pre-Roman Celts, especially in an age of increasing Romanticism, was a claim for the native dignity and worth of British culture. Stukeley claimed that eighteenth-century Anglicanism was the direct descendant of 'primitive' (Celtic) Christianity, which in turn derived from druidic religion, which was ultimately imported directly from Palestine by Hercules and the Phoenicians, and that thus the druids 'were of Abraham's religion entirely' (Stukeley 1740, 2).

As I have argued elsewhere at greater length (Jones 1998), the ultimate effect of such a religious pedigree was to provide post-Catholic Britain with a lineage that bypassed the Pope and went straight to Jehovah himself. Likewise, 'druidic' Stonehenge, Avebury, Rollright Stones, Callanish, offered a Romantic pedigree for a British culture that preceded any outside influences from the Continent (Roman, Anglo-Saxon, French) or any internal minority claims to sovereignty (Welsh, Scottish, Irish, Cornish). The Celts were conceived as the aboriginal inhabitants of Britain, and stone circles became an easily identifiable icon of their role as the guardians of the archaic and Pagan (but almost Christian) British past.

This image of Stonehenge continues to surface in contemporary visual media not because it makes reference to historical reality, but because it makes reference to the immemorial past, particularly in its more sensational aspects. Just as the medieval Irish compilers of the *Lebor Gabala* inserted their local cosmogony of Ireland into the world cosmogony of the Old Testament, the image of a druidic Stonehenge stands as an icon of a British cosmogonic myth that precedes and in some ways even creates the historical continuum. But because our scientific understanding of the prehistory of the British Isles has multiplied a hundred-fold over the past century, a strange reversal has taken place. Whereas the iconography of the stone circle and druid was originally intended to create distinctions between the various ethnicities inhabiting the island, locating a Celtic stratum underlying Roman or Germanic strata, now the British Pagan past is, in the mythical history of Britain, implicitly or explicitly monolithically Celtic. And as intellectual relics of the Neo-Druidic manias of the eighteenth century, stone circles are associated particularly with the darker side of Paganism, with hostile magic and human sacrifice. The stuff that films are made of.

Wicca, which is possibly the largest of the Neo-Pagan religions, is often regarded by both members and outsiders as being in essence a 'Celtic' Paganism, mystical and otherworldly, that is inspired by Western folk traditions and the pre-Christian religion of the Celtic regions. As Wicca and Neo-Paganism have developed in the late twentieth century, the stereotypes of the Visionary Celt contributed greatly to an initial polarization of Pagan versus Christian, a polarization which rapidly made its way into film. Gerald Gardner published *Witchcraft Today*, the book that announced Wicca to the world, in 1954. Only three years later, in 1957, the film *Curse of the Demon* was made as an adaptation of M.R. James's short story 'Casting the Runes'. Already the influence of Gardner's revelations of witch covens preserved through family tradition could be seen in the popular media. James's original story, set in 1899, concerns a mysterious Mr Karswell, who submits a paper on 'The Truth of Alchemy' to some type of academic society, and when his paper is rejected he wreaks terrible retribution on those who would deny his discoveries. Ten years previously, Karswell had published a *History of Witchcraft*, which was 'an evil book. The man believed every word of what he was saying, and I'm very much mistaken if he hadn't tried the greater part of his receipts' (James 1992, 242). Karswell is presented as a completely evil man, and, as events bear out, a powerful sorcerer working alone. In this context 'casting the runes' is a simple piece of folk magic, useful both for cursing an enemy and bewitching a lover.

While the basic plot of the short story is retained in the movie, *Curse of the Demon* recontextualizes Karswell's practices in the form of a cult of 'devil' worshipers. The movie opens with shots of Stonehenge, as a voice intones:

> It has been written since the beginning of time, even onto these ancient stones, that evil, supernatural creatures exist in a world of darkness. And it is also said, Man, using the magic power of the ancient runic symbols, can call forth these powers of darkness: the Demons of Hell.

The Nordic runes, the Christian Devil and Neolithic Stonehenge, with its later druidic associations, are all linked together as one universal and generic 'Paganism'. The organization of Karswell's cult in the film is similar to that of a Gardnerian-style witch coven, in contrast to the short story's depiction of a ceremonial magician. However, unlike Wiccans, who honour a Horned God as their principal male deity, this group's horny deity is the Christian Devil, an evil spirit whose representation, as the scholars gathered for a convention into the Investigation of International Reports of Paranormal Phenomena realize, has remained consistent from the beginning of recorded time and throughout the world, as an assortment of vaguely Elizabethan antiquarian prints proves beyond a shadow of a doubt.

Curse of the Demon draws upon the idea of a persistent and world-wide belief in and worship of demons, and on the philosophical position, maintained since the early days of the Christian church, that other people's gods are understandable as Christianity's demons, as well as on the Frazerian paradigm of magic as bad science (bad morally *and* intellectually). One of the more inventive applications of the Frazerian thesis that magic is misunderstood science is the British television series *Dr Who*. Particularly in the Tom Baker years, it seems that the Doctor constantly encounters examples of British folklore which invariably turn out to derive from the machinations of hostile aliens bent on world domination. Naturally, druids had their turn for the Doctor's attention in the three-part 'The Stones of Blood'. A stone circle, called the Nine Travellers, in Boscawen, Cornwall (a clever combination of the Merry Maidens and Boscawen Un stone circles in west Cornwall), turns out to contain three rogue megaliths, silicon-based, globulin-deficient life forms called the Ogree, from the planet Ogros. Ogree need periodically to be fed blood. They are under the dominion of an intergalactic criminal named Cessair (the original settler of Ireland in the Irish *Lebor Gabala Erenn*) of Diplos, who had engineered a jail break *en route* to her trial 4,000 years before and set up shop with the Ogree in Cornwall. Cessair, who seems to be immortal, has taken on the name Vivien Fay and is still hanging out in the neighbourhood.

The episode has a lot of fun with the past 200 years of Neo-Druidism. The Nine Travellers, for instance, are said to have been first surveyed by William Borlase in 1754 (who was an actual eighteenth-century Cornish surveyor of stone monuments), and Borlase is said to have met his demise when one of the stones fell over on him (or was it a hungry Ogree?). The story also incorporates the widespread legend, attached to many stone circles, that the number of stones changes every time someone counts them. The real reason, of course, is that one or more of the Ogree has wandered off for a snack. Likewise, the Ogree's need for blood is the real reason for all those accusations of human sacrifice made against the druids. The Doctor, who like Taliesin has been everywhere and met everyone, opines that John Aubrey invented druidism in the seventeenth century, much to the offence of Mr Devries, the head of BIDS, the British Institute of Druidic Studies. Before we discover her true nature, Vivien dismisses her worshippers by commenting: 'British Institute of Druidic Studies, nothing at all to do with *real* druids, of course, past or present. ... They all wear white robes and wave bits of mistletoe and curved knives. It's all *very* unhistorical!'

The Nine Travellers (like the real Boscawen Un on which it is based) is said to be one of the Three Gorsedds (*sic*) of the Island of Britain, one of the meeting places of prophecy. Stonehenge, naturally, is one of the others. Cessair is supposed here to have arrived in a spaceship rather than a boat. When intergalactic justice finally catches up with Cessair, she is charged with 'impersonating a religious personage, to wit, a Celtic goddess'. The notion that pre-Christian Celtic society was a matriarchy, or at least strongly feminist—often promoted in popular New Age literature about the Celts—is given play in the importance of Vivien, in the fact that the land on which the Nine Travellers stands has always been owned by a woman and had been the site of a convent.

The Whovian paradigm of apparent Earthly magicians as disguised outer-space common folk takes us back in the realm of Toland's fakir-priest druids. Religion itself is a sham; the supernatural is only our misunderstanding of the advanced technology of space aliens. There are two levels of understanding: the common, uninformed, superstitious viewpoint of the masses, and the enlightened insider's viewpoint exemplified by the Doctor, his current assistant, and any other space travellers who happen to be in the vicinity. Most space aliens who make it to the Whovian Earth are as interested in power and 'the art of managing the mob, which is called *leading people by the nose*' as any Tolandish druid or priest. Furthermore, the connection between Celts, druids and stone circles is reinforced. The idea that the Nine Travellers are actually beings from another planet comes close to the idea, promoted in several contemporary Neo-Druidic publications, that the druids are really the survivors of Atlantis.

The Wicker Man (1975) draws on other Frazerian notions of Paganism as essentially a fertility cult, and also on the idea of reconstructing Pagan religion. The story takes place in Scotland, and the Paganism so reconstructed is, naturally, a Celtic Paganism, comprised of elements from Caesar's *De Bello Gallico* and Martin Martin's *Description of the Western Islands of Scotland*, Celtic mythology and Scottish folklore. The film begins with a credit which implies that this is a 'true story' if not an actual documentary: 'The Producer would like to thank the Lord of Summerisle and the people of his island off the west coast of Scotland for this privileged insight into their religious practices and for their generous cooperation in the making of this film'.

The film concerns the investigation of Sergeant Howie of the West Highlands Constabulary into the disappearance of a girl named Rowan Morrison from her home on Summerisle, an island renowned for its abundant produce, particularly its apples. Howie is a rigid Christian with particularly strong views on sexual morality which are the subject of raillery even amongst his fellow policemen. On arriving at Summerisle, he discovers, to his intense horror, that the islanders practice a Paganism that seems to come directly out of the pages of *The Golden Bough*. They copulate in the fields, they dance naked around stone circles, they teach their children that the Maypole is a phallic symbol. The close similarity between Summerisle Paganism and late-Victorian theories of primitive religion are not coincidental, for we discover that the current Lord's grandfather had rehabilitated the sterile island through the wonders of Victorian agricultural science, and its spiritual sterility through a recreated Pagan religion, as Lord Summerisle explains to Sergeant Howie:

> In the last century, the islanders were starving. Like our neighbours today, they were scratching a mere subsistence from sheep, and from the sea. Then in 1868 my grandfather bought this barren island and began to change things. A distinguished Victorian scientist, agronomist, free-thinker, how formidably benevolent he seems. [Camera pans to portrait in a neo-folk-art style of an aggressively bearded gentleman surrounded by nature's plenty.] Essentially the face of a man incredulous of all human good. ... What attracted my grandfather to the island, apart from the profuse source of wiry labour that it promised, was a unique combination of volcanic soil and the warm gulf stream that surrounded it. You see, his experiments had led him to believe that it was possible to induce here the successful growth of certain new strains of fruit that he had developed. So, with typical Victorian zeal, he set to work. The best way of accomplishing this, so it seemed to him, was to rouse the people from their apathy by giving them back their joyous old gods, and that as a result of this worship, the barren island would burgeon and bring forth fruit in great abundance. What he did, of course, was to develop new cultivars of hearty fruits suited to local conditions. Well, of course, to begin with, they worked for him because he fed them and clothed them, but later when the fruit started bearing it became a very different matter. And the ministers fled the island never to return. What my grandfather started out of expediency my father continued out of love. He brought me up in the same way, to reverence the music and the drama and the rituals of the old gods. To love nature, and to fear it, and to rely on it, and to appease it when necessary. He brought me up ...
>
> [Howie]: He brought you up to be a Pagan!

To the 'free-thinking' Victorian scientist, replacing one religion with another is a mere trifle—it is the science that counts, and the results. Faith is merely a tool to be employed so that the ignorant peasants will be willing to work, truly an 'opium of the people'. Summerisle's grandfather in his role as Victorian scientist bears more than a superficial resemblance to Toland's druids who 'lead people by the nose' to maintain their own power and achieve their own ends and create a garden from a barren rock.

But all is not well in this Pagan Eden. Howie comes to suspect that the previous year's crops had failed, and concludes that the islanders intend to sacrifice Rowan at their May Day celebration in an attempt to win back the favour of their heathen gods. He infiltrates the May Day Morris Dance procession disguised as the Fool. But Rowan is *not* the intended sacrifice, and this whole mystery has been a ploy to lure Howie himself to Summerisle, there to be the perfect Pagan sacrifice himself:

> [Summerisle]: It is our most earnest belief that the best way of preventing this [repeated failure of the harvest] is to offer to our God of the sun and to the Goddess of our orchards the most acceptable sacrifice that lies in our power. Animals are fine, but the acceptability is limited. A little child is even better, but not nearly as effective as the right kind of adult.
>
> [Howie]: Right kind of adult?
>
> [Summerisle]: You, Sergeant, are the right kind of adult, as our painstaking researches have revealed. You, uniquely, were the one we needed.
>
> [Innkeeper's daughter]: A man who would come here of his own free will.
>
> [Miss Rose]: A man who has come here with the power of the king, by representing the law.
>
> [Innkeeper's daughter]: A man who has come here as a virgin.
>
> [Miss Rose]: A man who has come here as a Fool!

The film presents a set of moral and intellectual dilemmas. Howie believes that the islanders are all completely mad, especially when he realizes that they actually intend to kill him. Yet the islanders merely embrace their religion as whole-heartedly as Howie embraces his. From their point of view, they are as ethically bound to offer a human sacrifice to Nuada and Afallenau as Howie is bound to preserve his virginity until marriage. Furthermore, believing as they do in reincarnation and the transmigration of souls, for them the death of the physical body is not a thing to be feared. If Howie believes as strongly in the doctrines of his faith regarding the existence of heaven and the value of martyrdom, he should not fear death either. The final scenes counterpoint the islanders' rousing chorus of 'Sumer Is Icumen In' with Howie's defiant rendition of the 23rd Psalm, exemplifying the complete incompatibility of the two religions, yet illustrating the capacity of both to define completely their believers' world-views.

In contrast to the eighteenth-century belief in the consonance of druidism with Christianity, twentieth-century Paganism has emphasized the mutual hostility of Paganism and Christianity. *The Wicker Man* inverts the historical triumph of Christianity over Paganism by creating its own 'Burning Time'. The Paganism of Summerisle is native, productive, and, for its believers at any rate, joyous. Its rites seem to consist primarily of singing, dancing and sex. Yet it has its dark side as well, when the favour of the gods requires sacrifice. Given what we are shown of the islanders' life, it would seem that when a perfect human sacrifice is called for, he *must* be imported, for no representatives of the King or the law are permitted on the island, and thanks to the landlord's daughter it would appear that there are no adult virgins handy either (unless, as Howie suggests, the next step is to sacrifice the Lord of the Island himself). Therefore it would seem that the islanders are dependent upon the outside Christian world to provide their backup in times of environmental stress.

One of the origin myths of modern Paganism initially made popular by Margaret Murray is that pre-Christian religions have survived the millennia in secret enclaves in more or less operative form. Summerisle is a perfect candidate for such a survival: isolated, marginal and Celtic. Yet the religion of the islanders is not a survival but a reconstruction. When the first Lord bought the island, the inhabitants were as Christian as the rest of Scotland. Howie's investigation into Rowan's supposed death leads him to the death records, where he finds that islanders with biblical names, rather than the Pagan nature names that everyone now bears, have only recently deceased. Is it the passing away of the last residually Christian inhabitants which has brought down the wrath of the Christian god on the island, rather than the disfavour of the new Pagan gods? We are left to wonder whether the next year's crops failed or flourished.

The relations of female and male, nature and culture, magic and technology are given a Celtic gloss in *Excalibur* (1981), which presents an

Arthurian environment in which magic is to nature as technology is to culture, and Merlin is the representative of the first part of the equation. Unlike most Arthurian films, which begin with Arthur's attainment of the throne as a young adult, *Excalibur* goes back a generation to his conception as the son of Uther and Ygraine. Uther is represented as an oafish thug who sees following Merlin's advice as the quickest route to satisfying his desire for political power. He does what Merlin tells him without understanding why ('Say the words ...' 'One Land, One King!'). Yet as much as he desires power, he cannot control his physical desire for Ygraine, and breaks his hard-won treaty in order to obtain his ally's wife. Just as his son is born, he finally realizes the value of something other than bashing people over the head until they yield, but then it's too late.

The Merlin of this movie is a man of the Old Religion; he dresses in a Pagan-priestly uniform which sets him apart from other men, and he carries a wand whose tip depicts the two fighting dragons whose actions Merlin interpreted for Vortigern when he was a youth. He advises Uther as Cathbad advises Conchobor; he incites men to war or brokers peace as he sees fit. He is a joker, a buffoon; he speaks, says Arthur, in riddles. He raises mists, and in the midst of a stone circle at the walls of Tintagel— a monument which does not, strictly speaking, exist at Tintagel castle—he presides over a rite of shape-shifting. The 'dragon' whose breath Merlin conjures to effect the transmutation is the essential spirit of the land of Britain. (It also seems to have some vague implicit connection with ley-line energies.) Later, at Arthur's wedding, which Merlin watches from a distance, not entering into the Christian church, he says to Morgana: 'The days of our kind are numbered; the One God comes to drive out the many gods; the spirits of wood and stream grow silent. It's the way of things. Yes, it's time for men and *their* things.' This Merlin is a priest of a Pagan earth religion. His explanation to Arthur of the meaning of sovereignty echoes all the medieval Celtic tales, and is formulated wholly in terms of the king's relationship to the earth: 'You will be the land, and the land will be you. If you fail the land will perish; if you thrive the land will blossom.' It is as simple as that.

The part of the movie concerned with Uther shows an age of mud and blood. People scream and yell and hit each other over the head with blunt instruments, lurching around in heavy, cumbersome armour. When they're not fighting, they scream and yell and pound each other on the back in good fellowship, lurching around with overflowing ale pots in their hands. Lancelot—the outsider, neither Celtic nor Saxon—is our first 'knight in shining armour' and at Arthur's wedding this shine and gleam seems to have become the fashion. Life becomes balanced. Arthur's Camelot is a sophisticated place, frequented by traders from all the known world, alchemists and entertainers in its halls, music played with the tones of the Near East. The castle is light and bright and colourful, but still close to the woods and the natural world. The primitive stone circle, where Merlin transforms bodies from one semblance to another, is replaced by the Round Table, where Arthur transforms the body politic. Unfortunately, as things turn out, it seems that Arthur's transformation is as illusory as Merlin's.

When things turn sour, when Lancelot and Guinevere betray Arthur and Morgana entraps Merlin in his cave, the balance of nature and culture goes out of whack again, this time in the direction of culture. We see the walls of Camelot are made of silver, unnaturally metallic. Arthur himself becomes the Fisher King, with a wound that will not heal, presiding over a dry and dusty wasteland. Sovereignty has abandoned him. Mordred—his bastard son born of an incestuous union, transgressing the laws of culture—wears armour completely shaped to his body, which turns him into an unnatural cyborg, a mockery of nature. It is only the final battle between Mordred and Arthur which returns the story to the realm of nature. Mordred and Arthur fight on the land, over the land, for the land. The sword is returned to the Lady of the Lake, like all the devoted swords deposited in lakes throughout the Celtic realms. Arthur's body is carried to sea by the four queens of Avalon. Everything is back where it began, in blood and mud.

In this pendulum swing between the extremes of nature and culture, the 'Celtic' equals 'natural'. The druid, the earth religion, the magical stone circles, are all associated with the stereotypical Celt, impetuous, superstitious, quarrelsome, divisive, passionate. It is a time ruled by sexual urges, not love; significantly, the archetypal Celt, Merlin, cannot know or understand love; when Uther finally feels love, it leads directly to his demise. When life is nasty, brutish and short, love makes you fatally vulnerable. The two extremes correspond to the Victorian stereotypical opposites of Celt and Saxon cited above. But as the world turns into a technological hell, as it becomes more 'Saxon', magic is dominated by Morgana, the Celtic woman. Merlin's magic worked in harmony with natural forces; Morgana's magic corrupts nature, suspending time, crossing the boundaries between human and machine, mutating the supernatural into the technological.

At the end, the only knight left standing is Perceval. He is the only one who is capable of transcending this dichotomy between nature and culture. When we first see him, he is even more primitive than Uther's men, a feral Wild Man of the Woods, a Holy Fool. He learns to acculturate to the court, but he never learns to play the game of courtly intrigue. Perceval alone sees the Grail, and his first vision of it comes while hanging on a tree, a vision of fertility in the midst of the wasteland. The truth that it reveals is the truth that Merlin told Arthur so long ago: the secret of sovereignty. Perceval is the one figure who is not a midpoint in the swing between extremes, as Camelot was at its height, but a figure who incorporates the entire spectrum within himself. As the sum of the completed cycle, he is the seed of the next regeneration.

While a generalized 'Celtic Paganism' is common in fantasy and horror films, and Celtic magic is often evoked in films based on Arthurian legends, druids *per se*, druids *en masse*, are not often met. When they do appear, there is little consistency in how they are treated. This is probably a consequence of the uncertainty in general about what druids are. One exquisitely bad druid movie is *Viking Queen* (1968), a film whose title is an immediate tip-off that we are inhabiting a historical never-never land, since the plot is loosely based on Boudicca's rebellion against the Romans, an event which predated the emergence of Vikings by a good 700 years. The film begins with a narration, in a very authoritative news-reel tone of voice, describing the rise and spread of the Roman Empire, and its conquest of Britain. At this point, in addition to the narration we get the words themselves on the screen, over a background of druids conducting a ritual between the two uprights of a trilithon.:

> This was a land where druid priests held sway over people's minds and prophesied that one day a woman would wear armour and wield a sword against the Romans. A woman who would be called …
> **THE VIKING QUEEN!**

This is a story of political intrigue rather than magic. The druids oppose the Romans because the Romans have usurped the druids' political power, and they conspire against the Romans and foment rebellion in order to gain back their power. They carry out their rituals in stone circles and they are dressed straight out of Smith and Meyrick's 1801 book of historical costumes of the British. They also worship Zeus and Dis, neither of whom are Celtic.

The blonde and strangely accented Viking Queen (*sic*) is Salina, daughter of King Priam of the Iceni. She has two sisters: Beatrice, a red-headed schemer who is thick with the outlawed druidic party, and Talia, a flighty brunette who loves Fergus, a hot-headed youth with druidic leanings. Like the historical Prasutagus of the Iceni, Priam signs a will dividing his kingdom between Salina and the Roman Emperor, hoping that joint rule will bring peace between conqueror and conquered. The Roman Governor-General, Justinian, and Salina are just and responsible rulers, passing judgements which take from each according to his ability and give to each according to his needs; when the two fall in love and wish to marry, it seems as though there is hope for a biological as well as a political assimilation between the two opposing cultures.

But it is not to be. The druids refuse to countenance the match: Maelgan, the Archdruid, sees in the stars and the clouds that Salina will never marry, and like Fedlimid in the *Táin*, he sees red, he sees blood. Octavian, Justinian's second-in-command, has his own axe to grind, and wishes to scuttle Justinian's rule and take over himself. And the merchants of Britain, who resent Justinian's taxes even though the money so raised provides them with safe roads to transport their goods, are eager to ally themselves with his enemies, Roman or druid. Justinian welcomes the revolt of the druids in Anglesey, seeing this as an opportunity to destroy the druids once and for all, and with their power broken, to marry Salina. But while he is away quashing that rebellion, Octavian destroys Priam's will, declares the Icenian government illegal, has Salina publicly flogged and rapes Talia. Priam's daughters have no option but to raise the Celts in rebellion in the east. In the conflict between love and queenly duty, Salina is forced to do battle with Justinian, and kills herself on the battlefield rather than surrender.

Although this plot is clearly based on Boudicca's rebellion, with a little love interest thrown in, the Celts are represented through something of an *interpretatio Graeca*. Prasutagus—which admittedly is a mouthful— becomes Priam. The druids call upon Greek gods. The initial conflict between Celt and Roman occurs when Justinian forbids a public druidic burial for Priam; Salina, like Antigone, defies official sanction and buries Priam privately, but druidically. With the Romans as the unchanging centre, Celt and Greek are interchangeable as the non-Roman Other. The movie was made in 1968, and in the context of the 1960s counter-culture the Celts are clearly hippies, the Romans the corrupt Establishment, and the anything-for-a-buck merchants the sleazy capitalist pigs. According to Dumézialian analysis, the summer of love envisioned by Salina and Justinian is overwhelmed by the combined forces of the druids, the Roman army and the merchants, representatives of evil aspects of the three functions of sovereignty, force and fecundity.

The druids in *Viking Queen* dress like druids, they prophesy and carry out ritual, they advise the ruler on matters of state and questions of war. These are druids whom John Toland would recognize, power-brokers who seek to bend the ignorant masses to their will. And they are no more nor less political than their opponents, who worship dead emperors as gods. However, these druids are interested in preserving the freedom of their people. When the revolt is raised in Anglesey, the druids are joined by Talia's lover Fergus, who with his shaggy shoulder-length hair and natural-fibre and fur clothing could have taken his place in an anti-Vietnam demonstration without anyone blinking an eye. The conflict of Roman and Celt, with the druids as the pivotal figures fomenting rebellion, is a clear calque on the social turmoil in Britain and America in the late 1960s. The classical comparisons of druids with brahmans here mutates into druids comparable to militant gurus of the counterculture.

The people who produce the popular television series *Xena, Warrior Princess* really must see *Viking Queen* if they haven't already. In an episode titled 'The Deliverer' (1997), Xena and Gabrielle find themselves in Britannia, allied with Boadicea (sic) against Caesar. While *Viking Queen* has only one major conceptual anachronism in calling a Celt a 'Viking', *Xena* not only has Boudicca fighting Caesar (a mere misplacement of a century or so, no big deal), but since other episodes have established meetings between Xena and characters from the *Iliad* and *Odyssey* (not to mention her relationship with Hercules, who is technically located a generation or so before the Trojan War), we are also evidently seeing a Mycenean Greek allied with a first-century CE Celt against a first-century BCE Roman. If we decide to throw caution to the winds and forgo historical accuracy, however, there is a certain poetic logic in the juxtaposition of Xena and Boudicca, fictional and non-fictional women warriors *par excellence*. The types of past atrocities which haunt Xena are cognate with the atrocities laid to Boudicca by the Romans—not just the unwomanly participation in battle, but the uncivilized disregard of the boundaries of battle to include the murder of women and children. And as in *Viking Queen*, Caesar, as a iconographic short-hand for 'rigid, domineering (masculine) Rome' is opposed by Xena and Boudicca, standing for 'tenuously controlled, freedom-loving underdog (female) Greek/Celt/not-Roman'.

Just as the figure of Xena, warrior and princess, plays with our assumptions about gender roles, this episode plays with the common Neo-Pagan assumptions about pre-Christian religions in Britain. Xena and Gabrielle have previously been mixed up in a revision of the story of Abraham and

Isaac, so they are certifiably familiar with the Judeo-Christian notion of monotheism (and we've decided to forget about historical accuracy, so we won't question the fact that Xena gets to hang out with heroes of the Trojan War, the founders of Judaism, and the founders of the Roman Empire). Here they encounter a monotheistic cult, seemingly gentle and kind, oppressed by the Romans and opposed by Ares (who in the past has always represented everything that Xena is trying to vanquish in herself). Their life-affirming message is particularly attractive to Gabrielle. It turns out they're really the worshippers of Dahok, whose monotheism is a metaphor for monomania, and who need a sacrifice of Gabrielle's 'innocence' in order for their god to become incarnate in this world. In the battle to prevent Dahok from materializing and consuming the mortal realm, his temple is blasted to pieces, leaving behind only a tattered wreckage of trilithons—you guessed it, Stonehenge.

Once again, the image of Stonehenge is connected with ideas of human sacrifice, of a 'perversion' of the tenets of Judeo-Christianity associated with religious rituals in stone circles. The need for a morally pure outsider to provide the sacrifice reinforces themes in *The Wicker Man*—where do you find an acceptable sacrifice when everyone who belongs to the religion is by definition unfit for the job? But the kind of plot twists used in this episode of *Xena* would not be possible—would not be 'twists'—if the writers could not assume that their audience already possessed a set of assumptions about the basically pacific nature of Pagan Celtic religion and a real or perceived continuity between that religion and early Christianity. If druids are considered to be shams and tricksters and nasty savages, then we would hardly be surprised that these Rome-opposing Brits would be interested in a little human sacrifice to while away the time. We would, in fact, expect it.

Tacit audience expectations are the only way to make any sense out of *Roar*, a replacement series on the American-based Fox network that appeared in the summer of 1997. Each episode begins with the statement, 'The last Celtic tribes struggle for survival ... Europe had fallen to the Romans, and this remote and untamed island was the final stronghold of the ancient ways ... Between history and myth, a great battle will be waged ...', and all I can say is that history is beyond all doubt the loser. As these words are intoned, the camera pans over a map of Europe, labelled with the date '400 A.D.', finally focusing in on the islands of Britain and Ireland. Literal-minded viewers might be forgiven for assuming that a series based on a conflict between invading Romans and Celtic tribes was taking place in Britain, although they might be a little confused that these Romans are represented as only getting around to invading the island at the time when they were, in fact, retreating from it after four centuries of rule. However, a quick search for discussion of the series on the Internet would show them the error of their ways. As Amy Hale and Shannon Thornton have noted, as far as American audiences are concerned, 'Celtic' equals 'Irish', (Hale, 1994, and see Thornton, Hale and Thornton this volume), and therefore these misguided Romans are not conquering Britain when they should be abandoning it to the ravages of the Saxons, but conquering Ireland when they have no historical right to be there in the first place. For as far as the Romans in this series are concerned, this island, whatever it is, is firmly established as a province of the Empire.

The representation of the Celtic tribes in this series is in keeping with the general New Age and Neo-Pagan image of the Celts as good guys, independent and open-minded, only fighting when attacked, in touch with the harmonies of the natural world. The 'roar' of the series title is a kind of aural Force, 'the voice that echoes in every living thing, the power that binds us together. It can give you a strength and clarity like you've never known', as the druid Galen puts it. This empowering roar is a stark contrast to the kinds of roars that occur in medieval Celtic literatures, the screams of the Coraniaid and of Culhwch which cause women to spontaneously abort, the tumult of the mysterious Claw that pulls Teyrnon from his bed, the wails of the mourners for the Black Knight that make Owein think the sky would fall down with the reverberations. Loud noises are often offensive weapons in Welsh and Irish medieval literature.

On one level the series is pure action/adventure, relating a story of scrappy, freedom-loving underdogs battling against an evil, power-mad Establishment—the same basic plot structure appears in movies about spunky battalions fighting Nazis, bugs from outer space, Communists, the army of George III, the minions of King John, Big Brother. However, beside this basic plot runs a story of religious conflict. The main villain is Longinus, the centurion who speared Christ on the cross and who is now condemned never to die.[2] The Celts themselves seem uniformly to worship Brigit, and repeatedly refer to Christ as 'the Roman god', a misapprehension which is never corrected by the one covert Christian among them. The theological assumptions of the series are rather foggy—in an interview in the *Los Angeles Times* television section (13 July 1997) the creators of the series claim to have been inspired by Thomas Cahill's *How the Irish Saved Civilization*, in which case one can only say that they may have read the book but they seem to have completely misunderstood what it was saying. Nonetheless, it appears that the Roman Empire is officially Christian, but only in the most opportunistic sense. The figure of Christ seems to have been appropriated as a means of obtaining power over the masses, Christianity a means of spreading propaganda that will keep the imperial power structure in place without challenging it.

There is a peculiar lack of ritual in this Roman Christianity—while the Romans talk about Christ, none of them seem to do anything to worship him. In contrast, the Celts seem to take belief (theirs and the Romans) for granted and cede the practice of ritual to their druids, who live separately headed by a (child) king.[3] The druids decide what rituals need to be performed to maintain the balance of nature, and call upon the lay folk to take part when appropriate. Otherwise, aside from the constant swearing by Brigit, the Celts go on their merry way without the need of organized religion because, evidently, they are so completely at one with nature. As such, they appear to be more open to the 'truth' of Christianity than the ostensibly Christian Romans.

The episode 'Red Boot' deals most explicitly with the religious message of the series. The Red Boot is a secret organization, the emperor's inner circle, who are charged with 'documenting' the history of Rome. Their motto is, 'control the truth, you control the masses'. This written history is contrasted with the Celtic, druidic oral tradition. The druid king comments, 'The Romans lie, they lie about us, and they write down their lies with marks that last forever. No long poems, no songs, only marks that hide their deeds.' The lying, third-person writings of the Romans are also contrasted with the scroll which is the focus of the episode, a letter written by Jesus himself to his brother James. The good (Celtic) Christians must preserve the scroll to contradict the propagandistic writings of the Red Boot leader Pasolinus, who wants to destroy the scroll and thus the truth. His corruption is made clear when he makes a deal with Longinus to portray the centurion as, explicitly, a saint. The tension between the authority of the written versus the spoken word runs throughout this episode. Pasolinus, the writer, is a liar. He manipulates texts to make them say what he wants. Against his written lies stands the testimony of Jesus, which is itself a text, a written document but one whose authority lies not in its textual nature, but in the fact that it is written *in his own hand*. The Derridian authority of the word over the text is displaced from the mouth to the fingers, from breath to flesh.

The scenario of a corrupt and secret governmental organization which seeks to preserve its power through the manipulation of 'the Truth' has a curiously familiar ring, and one is not surprised to discover that the 'Red Boot' episode was written by Larry Barber and Paul Barber, who wrote several early episodes of *The X Files*. Conspiracy is timeless, at least in TV-land. In fact, the confusing representation of the Roman Empire in *Roar*, so completely at odds with the actual history of the Roman presence in Britain and Ireland, becomes much more comprehensible in the context of post-colonialism, contemporary American assumptions about governmental conspiracy and corruption, and the legacy of post-Reformation and Enlightenment ideas about the necessity of a personal relationship with one's deity rather than a reliance on the mediation of priests.

What is interesting in light of the common assumptions of academics that the 'romantic Celts' are stereotypically contrasted with the 'pragmatic Anglo-Saxons' is that television series such as *Xena* and *Roar* demonstrate a shift in the stereotypical oppositions. In a world where Neo-Paganism is increasingly vocal, Angles, Saxon, Jutes and Vikings inhabit the same Pagan periphery as the Celts (although they may clump on the bloodier end of the spectrum). The centre is now inhabited by 'Rome', which stands for both (over-) organized religion and imperialism, for rigidity, narrow-mindedness, mindless ritual, the letter of the law rather than its spirit, bureaucracy, the absolute power that corrupts absolutely. 'Celt' stands for freedom, openness, understanding, acceptance of others, tolerance of diversity, personal spirituality. While the human mind may inevitably organize the world around it in terms of binary oppositions, the terms that are opposed are subject to shift and mutation. Likewise, a sort of anthropological Uncertainty Principle operates: who occupies the centre and who occupies the periphery depends on where the observer is standing at the moment of observation, and what she or he is trying to measure.

I have argued previously (Jones 1998) that in much of the Enlightenment writing about druids, 'Rome' stands for '(Roman) Catholicism' in opposition to Anglicanism. The 'primitive' religion of the druids, which was almost but not quite Christianity, returned in its pristine and completed form in the Church of England. Enlightenment druidism was a discourse about the relationship between science (all those stone circles) and religion. Twentieth-century mediated images of early Celts and druids have become a discourse about colonialism and spirituality, played out with the same linguistic and iconographic markers. The images of stone circles and druids that appear in the movies and television series discussed here are meant to telegraph the idea of 'primordial truth', 'primal wisdom'. Power is inscribed upon them, magic is performed within their ambit. But the message always changes with the times.

Notes

1. Permutations of some of this material have appeared in Jones (1998), and in presentations at the American Folklore Society meeting in Milwaukee, October 1994 (Jones 1994) and the UCLA Celtic Colloquium/Celtic Studies Association of North America meeting in Los Angeles, April 1996 (Jones 1996). I would like to thank Susan Scheiberg for help with folkloric references, and Dave Walsh for help with Irish wisecracks.
2. Longinus usually looks like a man in his early prime, but on occasion reveals his real, 400-year-old appearance.
3. This seven-year-old druid-king is represented as a Celtic Dalai Lama, preternaturally wise, presenting the druidic doctrine of the transmigration of souls in a New Age guise.

References

Films and television episodes

Curse of the Demon. J. Tourneur, director. C. Bennett, screenplay. Based on M.R. James' 'Casting the Runes'. Columbia, 1957

Dr Who. Stones of Blood. D. Blake, director. D. Fisher, screenplay. BBC/Lionheart, 1978.

Excalibur. J. Boorman, director. J. Boorman and R. Pallenberg, screenplay. Based on Thomas Malory's *Morte D'Arthur*. Orion, 1981.

Knights of the Round Table. R. Thorpe, director. Based on Thomas Malory's *Morte D'Arthur*. MGM/UA, 1953.

Roar. Red Boot. T.J. Wright, director. L. Barber and P. Barber, screenplay. Sea Change Productions, 1997.

Viking Queen. D. Chaffey, director. Hammer/Seven Arts, 1968.

Wicker Man. R. Hardy, director. A. Schaeffer, screenplay. Republic, 1975.

Xena: Warrior Princess. The Deliverer. O. Sassone, director. S.L. Sears, screenplay. Pacific Renaissance Pictures, 1997.

Books

Bowman, M. Cardiac Celts: Images of the Celts in Paganism. In C. Hardman and G. Harvey (eds) *Paganism Today*. London, 1995.

Cahill, T. *How the Irish Saved Civilization: The Untold Story of Ireland's Heroic Role from the Fall of Rome to the Rise of Medieval Europe*. New York, 1995.

Chapman, M. *The Celts: The Construction of a Myth*. New York, 1992.

Frazer, J. G. *The Golden Bough: A Study in Magic and Religion*, abridged edn New York, 1922.

Hale, A. A Violent, Stormy People: The Role of Race in the Construction of Celtic Identity. Paper presented at the University of California Celtic Colloquium, Los Angeles, California, May 1994.

Hobsbawm, E. and Ranger T. (eds) *The Invention of Tradition*. Cambridge, 1983.

Hutton, Ronald. *The Pagan Religions of the Ancient British Isles: Their Nature and Legacy*. Oxford, 1991.

Ignatiev, Noel. *How the Irish Became White*. London, 1995.

James, M.R. *Collected Ghost Stories*. Hertfordshire, 1992 [1931].

Jones, L.E. The Bad Anthropology Film Festival: How the Other Sees Us. Paper presented at the annual meeting of the American Folklore Society, Milwaukee, Wisconsin, October 1994.

Jones, L.E. From *Viking Queen* to *The Wickerman*: (Mis)Representations of Celtic Paganism in Popular Film. Paper presented at the UCLA Celtic Colloquium/Celtic Studies Association of North America Joint Meeting, Los Angeles, California, April 1996.

Jones, L.E. *Druid-Shaman-Priest: Metaphors of Celtic Paganism*. London, 1998.

Kirschenblatt-Gimblett, B. Studying Immigrant and Ethnic Folklore. In Richard Dorson (ed.) *Handbook of American Folklore*. Bloomington, 1983.

Morgan, P. From a Death to a View: The Hunt for the Welsh Past in the Romantic Period. In E. Hobsbawm and T. Ranger (eds) *The Invention of Tradition*. Cambridge, 1983.

Piggott, S. *The Druids*. New York, 1975.

Piggott, S. *William Stukeley: An Eighteenth-Century Antiquarian*. New York, 1985.

Piggott, S. *Ancient Britons and the Antiquarian Imagination: Ideas from the Renaissance to the Regency*. New York, 1989.

Sims-Williams, P. The Visionary Celt: The Construction of an Ethnic Preconception. *Cambridge Medieval Celtic Studies*, 11, pp. 71–96, 1986.

Stukeley, W. *Stonehenge: A Temple Restored to the British Druids*. London, 1740.

3

Pre-Packaged Breton Folk Narrative

ANTONE MINARD

Most anthropology used to be conducted from the comfort of the armchair, not the field. In the not-so-recent past eminent scholars such as James Frazer and Edward Tylor sat in their libraries and contemplated people's quaint and strange behaviours, from the peasants in their own backyard to the so-called 'savages' in the far-flung outposts of the Empire, solely from the reports brought back by missionaries, travellers and the military. These scholars generalized about human universalities and social evolution without having to go out into 'the field' actually to converse with real people. Such out-worn practices from the infancy of the discipline were useful in their day, but they could not possibly have any relevance to the modern social sciences. Or could they? What can we learn about people simply from textual evidence?

Clearly the goals of the modern folklorist and anthropologist have moved beyond the eighteenth- and nineteenth-century pursuits involving the reconstruction of a Germanic mythology, fragments of which were to be rescued from the half-forgotten survivals of the ignorant folk. Yet, although our assumptions of the 'folk' and the subjects of anthropology have changed, the models for anthropological and folkloristic scholarship in practice still tend to assume that the groups under consideration are not quite our contemporaries in technology or literacy. This is not to say that we assume our subjects are ignorant: quite the contrary. It is merely to say that neither field has quite internalized the fact that the telephone is an essential tool of communication among 'the folk', not to mention e-mail and desktop publishing.

PRE-PACKAGED BRETON FOLK NARRATIVE

Both anthropologists and folklorists have taken hesitant steps towards creating a model for dealing with a relatively recent phenomenon: the publication of folklore and other types of anthropological data by the folk themselves. They may or may not have some academic training, but they are producing newsletters, books, websites, any number of materials, and not just aimed inwardly at the other members of their groups. This phenomenon is larger than the education reforms of the late nineteenth and early twentieth century, whose results (an inconveniently literate folk) led to the revision and expansion of the concept of 'folk' away from just 'them', i.e. 'not us scholars'. A folk group now can be considered to be 'any subset of everyone'.

This chapter will be a discussion of folk narratives and legends currently mass produced for consumption by tourists and other visitors to Brittany, and perhaps for the Bretons themselves.[1] Breton identity, like many expressions of modern national identity, involves a sense of shared community and history, usually manifested in shared language, custom and geographical space. Much of what is specifically Breton, i.e. shared but not French, is in the form of folklore: folk music, folk dance, legend, proverbial expression. The modern 'Breton Renaissance' began in the 1950s in the realms of art and music, and continues in the numerous public folklore festivals during the summers (Kuter 1994, 2). Although individual Bretons may or may not identify themselves as 'Celts', I consider the narratives I am examining here to be Celtic insofar as they are clearly and consciously linked with traditions from other Celtic regions, and are part of the artistic and narrative corpus which is redefining and re-creating the notion of Celtic identity in the Brittany of the 1990s.

By 'pre-packaged folk narratives', I refer to the narrative summaries, narratives, and collections of narratives which can be accessed or purchased by the public at large in Brittany, both tourists and interested Bretons. This material is to be found in newspapers, on radio and television, in books, and on compact discs, postcards and the Internet. I collected the examples I am using in this chapter at the Abbey of Landeveneg (Landévennec) and in Kemper (Quimper), Roazhon (Rennes), and Sant-Malo (Saint Malo) in July 1996, and from Internet websites in November 1996. All of the sites cited were active as of 1 February 2000. Whether the materials I collected are representative of folk narratives told in the community I cannot say, but there is remarkable consistency between the different sources, with the same few story cycles being repeated again and again.

With material conflated from several sources over a period of more than a century, it would be difficult, if not impossible, to analyse any performative aspects of these narratives. So, if these narratives are the productions, not the performances, of members of the folk group (in this case, Bretons), are they still to be classed as folklore? Some scholars would argue that because there is no direct interaction between the narrator and the audience, and because these postcard narratives now exist in static form, that they are not 'authentic' folklore. American folklorist Richard Dorson might have termed these manipulations of traditional tales 'fakelore', since they were literary renderings from printed sources and not actually representative of narratives collected in the field (1969, 60). Somewhat similarly to Dorson, German folklorist Hans Moser would have called these marketable treatments of traditional tales *folklorismus*, as they are not transmitted in a 'natural' context, and are adapted for commercial use, although his use of the term was ultimately less judgemental of the practice (Bendix 1988, 5–15).

However, these perhaps less conventional and emergent renderings of traditional tales can be argued as folklore for a number of reasons. First, the emic categorization of the material is as specific genres of folklore: 'légende' (legend), 'conte' (folktale), 'proverbe' (proverb), etc. Unfortunately, native characterization alone is no longer a firm indication of genre since some of these words have shades and varieties of meaning. For instance, in common American usage the words 'folklore', 'folktale', 'legend' and 'myth' all mean 'untrue' in popular usage. The *Geriadur Brezhoneg-Saozneg* (Breton–English Dictionary) contains the word *folklorach*, pl. *folklorachoù*, which, perhaps similar to Dorson's 'fakelore', means '(derogat.) an unscientific and cheap form of folklore used to attract tourists'. I assume this is a borrowing from French *folklorage*, but I have not seen this attested. Similar usages in French, the language of these narratives, are: *folklo* 'folklorique, qui ne peut pas être pris au sérieux' (folkloric, which cannot be taken seriously); *folklorique* '2. pittoresque, mais dépourvu de sérieux' (picturesque, but lacking in seriousness).

Furthermore, the field of folklore contains such emergent genres as xeroxlore and e-mail lore, both new forms of folklore in response to new technology. Every joke or personal experience narrative told over the telephone mocks the sometime definition of folklore that requires face-to-face interaction (Georges and Jones 1995, 1). These narratives exist in a variety of forms and formats. Following Claude Lévi-Strauss, all versions of a myth (read: narrative) are part of the myth, diachronically as well as synchronically. Thus, if the legend still exists in contemporary tradition, the pre-packaged narratives contribute to that legend. These pre-packaged narratives are in fact forms of traditional narratives which are specific to Brittany, put together and presented to an audience by inhabitants of Brittany. For some, they may be easier to comprehend as literature rather than folklore, since they are deliberate written products based on both oral and written sources. Although there is a long tradition of looking for folklore in literature (Zumwalt 1988; Rosenberg 1991), I am also concerned with the literary product as folklore itself.

With the narrator divorced from his or her audience, and the audience scattered throughout Europe, America, and elsewhere, we are left with only the physical evidence of the narratives themselves. And so we are back to armchair anthropology, a century after we thought we had left it behind. Can an outsider say anything about a culture, using only written narratives and supplementary material? Historians and literary scholars would say yes, with qualifications. And so, with qualifications, here is what Bretons are saying about themselves, through the medium of folk narrative, to themselves and the rest of the world, filtered through the impressions of one folklorist.

Selling Bite-Sized Legends

My first encounter with these pre-packaged narratives came when I travelled to Brittany in 1996 to a conference held at the Abbey of Landévennec. As an American tourist, I was both pleased and surprised to find a bookshop on the Abbey grounds. I had hoped to find a collection of Breton folk narrative, normally unavailable in America, and it looked like the conference site would provide me with the one-stop-shopping experience for which my native southern California is famous. Folkloric material was everywhere. Not only were there several books of this type, but posters and postcards as well.

The postcards included the standard images one would expect, with views of the Abbey and surrounding Crozon peninsula, but, surprisingly, an equal number of legend postcards. I continued to find these cards at every train station and souvenir shop in Brittany. The postcards are produced within Brittany, and therefore to a degree present an insider's view of the culture, or at least what an insider wants outsiders to take away. It is not knowable whether the postcard narrator identifies as a Breton in his or her heart of hearts, but the local preparation of the narrative and its presentation as Breton to the outside world must identify her or him as an anonymous Breton in the public sphere.

Normally, the material produced for tourists pictures a stereotypical Breton peasant arrayed in the distinctive local costume, with wooden shoes and lace coiffes in a variety of contexts, some of which are thematically similar to postcards from other areas. For example, contrast two postcards from America with their counterpart from Brittany. A Washington postcard is light grey on the top, and dark grey on the bottom. The top reads 'A Summer Day in Seattle', and the bottom reads 'A Winter Day in Seattle'. Along the sides, running through both colors, is 'A Spring Day in Seattle' and 'A Fall Day in Seattle'. A similar card from San Francisco is entirely grey and says 'San Francisco in the Fog'. Both of these cards contrast the stereotypical scenic postcard view with the notoriously foggy local weather, the joke being a postcard where you cannot see anything at all. The Breton postcard, drawn for Jos le Doaré by Philippe Luguy, shows a smiling grey-bearded man in wooden shoes, wearing traditional costume, standing before an impenetrable fog bank, saying 'Comment rester insensible devant une telle varieté de gris' (How can anyone remain unmoved before such a variety of grey). Unlike the American cards, here there *is* something to see: a Breton. He is elderly, and worth observing because of his costume and his quaint, queer attitude: he thinks fog is beautiful.

But while Breton peasants are in evidence on many of the postcards representing folk speech, and humour, curiously they are absent from the postcard representations of legendary narratives. While the peasant in folk costume may be out of date, he or she is still in the present. The legend cards of 'Coulours de Bretagne' gently reinforce the image that they are anchored in the past, unrelated to modern human habitation. The photos are of depopulated landscapes: a pool in the forest; a bay with a single house in view on a hill; and one rock formation with a dog perched atop the rock, presumably for scale. Other than the dog, the only 'human' to appear is King Gradlon, whose statue in Kemper (Quimper) is shown prominently. At the bottom of these images is a summary of the legend associated with the site.

The available postcard series have several legends in common, evidently those that they feel are most representative of Brittany. In the interests of space, I will focus on the most common legend cycles, those about the drowned city of Ys ('Lower' in Breton) and various Arthurian legends. Virtually the entire corpus of Breton folklore collected over the last 180 years is in print, in one form or another, but these two cycles are far more commonly represented than any other topic, including the famous megalithic monuments and *An Ankou*, the Breton personified Death.

There are at least three series of these cards put out by Éditions Jos le Doaré (two series) and Éditions Jack (Éditeur—Fabricant). Éditions Jack's cards are simple pictures of a legend site, labelled in clear white type in the upper left-hand corner, above the picture, e.g. 'LA FONTAINE DE JOUVENCE' (The Fountain of Youth) or 'LA VILLE D'YS' (The City of Ys). In the upper right-hand corner, a smaller version of the same font reads 'LÉGENDE DU PAYS BRETON' (Legend of the Breton country) in yellow or gold. All of this is on a blue background framing the picture. On the back, beneath the series title 'Couleurs de Bretagne' (Colours of Brittany), the words 'Légende du pays Breton' are repeated. Below that the title of the legend is repeated in French, English and German, the languages of the bulk of the region's tourists. Notably, it is not given in Breton. The framed picture is a photograph of a site associated with a legend. The postcards are distributed across Brittany, regardless of proximity or lack thereof to the place depicted.

The other two series, by Éditions Jos le Doaré, are much the same, except that one series forgoes the word 'légende'. Instead, the title is framed above the centre of the picture, and the text begins with a decorated initial. The pictures contain no evidence of human habitation, only (in one case) a megalithic monument. On the backs of both Jos Le Doaré series, the title is 'Le légendaire de Brocéliande, en Forêt de Paimpont' (The Legendary (Corpus) of Brocéliande, in the Forest of Paimpont). The only descriptions are in French.

The third series, by far the most prevalent, places the title within the frame of the picture. It is written in an exaggerated cursive. The word 'Légende' is written in a fancy font in the lower left corner, with the initial 'L' decorated in a very recognizably 'Celtic' style. The initial is blue, with a yellow beast (similar to one of the birds from the Lindisfarne Gospels) overlayed in yellow, with additional decorations in red and green. The style is that which has come to be associated with Irish art, and, by extension, as Celtic in general, although that style of manuscript illustration is not local to Brittany. A more appropriate design, for instance, would have been zoo-anthropomorphic, with an animal head atop a human body, historically quite popular in Brittany. I noted a similar use of 'Celtic' decoration everywhere in Brittany, from the logo of the popular folk-rock group Tri Yann to the bilingual street signs of western Brittany. The French-language information is presented in standard Roman type, while the Breton language is written in a font based on Irish uncial, as 'Le Faou **Ar Faou**'.

The Lost City of Ys

The Lost City of Ys is by far the best known of all Breton legends. It tells of a beautiful, utopian city, lost beneath the seas through the treachery of a godless woman, and despite the best efforts of Saints Corentin and Gwénolé, and the good King Gradlon. In Ys, Gradlon's daughter Dahut lived a life of pleasure, turning Ys into a kind of second Gomorrah, and drowned her lovers after seducing them. One day, she herself fell in love with a man, the Devil in disguise. He asked her for the key to the dike that held back the sea. She obtained it for him, he drowned the city, and only Gwénolé and Gradlon escaped.

Two postcards are simply titled 'La Ville d'Ys'. The Jack text is slightly longer than the le Doaré text, and less romantic. It shows a photograph of waves in the Bay of Douarnenez, with the city in the distance. The story begins with 'Ys, situated in the real-life Bay of Douarnenez, was the capital of [Breton] Cornwall' clearly showing the legend's ties to geographical reality. Le Doaré's photograph is taken at sunset or sunrise, with a plain grey sky. The view is slightly different, with two arms of rock in shadow, no signs of humanity to be seen. The text starts out, 'Under the waters of the Bay of Douarnenez, the ruins of the town of Ys sleep forever'. The style of the former is stark and factual, whereas the latter is fanciful, ornate and romantic.

The Jack text continues to present a factual representation with the use of such technical terms as 'polder', land reclaimed from the sea. The city was 'protected' from the sea, not 'defended' as in the other text. Dahut is 'heedless', as opposed to 'cursed.' At the end, Gradlon 'impotently attends the annihilation of the city and its inhabitants'. There is no mention of either Saint Gwénolé or Saint Corentin. In the le Doaré text, Dahut again steals the keys to give to her lover, and the city is drowned. Only the king escapes, warned by Saint Gwénolé. There is no mention of the king's attempt to save her. The only common language to the two texts is the description of Dahut's lover, 'who was none other than the devil'.

Contrast these with another widely accessible Ys text, to be found on the Internet at www.bretagne.com, whose motto is 'Ici, la legende est vraie. Il suffit d'y croire' [Here, legends are true. One need only believe). This text is approximately three times as long, and if anything is even more romantic than the postcard texts. It also has a visual, a reproduction of an 1884 oil painting by Evariste-Vital Luminais which is exhibited in La Musée de Quimper. The scanned image features King Gradlon, his daughter Dahut, and Saint Corentin, who are fleeing from the drowned city. Dahut is falling off the king's horse, and he is trying to hold on to her, while the saint admonishes him.

The story begins, 'At the great March tide, called the tide of St Gwénolé, the sea at Douarnenez pulls out far, so far that it uncovers the debris of a town composed of a palace in ruins'. Although this starts out in the same manner as the Jack text, emphasizing the physical reality underlying the narrative, its prose is more flowery than that on the postcard. Right away, it makes reference to other Breton folklore: the great equinoctal tides, especially famous at St Malo, and Saint Gwénolé, who appears later in this as well as other stories.

The Internet summary is clearly based on the version collected by Émile Souvestre in *Le Foyer Breton* in 1845, as the two share many details of plot and language. Even so, this version places more emphasis on the Celtic aspects of the narrative. Dahut is described as 'deeply attached to the ancient Celtic gods' and 'guardian of the heritage of the Celts'. In this narrative, she 'reigned there as absolute mistress', in a city that her father had had constructed for her. Like the postcards, there is a reference to the moral laxity in Dahut's behaviour. But unlike the other two narratives, the internet text sets up an opposition between Dahut and Corentin, ascribing to him the negative values of 'having made the city sad and tiresome'. Dahut, despite her grand ways, has given the city wealth and dreams of nothing but liberty and *joie de vivre*. She has made Ys the richest and most powerful city in Brittany—reminiscent of Eva Peron in Andrew Lloyd Webber and Tim Rice's *Evita*.

Dahut's persona as pre-modern Celtophile is echoed in the le Doaré postcard labelled 'La Marie-Morgane', which reads 'Marie-Morgane is the Breton Goddess of the Seas ... she is none other than Dahut, the damned daughter of King Gradlon'. The photograph is again one of indistinct rocks in crepuscular light, in a stormy sea. The card continues to relate that 'if you do not see a relative or friend return in the evening, it's Marie-Morgane who has becalmed his boat on the open sea', thus portraying her as an active phenomenon, but a relatively harmless one.

The sentiment is echoed by 'outsider' versions of this legend: Houghton-Mifflin's travel guide reports lightheartedly that 'Dahut became a mermaid known as Marie-Morgane ... [when her curse is lifted she] will cease to be an amphibious seductress'. More often, in Breton tradition, the Marie-Morgane will drown you if you catch her attention (see Sébillot 1968). The pre-packaged Marie-Morgane narratives downplay actual folk belief, whether past or present, in favour of producing an interesting survival of Celtic Paganism.

The earliest reference to Ys is from 1515, in Pierre Le Baud's *Histoire de Bretagne* (Bromwich 1950, 235). The legend appears in almost every folklore collection, and in many of the histories dealing with the sixth century. The king, Gradlon or Grallon, is semi-historical, as are the Welsh leaders mentioned in *Cantre'r Gwaelod*. The story has been told and re-told, from Edouard Lalo's opera *Le Roi d'Ys: Légende Bretonne* to Poul Anderson's science fiction. Edouard Lalo and lyricist Edouard Blau felt sufficiently familiar with the tradition to change the ending—here the king's daughter, instead of perishing tragically for her sins, repents at the last minute and saves everybody before throwing herself into the sea as a sacrifice. All the Breton versions, however, hold Dahut responsible. Ys is always specifically located, usually in the Bay of Douarnenez—a tangible folkloric artefact for tourists to visit.

Versions of the 'submerged city' legend are found throughout northern Europe and in other Celtic regions, with an especially close parallel in the ninth-century Welsh poem *Cantre'r Gwaelod* (The Low Hundred). The Welsh legends of Cantre'r Gwaelod and Llys Helig (Helig's Court) contain the same details of audible bells beneath the waves and ruins which are visible at the equinoctial tides, which are the anchors of credulity in the story. The Cornish legend of the submerged land of Lyonesse which is believed to lie off of Penzance also contains the motif of visible ruins under the water at low tides. The near literal parallels between *Cantre'r Gwaelod* and the nineteenth-century Breton ballad *Liñvadenn Kêr-Iz* (The Drowning of the City of Is) are probably due to an excess of enthusiasm on the behalf of the collector/author Kervarker (le Villemarqué), rather than to historical accuracy (Bromwich 1950, 232). There seems to be a parallel to Ys in an even more famous drowned city, Atlantis, although other scholars have denied it.

Morvan Lebesque uses legendary Ys as a metaphor for discussing perceptions of contemporary Brittany: 'You can discuss injustices in politics in Paris and abroad, but should you discuss Brittany, even so far as citing facts and figures, it is as if there were a revolution in the City of Ys. This is in part because no one thinks the City of Ys capable of saying *telephone* or *television*' (n.d., 14). However, there has been a tremendous effort to provide Breton with a complete technological vocabulary. As in Welsh and Cornish, words are carefully and conscientiously calqued from Greek and Latin. For example, to telephone is *pellgomz*, from *pell* (far) and *komz* (to speak, speech). In 1995, when the first monolingual Breton dictionary *Geriadur Brezhonek* appeared, it also contained words such as *adkaser douar* (satellite dish), and *skeudenroller* (video recorder). Video recorders and telephones, however, are a small part of the public image of Brittany. Tourists who come to Brittany want quaint. The hint of cities beneath the ocean, filled with ancient lore, and the connection with the newly rediscovered ancient druidic wisdom, is very appealing to the tourist trade, much more so than modern agricultural techniques.

The immense popularity of the story of Ys can be attributed to the fact that it satisfies the requirements for a quaint and romantic story intimately tied to the Breton landscape. Beyond that, for the Bretons themselves, it may be a coded message about the Breton experience, culturally and historically at the margin of France. Its historical time frame, the sixth century, coincides with the age of King Arthur and the Breton migrations to the European mainland, recalling Brittany's historical and cultural connections to the rest of the Celtic countries.

King Arthur in Brittany

No collection of Breton lore is complete without an Arthurian story. *Histoires et Légendes de la Bretagne mystèrieux* (Stories and Legends from Mysterious Brittany) contains a Merlin story, 'Merlin l'Enchanteur' from de la Villemarqué's *Myrdhinn ou l'enchanteur Merlin* of 1862. This version is not an 'authentic' representation of folk narrative as are some of the others in this volume, including 'Keris' (the City of Ys). The story in this volume is actually a borrowed tradition that the author superimposed on the actual Merlin lore in Brittany. Yann Brekilien begins his folktale collection *Autres Contes et Légendes du Pays Breton* with four Arthurian stories, in a section entitled 'In the Enchanted Forest of the Ancient Celts'. Interest in Arthurian material is certainly not a recent phenomenon: O.L. Aubert also included Arthurian and Ys material in *Légendes Traditionelles de la Bretagne* of 1928. He does not wax as romantic about the Celts as Brekilien, but he waxes in a similar vein about the lore of Classical Greece, from which he derives the Breton tales.

It is important to note the significance of Arthurian lore in the shaping of Brittany as a Celtic region. As in Wales and Cornwall, Arthurian material plays a role in Breton nationalist rhetoric as well: not only is there the linguistic and historical evidence linking Brittany with Britain, but clearly the people *feel* British. If not, how could they claim King Arthur, that most British of kings? This perception gives Brittany a dual citizenship: French, but also a phantom part of the British Isles, and of 'Celtia', a constructed community of several Celtic nations. The renewed interest in Brittany's Celtic historical connections to Ireland, Wales, Cornwall and the other Celtic countries is certainly partly responsible for the popularity of the Arthurian material on the available postcards. Scholars acknowledge that Brittany must have been a key in the transmission of the *Matière de Bretagne* from insular to continental tradition (Bromwich 1991). This material is part of the core of English, Cornish, French and Welsh medieval literature and culture. If the Arthurian cycle is important to these countries, especially France and England, then so too must Brittany be a central link.

However, the narratives about Arthur in Brittany tend not to be about Arthur himself. They focus more on Merlin, who is in fact a part of Breton popular tradition (Philippe 1986), or else they focus on the many local legends related to the Arthurian material, especially from the Forest of Brocéliande. The website, www.bretagne.com gives a brief summary of Arthur's life, based mostly on Mallory or the Vulgate, but has an entire page devoted to the Brocéliande legends. The references to legend take the form of descriptions rather than narratives, and are usually not given more than one sentence per location. The postcards, however, present numerous narratives about the forest and the Arthurian world in general. Some of these sites are peripherally related to the Arthurian corpus, such as 'Les Pierres du Ménez-Hom' (The Stones of Menez-Hom), under which king Marc'h (Mark) is said to be buried. Other sites are more central to popular Arthurian material, such as the 'Fontaine de Barenton' (Fountain of Barenton), where Yvain killed the black knight.

Constructions of Brittany: Myth v. History

Brittany itself is a mythological construction in many ways. In Benedict Anderson's classic work *Imagined Communities* (1983), the author discusses the ways in which all communities are to some extent imagined. This is certainly true of Brittany, where in fact there are two important conceptions of Brittany at the provincial level: Brittany as a mythological country, and Brittany as a political region. In one sense, Bretons are citizens of France inhabiting a political space called Brittany. However, there is also the Brittany that has been constructed as a 'Celtic land of myth'—an 'otherworldly' nation. Mordrel (1973), Mayo (1974) and McDonald (1989) have discussed nationalism and separatism in Brittany, including the role of the Celtic revivals and folklore in the context of these movements.

Claude Lévi-Strauss in *The Structural Study of Myth* suggested the notion that real communities are often discussed in mythic terms (in Sebeok 1955, 85). It is an ahistorical construction as well as historical; events reverberate throughout history, shaping both the events that came after and the interpretation of events that came before. 'Celtic' Brittany, as opposed to French Brittany, can be understood in this ahistorical fashion. Individuals as good 'Otherworldly Celts' may or may not believe in traditional characters such as *An Ankou* (personified Death), the supernatural, Merlin, mermaids, giants or dwarves. Even if they do, they may or may not admit it to outsiders. But everybody *believes* that Bretons believe this—or used to at any rate—and everybody believes in the imagined, constructed mythic Brittany. In truth, legends such as those of the drowned city of Ys and Merlin the Enchanter are less likely to be believed than contemporary legends such as the story of the individual whose kidney is stolen from him in an airport. But the former are considered uniquely Breton, and are discussed as such even in Upper Brittany, which may have no historical or cultural claim to them, while the latter are considered to be French or international.

Merchants, too, are capitalizing on the sense of Brittany as place of the unreal. Loïc Raison, a cider maker, advertises that his cider was 'born in this land of a thousand legends', presumably as opposed to its Norman rivals. In St Malo a shopkeeper uses local legend to advertise 'Le MacLow Fast-Food', with a signboard of a tonsured monk eating a hamburger. This is an elaborate visual pun on the historic version of Malo's name, Maclou, and the ubiquitous McDonald's, world-wide hamburger purveyors. It says to the customer; 'McDonald's, but local … the best of both worlds' where the spiritual and material collide.

How is a modern-day Celt supposed to cope with the influx of interest in his or her heritage, from both inside and outside the country? One natural result is to become more aware of one's own heritage, and possibly be moved to defend or advocate it. The Celtic revival over the last two centuries has brought about an increased awareness of what 'Celtic' is, and also more than a little bit of what it never was. Another natural result is to capitalize on this interest, and market it on postcards, books, stickers, posters, flags, music, etc. Folklore seems like such a little thing with which to try and stay afloat in the perceived rising tide of French 'monoculture', but it is certainly also a useful strategy in asserting a unique identity within a larger state.

Bretons, like all of us, have multiple identities and affiliations. If one is to have multiple identities, it is useful to be able to differentiate between them. Thus 'mythic Brittany' as opposed perhaps to 'rational

France' has been constructed, and in turn exploited. It is quite a marketable commodity. Legends in Brittany reinforce a sense of identity and continuity, while at the same time providing a source of income. But do the Bretons themselves actually believe that Brittany is the land of myth and legend that they are selling?

An important function of narratives within the preservationist ideology of much cultural nationalism is to maintain and reproduce the legend itself. These 'pre-packaged narratives' are an efficient means of disseminating information quickly and with an air of authority. The variation in the narratives indicates that there is some competition as to exactly how to describe the legendary Brittany, and how closely to reconcile that country with the actual Brittany. The narratives, though the products of individual, anonymous narrators, are in fact the representation of the collective perception of this fictional country by both Bretons and outsiders, as the entrepreneurs strive to satisfy their market by writing what the public wants to read. As we move further into the electronic age, we will see more of this 'Virtual Brittany', occupying the same physical space as Actual Brittany, where natives and tourists alike can move freely between the two.

Appendix: Texts Cited

Text A: Jack—'La Ville d'Ys'

Ys, située dans l'actuelle baie de Douarnenez, était la capitale de la Cornouaille. Cette ville bâtie sur des polders était protégée de la mer par une grande digue pourvue de vannes. Gradlon, roi bon et juste, régnait sur cette florissante cité. Mais sa fille Dahut ne se complaisait que dans la débauche. L'un de ses nombreux amants lui demanda, en gage d'amour, de voler à son père les clés d'or ouvrant les vannes. L'irréfléchie princesse les subtilisa et en fit don à son galant qui n'était autre que le Diable. Gradlon, voulant sauver sa fille de la brusque montée des eaux, la prit en croupe sur son cheval. Mais pour échapper aux

Ys, situated in the real-life Bay of Douarnenez, was the capital of [Breton] Cornwall. This town, built on land reclaimed from the ocean, was protected from the sea by a great dike provided with sluice-gates. Gradlon, a good and just king, reigned over this flourishing city. But his daughter Dahut delighted only in debauchery. One of her numerous lovers asked her, as a pledge of her love, to steal from her father the golden keys which opened the sluices. The thoughtless princess took them by deception and made a gift of them to her galant, who was none other than the Devil. Gradlon, desiring to save his daughter from the

flots puissants, il dut sacrificier sa fille et assista impuissant à l'anéantissement de la cité et de ses habitants.

sudden rising of the waters, took her on the crupper of his horse. But in order to escape from the powerful torrent, he had to sacrifice his daughter and impotently attended the annihilation of the city and its inhabitants.

Text B: Jos le Doaré—'La Ville d'Ys'

Sous les eaux de la Baie de Doarnenez, dorment à jamais les ruines de la ville d'Ys. Le roi Gradlon en était le maître, et sa fille Dahut, la princesse maudite. La ville était défendue contre la mer par une dige, et des écluses la protégeaient du flot de la marée. Dans Ys, Dahut menait grande vie. Un soir de fête, un prince qui n'était autre que le Diable, obligea Dahut à voler à son père la clé des écluses. Le Malin ouvrit toutes grandes les portes. La cité fut engloutie en un instant. Seul Gradlon, prévenu par saint Gwénolé, échappa à la noyade.

Beneath the waters of the Bay of Douarnenez, the ruins of the town of Ys forever sleep. The king Gradlon was its master, and his daughter Dahut, the cursed princess. The town was defended against the sea by a dike, and locks protected it from the surge of the tide. In Ys, Dahut lived the high life. One festival evening, a prince who was none other than the Devil asked Dahut to steal from her father the key to the locks. The Evil One opened wide the gates. The city was drowned in an instant. Only Gradlon, warned by Saint Gwénolé, escaped the drowning.

Text C: www.bretagne.com

La légende de la ville d'Ys en baie de Douarnenez

The legend of the town of Ys in the Bay of Douarnenez

A la grande marée de Mars appelée marée de Saint Guénolé, la mer de Douarnenez se retire loin, si'loin qu'elle découvre les décombres d'une ville composée de palais en ruines, de murs effondrés et les vestiges des chaussées de pierre reliant l'Ile de Sein à la terre. En ce temps là, Gradlon le

At the great March tide called the tide of Saint Guénolé, the sea at Douarnenez pulls out far, so far that it uncovers the debris of a town composed of a palace in ruins, sunken walls and the vestiges of stone causeways linking the isle of Sein to the

Grand, roi de Cornouaille, fit construire pour sa fille Dahut, la merveilleuse cité d'Ys. Elevée plus bas que la mer, la ville d'Ys en était protégée par une puissante digue. Une écluse fermait le port et seul Gradlon pouvait décider de son ouverture ou fermeture, permettant ainsi aux habitants d'aller pêcher. Dahut, profondément attachée aux anciens Dieux celtiques, accusait Cotentin [sic: leg. Corentin], évêque de Quimper, d'avoir rendu la ville triste et ennuyeuse. Elle rêvait d'une cité où seules règneraient richesse, liberté et joie de vivre. Aussi, Dahut donnatelle à chacun des habitants un Dragon qui s'empara de tous les navires marchands. Ainsi, la ville d'Ys devintelle la plus riche et la plus puissante de Bretagne. Dahut y régnait en maîtresse absolue, gardienne de l'héritage des Celtes.

Chaque soir, elle faisait venir un nouvel amant au palais, l'obligeant à porter un masque de soie. Mais le masque était enchanté et à l'aube il se transformait en griffes de métal, tuant ainsi ses amants dont le corps était jeté du haut d'une falaise dans l'océan. Un beau matin, un prince, tout de rouge vêtu, arriva dans la cité. Dahut tomba aussitôt amoureuse de l'étranger. Or, c'était le diable que Dieu envoyait pour châtier la ville pécheresse. Par amour pour lui, elle lui donna la clé de l'écluse qu'elle déroba à son père pendant son sommeil. Le prince ouvrit l'écluse et l'océan en furie envahit la ville en déferlant dans les rues et étouffant ainsi les cris d'horreur des habitants. Seul, le bon roi Gradlon réussit à s'échapper de cet enfer avec l'aide de St Gwénolé. Sur son cheval marin, il

mainland. In that time, Gradlon the Great, King of [Breton] Cornwall, had the marvellous city of Ys constructed for his daughter, Dahut. Built lower than the sea, Ys was protected by a powerful dike. A lock closed the gate and only Gradlon could decide its opening or closing, thus permitting the inhabitants to go fishing. Dahut, deeply attached to the ancient Celtic gods, accused Corentin, bishop of Kemper (Quimper), of having made the city sad and tiresome. She dreamed of a city where only wealth, liberty, and joie de vivre would reign. Also, Dahut gave each of the inhabitants a dragon which seized all the merchant ships. Thus, the city of Ys became the richest and most powerful city in Brittany. Dahut reigned there as the absolute master, guardian of the heritage of the Celts.

Every evening, she had a new lover come to the palace, having him wear a silk mask. But the mask was enchanted and at dawn it transformed into metal claws, thus killing her lovers, whose corpses were thrown from the height of a cliff into the ocean. One fine morning, a prince, dressed all in red, arrived in the city. Dahut at once fell in love with the stranger. However, it was the Devil whom God had sent to punish the town sinner [possibly an error for vieille, 'old']. Through her love for him, she gave him the key to the lock which she stole from her father during his sleep. The prince opened the lock and the ocean invaded the city furiously, bursting into the streets and stifling the inhabitants' cries of horror. Alone, the good king Gradlon managed to escape from

se mit à chevaucher péniblement dans les vagues, alourdi par un poids qui n'était autre que sa fille. Sommé par Saint Guénolé, il abandonna sa fille et parvint à regagner le rivage.

Aujourd'hui encore, il arrive que par temps calme, les pêcheurs de Douarnenez entendent souvent sonner les cloches, sous la mer et disent qu'un jour, Ys renaîtra plus belle, car elle n'est qu'engloutie.

this hell with the aide of Saint Gwénolé. On his waterhorse, he began riding weakly through the waves, made heavy by a weight that was none other than his daughter. Called upon by Saint Gwénolé, he abandoned his daughter and succeeded in reaching the bank.

Still today, in calm weather, it happens that the fisherfolk of Douarnenez hear the bells sound under the sea and they say that one day, Ys will be reborn more beautiful than when it was drowned [lit. 'because it is but drowned'.]

Notes

1. For the purposes of this study I consider anyone who lives in Brittany to be Breton regardless of language usage.

References

Anderson, B. *Imagined Communities*. London, 1983.
Ar Porzh, R. *Geriadur Brezhoneg-Saozneg*. Lezneven, 1993.
Aubert, O.L. *Légendes Traditionelles de la Bretagne*. Saint Brieuc, 1946.
Bendix, R. Folklorism: The Challenge of a Concept. *International Folklore Review*, 6, pp. 5–15, 1988.
Brékilien, Y. *Autres Contes et Légendes du Pays Breton*. Spézet, 1994.
Bromwich, R. Cantre'r Gwaelod and Ker-Is. In C. Fox and B. Dickens (eds) *The Early Cultures of North West Europe*. Cambridge, 1950.
Bromwich, R. First Transmission to England and France. In R. Bromich, A.O.H. Jarman and B.F. Roberts (eds) *The Arthur of the Welsh*. Cardiff, 1991.
Dorson, R. Fakelore. *Zeitschrift fürVolkskunde* 65, pp. 56–64, 1969.
Georges, R.A. and Jones, M.O. *Folkloristics: An Introduction*. Bloomington, 1995.
Kuter, L. Breton Identity and Language—Three Surveys. *Bro Nevez* 50, p. 2. 1994.
La Villemarqué, T.C.H.H. *Myrdhimm, ou L'Enchanteur Merlin: Son Histoire, Son Oeuvres, Son Influence*. Paris, 1862.
Lebesque, Morvan. *Comment peut-on etre Breton? Essai sur la democratie Francaise*. Paris, 1970.

Le Scouëzec, G. *Histoires et Legendes de la Bretagne Mystereuse*. Paris, 1968.
McDonald. M. *We are not French!: Language, Culture and Identity in Brittany*. London, 1989.
Mayo, P.E. *The Roots of Identity: Three National Movements in Contemporary European Politics*. London, 1974.
Mordrel, O. *Breizh Atao: Histoire et Actualité du Nationalisme Breton*. Paris, 1973.
Philippe, J. *War Roudoù Merlin e Breizh*. Lezneven, 1986.
Rosenberg, B.A. *Folklore and Literature: Rival Siblings*. Knoxville, 1991.
Sebeok, T.A. (ed.) *Myth: A Symposium*. Bloomington, 1955.
Sébillot, P.Y. *Le Folklore de La Bretaigne, Tome Second*. Paris, 1968.
Zumwalt, R.L. The Literary Folklorists. In *American Folklore Scholarship*. Bloomington, 1988.

4

Contemporary Celtic Spirituality

MARION BOWMAN

The Celtic mists are swirling again. As this volume testifies, we are once again in the throes of a Celtic revival. It might be argued that it is essentially similar to its predecessors, but whereas Celts have in the past captured the imagination of antiquarians, Romantics, popular folklorists, artists, poets and minority interest groups, the present phenomenon is significantly more varied and broadly based.

This mass appeal and the extent of the commercialization and commodification of Celtic people, things and places (Bowman 1994) mean differences in scale and content. The *spiritual* aspects of this revival are also considerably more developed and varied than ever before (Bowman 1993, 1996), though the seeds of contemporary Celtic spirituality were sown at different points in the past. In this chapter I shall examine current views of what 'Celtic' means, set the spiritual scene to explain why it is particularly popular at this time, give some examples of the variety and vitality of contemporary Celtic spirituality and examine some of the issues raised by it, in particular 'authenticity'.

We know that a major reappraisal has been taking place, broadening the definition of 'Celtic' and what Celticity entails (e.g. Chapman 1992; Collis 1996). Historians, archaeologists, linguists, Celticists and other scholars may agonize and argue over this, but who or what constitutes Celtic at present is fluid, one might even say 'up for grabs'. The great Celtic Exhibition in Venice in 1991 presented the Celts as the first Europeans. Tim Sebastian, Chosen Chief of the Secular Order of Druids, is of the opinion that ultimately everyone in Britain is of Celtic descent;

but anyway, he claims, as Celtic describes culture not ethnicity anyone can 'tap into' Celticity. There has generally been an expansion of who or what might be perceived as Celtic, the term popularly embracing *all* Scots, Irish, Welsh, Manx, Cornish, Northumbrians, people from the West Country, Bretons and Galicians. Many people are rediscovering or actively searching for Celtic roots, or simply becoming what I have referred to elsewhere as 'Cardiac Celts'—people who feel in their hearts that they are Celtic (Bowman 1996). For increasingly, Celtic is coming to signify a quality, rather than a linguistic, ethnic or geographical connection. As one New Age magazine put it, 'Being a Celt is like nobility—a thing of spirit not of heritage'.

The current scramble for Celticity provides a fascinating example of 'elective affinity'. Of particular interest to me is the phenomenon of people regarding themselves as Celts for spiritual purposes, for the call of the Celts is being felt by a variety of spiritual searchers: Pagan, New Age and Christian. Writing as a scholar of contemporary religion, with an academic background in both Religious Studies and folklore, my focus is what people believe, and how those beliefs affect outlook and behaviour in everyday life. In making this point, I am signalling that in describing some aspects of contemporary Celtic spirituality, my role is neither justifier nor debunker, simply reporter. My examples are based on fieldwork and 'insider' literature. Much of what is said of Celts within Druid, Pagan, New Age and Christian circles would be unfamiliar (and possibly unacceptable) to scholars in Celtic Studies, linguistics, archaeology and related disciplines. Likewise, it is perhaps good for academics to remember that, particularly in the realms of belief, our 'expertise' is not necessarily valued. This is a context in which the Religious Studies usage of 'myth' as 'significant story' (regardless of considerations of truth) is particularly useful.

A frequently quoted maxim in Religious Studies is that 'God is real for Christians whether or not he exists' (Smart 1973, 54). Similarly, we might now say that the 'spiritual Celt' is real for a great variety of believers, whether he or she existed/exists. Celtic spirituality may be dismissed by experts as 'inauthentic' but it is nevertheless gaining considerable popularity. The interesting question is 'why?'.

Contemporary Spirituality

Increasingly, for a variety of reasons and in varying ways, the Celts are being seen as providers of a particularly attractive 'brand' of spirituality.

CONTEMPORARY CELTIC SPIRITUALITY

Many people in Britain, Ireland, Western Europe, North America, New Zealand, Australia and elsewhere are now putting considerable and genuine effort into being restorers, reclaimers, rediscoverers, re-establishers, reinventors of Celtic spirituality, or 'innovators' within it. To understand why this should be so, it will be helpful to look very briefly at some trends within contemporary Paganism, New Age and Christianity.

While many in the West are dissatisfied with conventional religion, considerable numbers nevertheless seek a spiritual element in their life. Terms like 'spiritual supermarket' and 'mix and match religion' are frequently used by commentators on late twentieth-century religiosity to indicate both the considerable choice available to the spiritual seeker and the trend towards individuals 'customizing' their religion. Never before have people had access to such a variety of religious beliefs, practices, traditions and artefacts *simultaneously*. Global communications and commodification allow us to browse in this spiritual supermarket where Hinduism, Buddhism, Islam and Christianity (each internally and geographically varied) appear on the shelf with new religious movements; contemporary Native American and Australian spiritual traditions sit alongside ancient, medieval and modern esoteric beliefs; Celtic, Norse, Greek and Egyptian gods and goddesses jostle for attention beside Jungian archetypes; dreamcatchers, didgeridoos, silver boughs, ritual knives, crystals, chalices, specialist books, magazines, tapes and videos all await consumption. In this post-modern emporium, Irish Catholic nuns 'spice up' their devotions with Buddhist meditation, Anglicans learn spiral dances, and Druids teach Neuro-Linguistic Programming.

In sharp contrast with the end of the nineteenth century, when there was considerable optimism about 'progress' and the coming triumphs of science and technology, there is a widespread sense at the end of the twentieth century that we have misused our resources, technology and opportunities to the detriment of society and the environment. However, there are those who feel sure that in the past our ancestors understood the symbiotic relationship of people and planet, were in tune with nature and each other, cherished the earth, were aware of the sacred in everyday life, and knew their place in the great scheme of things.

Contemporary western Pagans, for example, are now seeking to recover, reactivate or capture the spirit of their ancestral, pre-Christian 'native' traditions. A Canadian Pagan commented: 'I think of Wicca (contemporary witchcraft, also known as the Old Religion) as being European aboriginal, and I relate to that in a way that I think there's very much of a racial memory thing, I think it is there for us to reach out to'. There is also an element of the Western tradition reasserting itself. As one group of Scottish Pagans writes: 'We feel it is important to make people aware of the indigenous deities of these lands, rather than looking to foreign lands' (Clan Dalriada leaflet).

Although contemporary Paganism is immensely diverse (Harvey and Hardman 1996; Harvey 1997), many would empathize with the three principles of the Pagan Federation:

1. *Love for and kinship with nature*, rather than the more customary attitude of aggression and domination over Nature; reverence for the life force and its ever-renewing cycles of life and death.
2. *The Pagan ethic*: 'Do what thou wilt, but harm none'. This is a positive morality, not a list of thou-shalt-nots. Each individual is responsible for discovering his or her own true nature and developing it fully, in harmony with the outer world.
3. *Honouring both the female and the male aspects of the divine reality*, which transcend gender, without suppression of either the female or the male principle.

Undoubtedly one of the great attractions of Paganism is as 'green' religion. At a time when social and geographical mobility is at its greatest, there is a new topophilia which leads many to feel drawn to what are perceived as significant or sacred places, and (as, for example, in the case of road protest) to protect the earth from further ravages.

The New Age is another trend of considerable importance in the Celtic spiritual revival, although it is variously characterized (e.g. York 1995; Heelas 1996) and is notoriously difficult to define. Nevertheless, for our purposes, a number of key ideas can be outlined, which are influential within specifically New Age circles but which are also gaining acceptance in mainstream society and within various religious traditions. Many so-called 'New Age' ideas are not new and do not claim to be so. The most basic concept is that of a New Age, though when it will commence (if it has not already done so), how it will be brought about, and what it will be like are all matters for debate. Some, for example, see significance in the astrological move from Pisces (which, like early Christianity, has the fish as its symbol) to the Age of Aquarius. There is a view that we are at a time of incredible significance in the history of the world, a time of spiritual renaissance, when, having evolved physically, humanity is ready to evolve spiritually. It is claimed that ancient esoteric teachings are coming to light and new knowledge is reaching us from a variety of sources (including science, the paranormal, inspiration, channelling, past life memories, extra-terrestrials). A frequently quoted saying is that in Judaism we had 2,000 years of God the Father, in Christianity we had 2000 years of God the Son, and we are about to move into the age of the Spirit.

Of paramount importance in New Age thinking is the idea that each individual must take responsibility for his or her own spiritual wellbeing, and embark on his or her own individual quest. Religion cannot be left to religious professionals; this is the age of spiritual DIY (Do It Yourself), using whatever 'spiritual tools' (as religious artefacts, ideas and practices are referred to) 'work' for you. A corollary of this is that, as you are on a progressive journey, your quest is dynamic; what 'works' for you at one point may not always do so, or you may simply wish to keep adding to your spiritual toolbox.

Other influential ideas which recur in New Age discourse but which have also gained wider currency include 'interconnectedness' (between all beings, seen and unseen; between people and planet; between past and present); synchronicity or meaningful coincidence; a particular understanding of reincarnation ('in every life a lesson' is a common maxim); the need for healing at both microcosmic and macrocosmic level; the notion that spirituality and money need not be mutually exclusive. It is vital to do what 'feels right', for, it is believed, intuition has been undervalued, ignored or over-ruled for too long and to humanity's detriment.

Turning briefly to Christianity, many feel that the millennium is of considerable significance, either as a marker of the last days, or as a time of potential spiritual change and renewal. The growth of the charismatic movement and phenomena like the 'Toronto Blessing' (reminiscent of the early days of the Quakers and Methodists) indicate a desire for more experiential forms of Christianity, and a return to the early Church. While some Christians are attracted to fundamentalism, there is growing Christian participation in both ecumenical and interfaith activity. Nevertheless, many mainstream denominations have been losing members, in the wake of social change or scandals, or because the Church simply has not seemed relevant to modern life; this is part of the trend towards 'believing without belonging' (Davie 1994). However, even Christians who have stayed within different branches of the Church have been feeling some dissatisfaction on various counts, because the Church seems too remote from everyday life, too impersonal, too ritualistic, too institutional, too 'worldly', too hierarchical, too patriarchal, not 'green' enough or whatever. Many Christians feel that somehow the 'vital spark' has been lost, and that, although they maintain their traditional denominational allegiance, they feel the need for some sort of revival, to recapture the purity and vitality of 'authentic' Chrisitianity.

Piggott writes, in relation to the history of ideas, of 'a recurrent series of speculations which seem to arise in civilized communities as the result of a subconscious guilty recognition of the inadequacy of the contemporary social order, and involve the concept of simpler and more satisfactory systems, remote either in time (Golden Ages in the past), or in place (Noble Savages at or beyond the edges of contemporary geographical knowledge)' (1981, 30). Many contemplating late twentieth-century life in the West are undoubtedly recognizing such 'inadequacy', whether for social, humanitarian, economic, environmental or religious reasons. Enter the Celts.

Celts—traditionally people on the fringes, patronized, pitied, insulted, laughed at for being outside the mainstream—have increasingly become regarded as Noble Savages, less tainted by the ills of modern life, repositories of a spirituality, a sense of tradition, a oneness with nature that has elsewhere been lost. The Celtic period (however it is dated) has become a Golden Age, the Celtic areas looked to as havens of spirituality. In order to deal with contemporary malaise, some people seek to model themselves on the Noble Savages and recover that Golden Age. The stereotypical Celt has once again emerged as more spiritual, more intuitive, more in touch with hidden realms, more in touch with nature, more egalitarian than others; as we know, this stereotype is not new, but it is certainly influential.

There are different ways of seeking and participating in this Celtic idyll. At the popular/commercial level, there is Highland Mysteryworld in Scotland, 'where the ancient mysteries of the Highlands are energised before your eyes', and you can make a wish at a newly constructed Cloutie Well. In Wales, at Machynlleth you can 'Experience the Mysterious and Magical World of the Celts' at Celtica. In the present climate, Celtic sells. A spokesman for the bookstore chain Waterstones commented in a radio interview that books with the word 'Celtic' in their titles simply 'fly off the shelves'. Shops such as Wilde Celts provide 'Pan Celtic Art inspired by the Golden Age of Celtic Creativity' in the form of books, cards, crafts, music and Celtic jewellery, featuring 'Designs from Wales, Ireland, Cornwall, The Hebridean, Shetland and Orkney Isles and wherever Celtic craftworkers continue the art of their forebears' (Advertisement, *Pagan Dawn*, 125 Samhain 1997, 33). The general market (including Celtic watches, Celtic mousemats, Celtic ties, and the wonderfully ambiguous 'Celtic Spirit Flask') overlaps with the specialist Celtic spiritual market (Bowman 1994), which includes any number of courses and workshops on different schools of Druidry, Celtic Paganism, Celtic Christianity and Celtic spirituality generally. Both provide people with means of expressing a love of or affinity with things Celtic.

The Creation of the Spiritual Celt

Glassie cautions that 'tradition is the creation of the future out of the past', and that history 'is an artful assembly of materials from the past, designed for usefulness in the future' (1995, 395). What we are witnessing in contemporary Celtic spirituality is an 'artful assembly of materials' not simply from the Celtic past (whenever and however that is dated), but from previous periods of interest in and speculation about Celts, as well as historical and contemporary religious trends.

In order to understand how different images of Celts are being constructed, the metaphor of the 'identikit Celt' might be employed. Just as in an 'identikit' different features are taken from a variety of pictures and are then combined to produce the image desired, so it is useful to review a variety of the 'snapshots' of the Celts and Celticity which are currently being used to provide some of the elements of the 'identikit Celt'.

Many scholarly summaries of the classical sources on Celts have appeared in recent years (e.g. Chapman 1992; Collis 1996; Piccini 1996; Green 1997). Of interest here, however, are the many stereotypes taken from this literature which have contributed to the present view of the Celts, including their passionate nature, their love of ornamentation, their bravery and bravado, their high-spiritedness, and so on. However, it is probably the Druids, their priestly caste, connected with mistletoe, oak, golden sickles, esoteric learning and (rather more controversial, and variously interpreted) human sacrifice,[1] who are most eagerly sought from this literature. I have been assured by a Druid that in the 1980s a hoard of golden sickles was uncovered at Stonehenge, 'proving' the connection between Druidry and Stonehenge; this was 'hushed up' by the authorities opposing the rights of Druids to have free access to the site at festival times for ceremonial purposes. There are estimated to be more than twenty different Druid groups active in Britain and Ireland today, with many more in Europe, North America and elsewhere. The Druids of Ecole Druidique des Gaules 'believe that, on the deep roots of Druidry,

Europe could be rebuilt, and that the spirituality of the Celts is the only one which represents the collective Indo-European heritage common to all Europe' (Shallcrass 1995, 22).

Another contribution to the identikit Celt emerges in relation to native peoples. Piggott (1989) argues that many sixteenth- and seventeenth-century views of ancient Britons and Celts were gained not from looking at contemporary Celts but from accounts and illustrations of Native Americans and other encounters with indigenous peoples. He demonstrates how pictures of native peoples influenced artists' impressions of ancient Britons. Here we have an important element in the current construction of Celts and Celtic spirituality: the assumption that Britain's native religion was and is akin to the beliefs and practices of Native Americans and Australians, and indeed any other indigenous or tribal group.[2] There is an assumption in some circles that whatever is present among contemporary native peoples must have been part of Celtic spirituality. Thus Celtic shamanism enjoys great popularity, with related books (e.g. Matthews 1997), workshops and training sessions,[3] and there are Druidic sweat lodges. The groom at a Druidic handfasting at Avebury wore a long white robe with a didgeridoo slung on one shoulder throughout the ceremony. As an English informant 'with Celtic blood' who attended a Native American weekend workshop commented, it is 'very close to the Celtic thing'; 'When it comes to spirituality, it's all the same in the end'. Whereas in the past this connection between native peoples and ancient Britons was made largely to help reconstruct the past for historical, antiquarian or archaeological purposes, the present connections are being made to expand and enrich the practice of what is perceived as Celtic native spirituality.

The eighteenth century was of course a great era of speculation about Druids, Celts and ancient Britain. The current explosion of interest in Druidry and Druidic activity undoubtedly owes much to such characters of that era as William Stukeley (with his *Stonehenge: A Temple Restor'd to the British Druids* of 1740 and his theories of Druids as proto-Christians), architect John Wood the Elder (with his attempted 'reconstruction' of the ancient British city of Bath, the 'Metropolitan Seat' of the British Druids), and William Blake, for whom 'All things Begin and End in Albion's Ancient Druid Rocky Shore'. There are those who see in the current Celtic and Druidic revival the trickle down to popular level of ideas which started to be 'revealed' in the eighteenth century. Some have been attracted to the city of Bath, for example, because of its Druidic connections. In 1997 on 28 November (William Blake's birthday) a ceremony organized by the Secular Order of Druids was performed in John Wood's Circus, which, it was explained, was based on the dimensions of Stonehenge and Stanton Drew (Mowl and Earnshaw 1988) and intended for such ritual; an Archdruid, Bard and Ovate of Caer Badon (Bath's 'Celtic name') were declared at this Gorsedd.

An important but frequently overlooked contribution to the image of Celts and Druids has been made by Theosophy. Among the ideas put forward by H.P. Blavatsky and her followers were the existence of an ancient wisdom tradition, esoteric in character but manifest through exoteric religious traditions; the existence of adepts or masters of the wisdom; channelling of this wisdom to those attuned to receive it; reincarnation and Karma; an evolution of the spirit undergirding physical evolution; a vision of universal brotherhood (Tingay, 1998). Many of the figures involved in the Celtic revival of the late nineteenth and early twentieth centuries had Theosophical connections, including W.B. Yeats, George Russell (pseudonym 'AE'), John Duncan, William Sharp (pseudonym Fiona Macleod) and Patrick Geddes. Michael McGrath, Archdruid of Tara and Ireland, has written of the Druids:

> Some were sent on across fifteen centuries on a sacred mission to this time and place for the benefit of humanity, bearing the Holy Grail of Druidry just hidden, never quite lost, to a whole new generation. The Door of Druidry is now open to all across the planet. You have only to step through to find out. It is significant that after fifteen centuries the Spirit of Druidry is revived universally. Once again the sacred flame is lit and sitting around it we can hear those Masters of the Universe whisper in our ear. (*The Druids' Voice*, Summer 1997, 35)

The reasoning and comparisons which equated contemporary 'primitives' with Celts received renewed impetus in the nineteenth century with ideas of cultural evolution and the 'survivals' theory of folklore, a legacy which continues in contemporary religiosity (Bowman 1995). Of considerable importance was the revived interest in Celtic legend and folklore. Irish, Scottish Gaelic and Welsh texts had been the object of study (and occasional forgery) in previous centuries, and the curious ways of the folk had been commented on by antiquarians. However, the conscious search for 'survivals' and active desire to 'reconstruct' led to a new bout of confident assertions (as opposed to tentative suggestions) about the beliefs and lifestyle of the Celts, and for some reinforced the desirability of a Celtic revival. As one Pagan group asserts, 'Writers such as AE, W.B. Yeats, Lady Gregory and Fiona MacLeod painstakingly worked on translations of manuscripts, collected folklore and helped to piece back together the Celtic system' (Clan Dalriada leaflet).

Alice and Lawrence Gomme, writing on British folklore, remarked:

> in every society there are people who do not progress either in religion or in polity with the foremost of the nation. They are left stranded amidst the progress. They live in out-of-the-way villages, or in places where general culture does not penetrate easily; they keep to old ways, practices, and ideas, following with religious awe all their parents had held to be necessary to their lives. These people are living depositories of ancient history—a history that has not been written down, but which has come down by tradition. Knowing the conditions of survivals in culture, the folklorist uses them in the ancient meaning, not in their modern setting, tries to find out their significance and importance in relation to their origin, and thus lays the foundation for the science of folklore. (1916, 10)

The academic study of folklore may have moved on, but such reasoning is very evident in much of the current literature on and discussion of Celtic spirituality, and many of the books cited tend to be reprints of works from the late nineteenth and early twentieth centuries, particularly early Celtic mythology collections.

This by no means exhaustive survey of sources of images of the Celts is intended to underline the fact that what we are seeing in contemporary Celtic spirituality has elements from a number of disparate standpoints, and that we have to some extent been here before. Such images, coupled with the late twentieth-century religious trends already outlined, provide any number of options for the aspiring spiritual Celt. Space forbids detailed examination of the many different forms of contemporary Celtic spirituality, but a brief overview of some aspects of it will demonstrate the immense variety of practice, theory, outlook and assumptions involved in it, and why Celtic scholars are almost inevitably bound to have problems with it.

Celtic Paganism

For many Pagans, pre-Christian, Celtic Europe generally is regarded as a Golden Age. However, not only is contemporary Paganism diverse, Celtic Paganism itself is very varied, including Wicca, Druidry, the

Western Occult Tradition, specialist groups such as Clan Dalriada (a Pagan group on the Scottish island of Arran, who have 'dedicated their lives to living and working the Celtic Gaelic system of the Bronze Age'), and individuals who mix their own Celtic cocktail.

Wicca, also known as witchcraft or the Old Religion, is one of the largest groups within contemporary Western Paganism. Many Wiccans believe that they are practising the 'Old Religion' which preceded Christianity in Europe and was preserved (though persecuted at the time of the witchcraft trials) to be revived by Gerald Gardner in the 1940s. Although this claim of an unbroken tradition is challenged both by scholars and some Wiccans (Harvey and Hardman 1995; Crowley 1989; Hutton 1991), what is important is the practitioners' perception that they are involved in ancient Celtic religion.

Most Celtic Pagans try to reconnect both with the Celtic past and with nature through keeping what is known as the '8-fold' or Celtic calendar. This 'Wheel of the Year', as it is frequently known, consists of Samhain (31 October), winter solstice, Imbolc (1/2 February), spring equinox, Beltane (30 April/1 May), midsummer solstice, Lughnasadh or Lammas (31 July/1 August), and autumn equinox. Customs and rituals are being 'revived', rediscovered or invented in observing this calendar: in Glastonbury, for example, some women celebrate Imbolc, 'the festival of Brighde, the Triple Fire Goddess' by making 'traditional Brighde Crosses' and 'Brighde Dolls', Pagan well-dressing has been introduced at Beltane, and a Mother Goddess figure is taken on a ceremonial journey round town at Lughnasadh. 'Celtic camps' and courses are often also held at these significant times.

Druids

For many, Celtic spirituality 'par excellence' is to be found in Druidry, which is likewise immensely varied, ranging from the Cotswold Order of Druids who declare that 'Druidry is not a hobby; it is a vocation' (*The Druids' Voice*, Summer 1997, 33), to the Berengaria Order of Druids 'dedicated to the aims, ideals and whatever else of Star Trek ... and Babylon 5 ..., plus any other sci-fi that takes our fancy' (*The Druids' Voice*, Summer 1997, 31).

Naturally the Celtic past is important to Druids. One of the aims of the Insular Order of Druids (whose founder 'practices the shamanic arts of body piercing and tattooing at Labyrinth, a New Age gift shop and centre for Celtic spirituality in Portsmouth') is 'to spread and encourage interest in Celticism, and the general knowledge of our heritage and lore, poems and myths and anything Celtically cultural'. However, as Druidry is seen as a living phenomenon, another aim is 'to recreate to the best of their knowledge authentic Celtic ritual, minus the bloodshed, within the framework of 20th century law and ethics, in a working form relevant for today' (Shallcrass 1995, 26).

The Charnwood Grove of Druids

> see Druidry as a modern adaptation of our native British spirituality which addresses contemporary problems and dilemmas in a manner that is uniquely suited to our needs.... We believe that people working together are capable of raising power which can balance and heal the Earth. We focus our energy at local sacred sites and we honour the Celtic god and goddess forms as personifications of the land and the seasons. We seek inspiration from our ancestors and we work with traditional Celtic symbols, myths and the tree ogham to reveal the power of our inner guides and totems. (*The Druids' Voice*, Summer 1997, 33)

The Secular Order of Druids 'seeks to enhance the modern-day relevance of Druidry by reviving folk traditions and by taking Druidry to "raves"' (*The Druid's Voice*, Summer 1997, 35–6). While the scholarly view of Druidry tends to be of something that existed in the past about which we have some information through particular sources, for many practising Druids it is a living tradition. As the British Druid Order declares:

> We draw inspiration from the sacred land and from our ancestry; the mud and blood of Britain, whose myths and mysteries are the well-spring of our tradition.... Although we work with the long spiritual and cultural heritage of Britain, we are not bound by any one aspect of it. We are not seeking to recreate a Druidry that may have existed 5000, 2000, 200 or 50 years ago. We see Druidry as a process of constant change and renewal whereby the tradition is continually recreated to address the needs of each generation. (*The Druid's Voice*, Summer 1997, 31)

Moreover, not only is 'post source' Druidry a matter for speculation and experimentation, but 'pre source' Druidry is reflected upon to help our understanding of it. As one OBOD (Order of Bards Ovates and Druids) publication records:

Some say that the Druids came from Atlantis—that the white magicians, sensing impending destruction, travelled westwards to the Americas and eastwards to the shores of Ireland and Britain. Here, blending with the megalithic culture, whose stone circles continue to inspire us, their wisdom was carried through to the celtic peoples who enabled Druidry to develop in a way that has been reported to us by the classical scholars. (OBOD *Gwyers Two*)

Druids and Christians

In many circles, it is part of contemporary belief that the unique nature of Celtic Christianity owed much to the fact that it preserved a body of esoteric wisdom, known to Druids but unknown to other branches of Christianity; some claim, for example, that Celtic Christians, like Druids, believed in reincarnation. Many maintain that the Druids anticipated the coming of Christianity, and that in certain Celtic areas the transition from the Old Religion to the new was essentially smooth. There is frequently the assumption that wherever there is evidence of Celtic Christianity, it would have been preceded by Druidry. Tim Sebastian of the Secular Order of Druids has commented:

> if you go to the history of Iona, yes, you could say that Druidism, or the old Pagan spirit, the spirit of Albion, died there, but really that's not true; the Druidic colleges were merely replaced by Christian cells.... There was, it would appear, absolutely no conflict between the early Celtic Christian tradition and the Pagan, or Druidic tradition. (Shallcrass 1995, 39)

Kaledon Naddair, through his Edinburgh-based College of Druidism, offers to train people as Druids/Druidesses or Culdee Priests/Priestesses.

It has become 'common knowledge' that Glastonbury was a great Druidic centre of learning. John Michell, describing Glastonbury as 'the citadel of Celtic esotericism' (1978, 167), not only claims that 'Glastonbury Abbey was built as the spiritual successor of Stonehenge, to exactly the same hidden plan as the monument on Salisbury Plain' (1969, 31), but that this was 'the same plan and to fulfil the same function as the archetypal "holy city" described by Plato and St John [in Revelation]' (1978, 163). He adds that St John 'is said to have been an initiate into the Celtic mysteries' (1978, 166).

Celtic Christianity

For many Christians, Celtic Christianity tends to be seen as more spiritual, more intuitive, more egalitarian, more in tune with nature than other brands of Christianity—all qualities that are felt by many to be missing from the institutionalized Church. Just as early Protestants wanted to recover 'pure' Christianity, many now want to 'recapture' the 'authentic' Christian spirituality of the Celtic Church. How that Celtic Christianity can best be recaptured, exactly what it was, and who can rightfully claim to be the heirs of Celtic Christianity are, however, all matters for debate (see Meek 1992, 1996, 1997).

Celtic Christianity tends to be characterized as gentle, 'green', meditative, holistic Christianity. Shirley Toulson, for example, claims that 'if we want to understand the depths of Celtic spirituality we shall find the nearest parallels in the Buddhist teaching[4] of today as well as in the creation spirituality of such Christian teachers as Matthew Fox' (1996, 15). Celtic paraphernalia (such as Celtic crosses, Celtic prayers and merchandise decorated with Celtic motifs and Celtic lettering) have become increasingly popular in British cathedral and church shops. In Christian denominations which have robes or ecclesiatical embroidery, Celtic motifs (particularly Celtic crosses) are increasingly appearing.[5] There is undoubtedly an element of religious Euroscepticism in this: a number of people have spoken to me of the Celtic Church as 'our roots' or 'our native Christianity' before Roman Christianity 'was imposed on us'. A staunch Presbyterian commented 'You and I both know that if the Church of Rome hadn't taken over the Celtic Church, there probably would have been no need for the Reformation'. I was recently told by a lapsed Anglican that Henry VIII's 'real plan' was to restore the Celtic Church, but it all got horribly subverted.

Indicative of the topophilia already mentioned, Iona has become important for a great variety of Christians, a place of spiritual refreshment and a protestant pilgrimage destination. For many, the Iona Community seems to have become an icon of Celtic spirituality. Iona provides 'a kind of corridor between Presbyterianism and Anglicanism' (Meek 1992, 22); its ecumenism is taken to be a reflection of Celtic Christianity which is perceived as relaxed and gentle, not bogged down in internal division. An ecumenical group in Glastonbury was 'inspired' by the Iona Community, as an example of 'true British Chrisitianity'. The use of Iona Community songs, prayers, etc. is felt by a variety of denominations to add 'a Celtic flavour' to worship. Thus in Bath, Manvers Street

Baptist Church has its Tuesday lunchtime 'Iona Worship', advertised by notices decorated with a Celtic cross, and parties from the church visit Iona every year.[6]

Language and Nationalism

Some see language as one of the main indicators of Celticness, and, obviously, much of the literature drawn upon by the various spiritual searchers in Celtic spirituality was originally in Celtic languages. It is therefore unsurprising that issues of language and nationalism can become contentious. Kaledon Naddair of the Scottish College of Druidism deplores most English Druidry, dismissing it as 'an English cover version' of the real thing, for example, while one English Druid described Welsh Druidry as 'racist' because of its insistence on the use of Welsh language.

It is acknowledged in Wales that while for many Welshness/Celticity is deeply rooted in the Welsh language, English-speaking Welsh people are left in an ambivalent situation. This can be further exacerbated by outsiders with strong views on the role of language, such as one American Pagan Welsh-language enthusiast who claims that the non-Welsh-speaking Welsh are not 'real' Welsh: 'They have forfeited their heritage'. Similarly, if there are certain Celtic expectations of Scotland, some natives will find themselves judged not to be 'real' Scots. One recent example of this potential confusion between language, Celticity and Scottishness occurred in an interview with Peter Berresford Ellis in which he is reported as saying:

> I would say, if you're interested in things Celtic, you've got to start with being interested in the culture ... you've got to see where this is coming from and not go down the bypath of 'Celtic' without reference to the Celtic people. Anyone can set themselves up and buy a kilt and wander about saying 'I'm a Scot,' but unless you speak Scots Gaelic, unless you're interested in things culturally Scottish, then, you know, you're just a joke. (*Keltria* 27, Fall 1995, p. 11)

The majority of Scots can quite legitimately say 'I'm a Scot' and be interested in things culturally Scottish without any reference to the Gaelic language.[7]

While language may be an issue for some, and many are learning Celtic languages to enable them to read material in the original or to express solidarity with the Celtic people, for the most part it is the message not the medium which is considered important. To some extent, Celtic-language material is being regarded in the same way as other previously 'hidden knowledge' which is now surfacing. Meek uses the example of the cover notes of Robert Van de Weyer's *Celtic Fire* (1990)—'Composed in languages long extinct, Celtic literature has been inaccessible for many centuries'—to make the point that 'Both these claims—about the extinction of the Celtic languages and the inaccessibility of the literature—are manifestly incorrect. What they do tell us is that Celtic literature is falling into the hands of some people who know nothing about its background, and assume that nobody else does either' (1992, 14). As one informant in Glastonbury said:

> There's something there, a wonderful ambience, and we can localise it as no one is sure who the Celts really were. It doesn't matter about strict historicity—it sets up a wonderful warm glow of hope, helps you feel more integrated. What we need in the West is a Celtic renaissance.

Centre and Periphery

It has frequently been argued that classical authors frequently tell us as much about themselves and their attitudes to 'others' as the people notionally described. As Piccini (1996, 88) comments, 'Characteristic of many of these descriptions is the way in which the Celts are always cast in opposition to the dominant cultural personae of Greece and Rome'. Chapman (1992) has also made the point that much of what has been said of the Celts at various periods is the designation of the centre on the periphery, and we can undoubtedly see elements of that now in relation to Celtic spirituality. Ian Bradley writes in *The Celtic Way* (1993, 30)

> The great upsurge of interest in Celtic Christianity in recent years can be compared to the re-evaluation of the religious beliefs of other peoples who have lived on the margins like the Australian Aborigines and the Native Indians of North America. It reflects a realisation that what is primitive and simple can also be profound and highly original.

Pamela Constantine, of the New Romantic Movement, has written:

> I think the reason there is such a Celtic Revival is because the human

spirit has been restricted so long by a society in which science and materialism and profit motive predominate. It has been dammed up and is now urgent for expression. It seems to me the Celts have a natural ability to reopen the 'magic casements' and to help people reconnect with the lost dimensions of themselves.

People who write or think in this way are honouring the people and traditions of which they speak; there is an extent to which the Celts are being looked to as spiritual midwives and role models. But might there not be the implication that Celts ('stranded amidst the progress') have not been exposed to science, materialism and profit motive? Would Celtic Christians, as Donald Meek (1996) points out, really have seen themselves as marginal, primitive and simple? The remedy for dissatisfaction with the present is being sought in a particular (some would say distorted) reflection of the past; the antidote to dissatisfaction with the mainstream is being sought in the margins.

However, although Celtic is being used in some contexts as code for 'long ago and far away' and Celts are being honoured as Noble Savages, Celtic lands and those being designated Celts are not distant in time and space. Indeed, many people are flocking to 'Celtic' destinations. At the intersection of 'Cardiac Celt' and conventional Celt, there is the possibility of friction; one may see a kindred spirit, the other a cultural imperialist or cultural transvestite. John Davies, a Welsh Pagan, has forcefully expressed some of his reservations and exasperation in this respect:

> I do not wish to see Ireland marketed for its sad air of the uncanny, when that is because it is full of ghosts; the ghosts of the million who starved to death in the famine of 1846/7, while the English went on exporting corn from Ireland.... I do not wish to see the empty landscape of the Hebrides extolled for its beauty, when it is empty because of brutal clearances.
>
> I do not wish to see you create a homogenised pabulum of Celtic culture, first ignoring the difference between the Goidelic and Brythonic strains, then going on to ignore every other important distinction....
>
> I do not wish to encounter hordes of eager-eyed acolytes who don't know the first thing about the reality of Wales. I do not wish to meet their teacher; some self-appointed Saxon expert on Celtia, whose tongue stumbles over the simplest Welsh place-names.

> I do not wish to see the less acceptable aspects of my ancestors glossed over, in order to create yet another sanitized 'noble savage' for your consumption....
>
> Worst of all, if you lecture us earnestly about our own heritage you will offend us badly. I wonder if that matters to you?

Authenticity

There is no doubt that a great number of people consider their spiritual lives enriched and enhanced by Celtic spirituality. Some of those attracted by and involved in it are interested in original sources, and do serious research on the archaeological evidence, languages, literature and cultural traditions. Others, however, would find such activity pointless. One of the major problems some scholars have with contemporary Celtic spirituality in its myriad forms is that they see it as inaccurate and inauthentic. However, from the foregoing it should be becoming obvious that ideas of authenticity will be tricky or impossible to pin down, for the criteria of authenticity and modes of authenticating which are operating in the various forms of contemporary Celtic spirituality are not necessarily located in the Celtic past nor available for empirical scrutiny. They are more often situated in the traits of late twentieth-century religiosity outlined above.

Caitlin Matthews writes of practitioners of Celtic spiritual traditions:

> Celtic ethnicity is not necessarily a prerequisite, as might be imagined. We have entered a phase of maturity wherein *spiritual lineage* transcends blood lineage. The impulse for joining such groups often springs from exposure to the lands of Britain and Ireland, or from reading stories and myths deriving from Celtic tradition. A sense of belonging is also often felt from perceived memory of previous incarnation. (1993, 7)

Being or feeling Celtic is something that can be acquired, from contact with the land, or from encountering some aspect of Celtic cultural tradition—a sort of contagious Celticity.

People visiting what are perceived to be 'Celtic' destinations, whether Ireland, Scotland, Wales and Cornwall in general, or more specifically Iona, Glastonbury, Lindisfarne, Stonehenge, Bath and Avebury, often comment on the 'feel' or 'energy' of such places. There is thus the authenticating nature of the experience of place. 'Spirituality is inherent in nature', Pennick claims, 'It has not gone away; it is still there for anyone who seeks it. Where it continues in existence, the Celtic sacred landscape serves to remind us that there are viable alternatives to the spiritual Wasteland' (1996, 180).

Matthews's comment on the perceived memory of previous incarnation is also extremely significant. Ideas of reincarnation are being used by some to explain or express their current feelings of Celticity. One American told me that as soon as he went to Scotland, he realized he had been a Scot in a past life. At what was presented as a 'Traditional Celtic Wedding' in Glastonbury, the groom, who wore stylized Highland dress,[8] declared that as soon as he had put on his costume, he felt strongly that he had looked liked this in a previous existence.

There is also a belief in 'karmic clusters', which implies that people who were together in a previous existence reincarnate together in later lives. Thus the Loyal Arthurian Warband (LAW), a group which campaigns for open access to Stonehenge, is led by Arthur Pendragon, who feels he is a reincarnation of King Arthur. Of the three degrees within LAW—Shield, Quest and Brother Knight—the Shield Knights 'have reverted to their once, true and former name, being the Fellowship of the Table Round, reincarnated Dark Age Celtic warriors, renewing their brotherhood to reunite the Celtic nation in its time of greatest need' (Shallcrass 1995, 29–30).

If reincarnation is connected with going back to the past for an explanation of the present, we should remember that much of what is being said about the Celtic past is the result of channelling, which is largely about the past coming to the present, a way of being authoritative about the past in the present, and experiencing the past in the present. The Insular Order of Druids believes that 'As Druidry is a growing movement ... the channelling of new Druidic information is of paramount importance'. Thus, at their meetings, you will not only 'hear genuine Celtic stories told in the Bardic way. You will hear new channelled material' (Shallcrass 1995, 27). Channelled material tends to come in the language of the receiver, regardless of the supposed transmitter.

For the scholar of Celtic literature there are concerns of dating, provenance, authorship, authenticity and so on. For the practitioner, Celtic myths and legends, or material derived from them, are read for clues to the beliefs, lifestyles and world-views of the Celts. They can also have a far more active role. Matthews compares the use of such material to Ignatian Spiritual Exercises:

traditional stories and myths are memorised and retold, not in any pretentious folkloric way, but as living pathways of spiritual wisdom. The spiritual beings encountered in these scenarios give actual teaching and often provide otherworldly and ancestral guidance to those bereft of ordinary reality tutors. By meditative interface with these stories, the Celtic tradition is passed on. (1993, 7)

This internalized, interactive transmission is not something which lends itself to scholarly checking, nor can we 'ordinary reality tutors' expect to be regarded as authoritative when Kaledon Naddair says of his Keltic Shamanistic Calendar that it 'represents many years of Research into our Native Tradition, plus personal Initiation by the Faerie Wildfolk'.

Conclusion

A variety of spiritual seekers consider that the Celts are providing inspiration, motivation and exhilaration in their religious lives. The 'spiritual Celt' is real, whether or not he or she exists/ existed. However, this 'spiritual Celt' has many and varied roots and takes myriad forms, being a product of the 'collage' approach of late twentieth-century religiosity.

Among the issues raised by this phenomenon are the post-modern approach to history and religion and the perception that there is no one version of 'Truth'; the tension between nationalism and globalization; the relationship between centre and periphery; perceptions of cultural imperialism and 'transvestism'; the creation and recreation of the self. Celtic has moved from being 'out there' to 'in here'.

Scholars may find many aspects of contemporary Celtic spirituality non-authentic or non-empirical but that does not negate it as a *religious* phenomenon. Myths remain significant stories, regardless of whether they are true or false. What needs to be understood is that it is not about then (the Celtic past), it is about now; it is not about them (the Celts), it is about us. Celtic spirituality is a complex, colourful and contentious part of the contemporary spiritual scene.

Notes

1. Some modern Druids simply deny that there was ever any human sacrifice, claiming stories of it were 'smear tactics' to discredit enemies. Others claim that the sacrifice would have been of a willing victim, for whom it was a great honour.

2. At the popular level this has been reflected in films like *Braveheart*, with Wallace and his followers in warpaint, and *Rob Roy* with its introductory music sounding suspiciously like Native American chant. Meanwhile, in addition to the workshops on fiddling and traditional dance offered at the 1997 Celtic Connections Folk Festival, there was one on 'How to decorate your didgeridoo'.
3. Welsh Pagan author John Davies does not share the current enthusiasm for Celtic shamanism, as demonstrated in this trenchant criticism:
   I doubt if it is possible to become a 'Celtic shaman', and it is a mistake to try. Because if you do; if you come to Wales (as I fear you may), wearing beads, and funny hats adorned with feathers and pieces of stick; if you come laden with rattles and spirit callers and suchlike paraphernalia; if you come following an expensive workshop leader who can't even pronounce, let alone speak, any Welsh; whose only qualifications are a set of distinctly cranky ideas, assembled from fragments torn loose from our heritage and a hotpotch of others; plus, of course, a fast line in chat to convince you that this system offers instant enlightenment at a price (the fast-food version of spirituality); then you will be obvious for the fool you are. (1993)
4. Connections between Buddhism and Celtic spirituality are often made, both directly and indirectly. The Tibetan Buddhists of Samye Ling monastery in southern Scotland have purchased as a place of retreat Holy Isle (off the Scottish island of Arran), said to have been inhabited by a Celtic saint. The FWBO (Friends of the Western Buddhist Order) in Ireland seem to be self-consciously 'Celticizing' with, for example, the wearing of green cloaks in the shrine room.
5. *The Grapevine* (official newspaper of the Anglican diocese of Bath and Wells) for January 1998 (8 (1) p.10), for example, reported 'A Celtic theme for new vestments for St. Andrew's, Cheddar was chosen by their designer Janet Knox to "compliment the Church and its very long history"'. They include a set 'embroidered with versions of the four evangelists described in the Revelation of St John and in the style of Celtic manuscripts'.
6. As Meek points out, 'Members of relatively old denominations and religious bodies such as Baptists, historically hostile to monasticism, wary of liturgies, and suspicious of symbols such as crosses, are prepared to accommodate these elements into their "Celtic" experiments' (1996, 153).
7. At the Stirling University conference 'Contemporary Innovations in Religion in Scotland' in 1998, one of the points made was that at this time of increasing pluralism in Scotland (with Moslem Scots, Scottish Buddhists, Hindu Scots, etc.) it is important that 'Scottishness' is increasingly *inclusive*, not narrowly exclusive. With examples of Scottish Sikhs, Muslims and even statues of Krishna dressed in tartan, this is not the time to be proscriptive as to who should feel free to wear a kilt.
8. The bride on this occasion wore a long cream lace dress, with a length of royal

Stewart tartan draped over one shoulder; the bridesmaid was dressed as a fairy, complete with wings.

References

Journals and Magazines
Keltria
Grapevine
Pagan Dawn

Books and Articles
Bowman, M. Reinventing the Celts. *Religion*, 23, pp. 147–56, 1993.
Bowman, M. The Commodification of the Celt: New Age/Neo-Pagan Consumerism. *Folklore in Use*, 2 (1) pp. 143–52, 1994.
Bowman, M. The Noble Savage and the Global Village: Cultural Evolution in New Age and Neo-Pagan Thought. *Journal of Contemporary Religion*, 10 (2) pp. 139–49, 1995.
Bowman, M. Cardiac Celts: Images of the Celts in Contemporary British Paganism. In G. Harvey and C. Hardman (eds) *Paganism Today*. London, 1996.
Bradley, I. *The Celtic Way*. London, 1993.
Chapman, M. *The Celts: The Construction of a Myth*. London, 1992.
Collis, J. The Origin and Spread of the Celts. *Studia Celtica*, 30, pp. 17–34, 1996.
Crowley, V. *Wicca: The Old Religion in the New Age*. London, 1989.
Davie, G. *Religion in Britain Since 1945*. London, 1994.
Davies, J. *Three Things There Are, That Are Seldom Heard: A Comment on Modern Shamanism*. House of the Goddess, 1993.
Glassie, H. Tradition. *Journal of American Folklore*, 108 (430) pp. 395–412, 1995.
Gomme, L. and A. *British Folk-Lore, Folk Songs, and Singing Games*. National Home-Reading Union, 1916.
Green, M. *Exploring the World of the Druids*. London, 1997.
Harvey, G. *Listening People, Speaking Earth*. London, 1997.
Harvey, G. and Hardman, C. (eds) *Paganism Today*. London, 1996.
Heelas, P. *The New Age Movement*. Oxford, 1996.
Hutton, R. *The Pagan Religions of the Ancient British Isles*. Oxford, 1991.
Kiberd, D. *Inventing Ireland*. London, 1995.
Matthews, C. A Celtic Quest. *World Religions in Education*, pp. 6–9, 1993/4.
Matthews, J. *The Celtic Shaman: A Handbook*. Shaftesbury, 1997.
Meek, D.E. Modern Celtic Christianity: The Contemporary Revival and its Roots. *Scottish Bulletin of Evangelical Theology*, 10 (1) pp. 6–31, 1992.
Meek, D.E. Modern Celtic Christianity. *Studia Imagologica: Amsterdam Studies on Cultural Identity*, 8, pp. 143–57, 1996.

Meek, D.E. Surveying the Saints: Reflections on Recent Writings on 'Celtic Christianity'. *Scottish Bulletin of Evangelical Theology*, 15, pp. 50–60, 1997.

Michell, J. Glastonbury Abbey: A Solar Instrument of Former Science. In M. Williams (ed.) *Glastonbury: A Study in Patterns*. RILKO, 1969.

Michell, J. Glastonbury-Jerusalem, Paradise on Earth: a Revelation Examined. In A. Roberts (ed.) *Glastonbury: Ancient Avalon, New Jerusalem*. London, 1978.

Mowl, T. and Earnshaw, B. *John Wood: Architect of Obsession*. Millstream Books, 1988.

Pennick, N. *Celtic Sacred Landscapes*. London, 1996.

Piccinni, A. Filming through the Mists of Time: Celtic Constructions and the Documentary. *Current Anthropology* 37, February Supplement, pp. 87–111, 1996.

Piggott, S. *The Druids*. London, 1981.

Piggott, S. *Ancient Britons and the Antiquarian Imagination*. London, 1989.

Shallcrass, P. (ed.) *A Druid Directory 1995: A Guide to Modern Druidry and Druid Orders*. British Druid Order, 1995.

Smart, N. *The Science of Religion and the Sociology of Knowledge*. Princeton, 1973.

Tingay, K. Madame Blavatsky's Children: Theosophy and its Heirs. In M. Bowman and S. Sutcliffe (eds) *Beyond the New Age: Alternative Spiritualities*. Edinburgh, 1998.

Toulson, S. *The Celtic Year*. Shaftesbury, 1996.

York, M. *The Emerging Network: A Sociology of the New Age and Neo-Pagan Networks*. Lanham MD, 1995.

PART TWO

THE CELTIC DIASPORA

This section addresses the increasing trend of people adopting a Celtic affiliation outside territories which have previously been defined as Celtic such as North America, Australia and New Zealand. While immigrants to these areas have often asserted an identification within a single specific cultural group, the Irish 'Green' diaspora is one well-researched example, these communities are increasingly being informed by wider pan-Celtic styles and ethics, which serves to forge new links between individuals and immigrant communities. The increase of 'New World' Celts can be attributed to a variety of factors. Of course there is the ethos of multiculturalism but perhaps there is also a response to a discourse of oppression which often identifies 'white' groups as 'oppressors'. We are also witnessing a sort of cultural feedback resulting from a heightened awareness of ethnicity within the Celtic regions themselves. As modern Celts strive to assert their identities and promote their own histories, learning about the often shared experience of emigration has created new opportunities for dialogue with the diaspora. Thus, the diaspora becomes as important to the country of origin as the reverse.

There has been a great deal of interest in the experiences of migration from the Celtic territories, and the shaping of distinctive ethnic identities in their new countries. Celticists have also focused on the role of the Celtic languages after migration, particularly in North America. However, very little research has addressed the effects of pan-Celticity and various aspects of pan-Celtic movements on immigrant identity-formation. In this section, the chapters by Hale and Thornton and by Payton examine this phenomenon, exploring why and in what ways Celtic identities have meaning for North Americans and Australians at the end of the twentieth century. The chapter by Curtis is a significant micro-study which reveals the processes by which one man, Curtis's father, constructed his own Scottish-American identity, thus focusing on the important relationships between the individual, tradition and creativity which are ultimately at the root of any identity-formation.

5

Pagans, Pipers and Politicos
Constructing 'Celtic' in a Festival Context

AMY HALE AND SHANNON THORNTON

Ethnic folklife festivals in the United States are designed to showcase and celebrate the cultural diversity that exists within American culture. They are generally organized by public-sector workers such as arts administrators in conjunction with government or local agencies. Sometimes, however, they are organized by immigrants, or more often by descendants of immigrants, to educate others, celebrate their heritage, and promote and preserve aspects of traditional culture perceived as somehow being under threat. These festivals are multi-faceted events which allow participants to experience food, dance, music, art and crafts that may be outside their own cultural experiences. Thus, some folk festival enthusiasts attend to 'broaden their cultural horizons' and to enrich their experience of the American 'mosaic'.

However, during the course of these events a particular portrait of a culture emerges. Participants see of a culture what organizers select and present, which ultimately informs their beliefs and experiences. Simultaneously, participants also shape the overall presentation through their own cultural expressions. For instance, at a German Oktoberfest organizers may schedule a polka band and serve sausages, but the participant who arrives wearing *liederhosen* contributes to the overall picture, or stereotypical picture, of what 'German' means or looks like to an

American audience. Thus, within the organized festival setting, producers and participants negotiate the terms of a particular ethnicity by establishing boundaries of acceptable expression throughout the course of the event. These festivals tend to present an uncomplicated, easily digestible picture of cultures relying mostly on nostalgia and dominant imagery that reinforces symbolic expressions of particular cultures.

Pan-ethnic events, such as 'Latino', 'Celtic' or 'Slavic' festivals, offer a different type of complexity as several distinct cultures are placed together under one roof, with participants and organizers forced to articulate connections between them for the purposes of the event. Celtic festivals often gather expressions of identity that are at once unified by their reference to a common perception of history, style and inherited culture, and the common goal of the festival to celebrate 'Celticness'; but are also quite disparate in individual conceptions of how and to what degree 'Celticness' is presented.

The events world-wide that could potentially fall into the category 'Celtic festival' are extremely varied. In Celtic countries events such as Scottish *mods*, Welsh *eisteddfodau*, and Brythonic *gorseddau* of Cornwall, Wales and Brittany function as fairly self-conscious, culture-specific expressions of Celtic ethnicity. Local festivals such as the Cornish 'Obby 'Oss are often believed by observers and participants to be 'Celtic' mainly by virtue of their longevity and the obscurity of their origins.

Pan-Celtic events such as the Festival Interceltique in Lorient, Brittany, and the Cornish Lowender Peran play a slightly different role from their diasporic counterparts in North America because they focus as annual rallying points for Celtic cultural activists in Celtic countries as well as enthusiasts from outside. Within the Celtic diasporas, group-specific festivals such as Scottish Highland games, which themselves have a long history in the United States and Canada, and Irish music festivals could also be considered within the larger category of 'Celtic festivals'. Yet, even predominantly Scottish or Irish festivals will often sell goods or present entertainment from other Celtic areas. For instance, the 62nd Highland Gathering we attended in Costa Mesa, California, also featured Irish and Welsh booths. However, there is a growing trend in the United States toward 'pan-Celtic' events which acknowledge an over-arching perception of Celtic culture and aim to be multicultural events rather than group-specific. One might observe, for example, the carving of Welsh love-spoons next door to a booth showcasing Scottish clan tartans. In this chapter we will address the ways in which various

Celtic identities are presented, negotiated and defined within a specific pan-Celtic festival setting in San Francisco, California.

The Celtic Music and Arts Festival in San Francisco is organized by the Irish Arts Foundation, and was conceived primarily as a forum to showcase contemporary Irish music. Contemporary folk music festivals are by now a recognizable feature of the American festival landscape, and many of the groups featured at this festival in 1994 routinely play several festivals throughout the country. Music is interestingly one feature which seems to unify the Celtic festival phenomenon on an international level: the individual festival events may serve the needs of particular and often localized communities; but it is often the musical performers who cross all national boundaries to play at several festivals throughout any given year. For traditional musicians, Irish and Scottish in particular, the route to a professional career often means touring the United States, Europe, and, more recently, Japan. Thus the motives for performing at a series of increasingly 'star-centred' festivals are understandably economic at base: to promote a new CD and/or expand an audience. That considered, these festivals also serve as an opportunity for musicians to meet one another, share material and generally revel in the experience of 'after-hours' or 'off-stage' sessions.

San Francisco's Irish and Irish-American community dates to the late 1800s and one local Irish journalist we interviewed thought the community to number between ten and twenty thousand. The organizers of the Celtic Music and Arts Festival, who are local arts promoters and Irish natives, informed us in 1994 that the decision to call the festival 'Celtic' was primarily logistical as another organization had already claimed the name 'Irish Arts Festival'. As a result, although the festival is called 'Celtic', the overriding and prominent imagery is Irish, and the festival serves the needs of the Irish and Irish-American community in San Francisco.

Yet the word 'Celtic' in the festival title insists that other-than-Irish expressions and interpretations of Celtic be permitted. In her study of the construction of Latinismo in pan-Latino festivals, Laurie Kay Sommers notes that when a pan-ethnic event is being shaped, one nation's traditions will often come to the forefront (depending upon, among other factors, the community in which the event is situated), yet not all nations can acceptably fulfil this role (Sommers 1991, 39). The result is that the symbols and traditions of a single group come to stand for those of many. In the case of the pan-Latino festival Sommers examined, the group identity of other Latinos was undermined by the dominance of San Francisco's

Mexican heritage and culture. The resultant tensions arise in the context of trying to establish a pan-Latino consciousness as an overt political strategy when other nations' expressive traditions were being subsumed (1991, 39).

In the case of the Celtic Music and Arts Festival, Irish served as the umbrella ethnicity for this pan-Celtic event. Not all groups or nations were on an equal footing and Cornwall and Brittany, for example, were not represented at all, either by vendors or by musical acts selected to perform. The omission of 'lesser recognized' Celtic areas is an almost typical feature of this type of pan-Celtic event in the United States, although the Oatlands Celtic Festival in Leesburg, Virginia, makes a concerted attempt to present representatives from Brittany, the Isle of Man, Cornwall and Galicia. In fact, some event participants in San Francisco, when interviewed, did not and could not distinguish between Irish and Celtic, and thought the two terms were interchangeable.

The size and visibility of the Irish community in San Francisco, aside from the initial intent of the organizers to have solely an Irish event, were prime factors in determining this dominance, with the effect being that misunderstandings arise from the cultural diversity that the term 'Celtic' can possibly encompass. Although other 'Celtic' affiliations were openly identified by variations on Highland dress and Scottish kilts, as well as green jumpers and shamrocks, other Celtic nationalities were not as clearly indexed. Wales was only openly identified by one Welsh vendor who displayed a red dragon banner, the same dragon as that on the Welsh flag, yet the booth was called Keltic Designs, and did not refer to Wales by name. The vendor displayed literature on the Welsh Arts Festival, a film-oriented event which took place the following weekend but was not in any way connected with or even cross-promoted by the Celtic Music and Arts Festival.

In considering which cultures were most likely to serve as the dominant Celtic cultures at a pan-Celtic event, we asked ourselves, 'Could Welsh possibly serve as an effective umbrella ethnicity for a pan-Celtic festival in the United States?' and concluded 'Probably not', mainly for two reasons. First, the strong and visible presence of the Irish and Scottish diaspora in the United States present identifiable 'Celtic' communities. Second, Tony Curtis has argued that the Welsh do not have the same recognizable sense of 'cultural style' as the Scottish or Irish; that the stereotypes of the Welsh do not exist in the same way (1986, 13). Jen Delyth of Keltic Designs told us that the local Welsh society did not realize the wider interest in Celtic history and thus has not capitalized on an interest that has led many people to conflate Irish (or Scottish) with Celtic. Furthermore, as Curtis argues, the primary cultural feature that distinguishes Welsh culture from English and other Celtic cultures is its language (and as Curtis maintains, Welsh is the significant marker for both speakers and non-speakers); as there are no longer major Welsh-speaking communities in the United States, the impetus to maintain the language has not emerged thus far as a struggle that has penetrated mainstream American consciousness. The fact is that Welsh culture is simply not as high-profile as Irish or Scottish culture in North America, and many Americans possess very little knowledge about Wales, not to mention the Isle of Man, Cornwall, Brittany and Galicia.

While affiliation with a national identity was one way of expressing Celticness, others, mostly vendors, appealed to a more pan-Celtic ideal through visual style of their products and accompanying texts that referenced the notion of a pre-Christian, unified European Celtic culture. Expressions of a pan-Celtic nature were represented as being rooted in a distant past that preceded individual nations. Jewellery and other decorative items featured designs that replicated or were inspired by Iron-Age European patterns and Hiberno-Norse knotwork. These stylistic markers were perhaps those most frequently correlated with vendors promoting a 'Celtic' rather than a specific national identity. Another feature of these vendors is that they displayed and often sold their products with a legend, either conveying the origin of the product or the symbolic significance of the design. One vendor had prepared a five-page handout for customers to take explaining the meanings behind each of the patterns on the products he sold. Next to a small knotted design is written:

> *The Iona Knot.* This symbol indicates achieving peace within oneself. This pattern is often used as a talisman, created by one continuous line forming four three-part triquestas which represent eternity, fidelity, and unity to a thought, person, or idea. The triquestra was used by the druids to indicate the three forces of nature: earth, fire and water. Each triquestra indicates one of the four seasons. It was later used by the Christians in the form of a cross to symbolize the holy Trinity. This made it easier to integrate Christian and Pagan beliefs. (McManus and Sons 1994, 1)

Product text not only gives the illusion of historicity, but also of continuity and ultimately meaning. This notion is extended further by the vendors whose products were aimed exclusively at a Neo-Pagan clientele, and who emphasized the 'authentic Celtic origin' of their product. In these cases, the products and legends were marketed in terms of their practical function, as well their aesthetic. Meanings and symbolism in this context are seen as of primary importance to the product; aesthetics alone will not suffice, and as one vendor's product sheet stated, the functionalism of the jewellery roots the design even further back in history and time:

> Symbols have power—they evoke images, and contemplating their meanings allows us to tap into that image—that power ... Jewelry was originally ceremonial, spiritual and meaningful beyond its purpose as adornment. We feel a return to this way is appropriate in these times. (Ancient Circles 1990, 1)

Many Neo-Pagans and New Agers believe that pre-Christian Celtic culture is the prototype or at least the inspiration for their contemporary practices and values. Marion Bowman has written about the commodification of the Celt in Pagan and New Age buying habits, and she mentions several factors that are relevant here. First, she notes that many New Agers in particular are affluent (Bowman 1994, 144). Thus, they can afford to make stylistic purchases that will assist them in proclaiming visible cultural allegiances, and making statements about their values and lifestyle—a lifestyle that requires a degree of economic commitment if the identity is to be maintained. Bob, co-owner of Moonblind Merchants, a vendor at the festival, was well aware of this. He said that the high admission price of the festival alone ($17.00) indicated that the attendants have 'surplus income'. He also stated that his clients are those who are 'really into alternative lifestyles ... into the New Age'. Furthermore, Bowman states that many Pagans hold Celtic artistry in particularly high esteem because of the belief that artists were central to Celtic society, and had special spiritual gifts; 'Craftwork is thus seen as a Celtic activity, which can increase the spirituality of the maker. However, by extension, the products of such craft can be seen as imbued with Celticity' (ibid., 149).

The association of Celtic with a particular lifestyle or lifestyles also implies an attendant set of values underlying many of the different expressions of 'Celtic'. Participants and vendors clearly articulated an overall sense that 'Celtic' is natural, pure, earthy, and tied to land and kinship. Bob from Moonblind Merchants says that 'The most important thing about Celtic is that it kinda symbolizes just people really getting back to what matters ... that the thing that keeps us all going, and in ancient times too, is just Mother Nature and all the things that She provides'. Brian, from Devine (*sic*) Celtic Sounds, a mail-order music company, considers that 'Celtic' was 'very politically oriented ... a whole attitude of being very down-to-earth ... very family oriented ... land oriented ... I guess what you would call a down-home-goodness kinda stuff'. Other music vendors played to the association of Celtic with nature in their display of categories for 'nautical' and 'environmental' musics.

On the other hand, some vendors were more nation-specific in their presentation, and offered recorded music and instructional guides for traditional instruments from most Celtic-speaking countries. This presentation perhaps attests to the fact that music vendors interpreted the event primarily as a music festival. Vendors' knowledge of their clientele is reflected in their presentation of tradition-specific categories, while they simultaneously take advantage of the broader reach of 'Celtic' as a music marketing term:

> People who come to this festival ... are very knowledgeable ... they know what kind of music they want and they know the people who are on the stage and they know all the different kinds of music so you don't have explain to them; it's a lot nicer not having to explain to people about the music; they come in knowing a lot about it. (Brian Westick, Devine Celtic Sounds).

Although festival organizers and some of the vendors representing community organizations were willing to acknowledge a wider pan-Celtic 'community' that had expression through the vehicles of music, culture and politics, those we spoke with also emphasized the desire to update the image of specifically Irish and Irish-American culture, and the Northern Irish political situation, to a wider public: as one participant put it, 'less doilies, more action', and another noted the absence of the older Irish-American generation at this year's event. The selection process involved in an immigrant community's showcasing of culture is based on the fact that immigrants represent a wide variety of interests and talents as well as localities and age groups. Recent immigrants may know more about recent cultural developments and what is 'current' back home. Trying to change the image of what being Irish or Irish-American means by presenting local and native *contemporary* culture was the official aim of this event, sponsored by a local Irish arts organization. This meant that the performative aspects of the festival were defined largely as Irish, rather than Celtic.[1]

As a music category, 'Celtic' is often viewed by musicians as too vague and too closely associated with commercial marketing strategies to hold any musical value. Viewed as a linguistic category, with extensions in expressive culture, it holds more credence with musicians whose playing practices are often specific in terms of a particularly Irish or Scottish repertoire. One Irish musician offered his interpretation of the distinction:

> I kinda' stay away from it [the 'Celtic' label], you know? I mean, what attachment would I have to someone in Brittany? In all honesty, we don't share the same language, or music or anything, but there is some kind of root there for it you know? But it doesn't mean that I should feel an affinity because we've been locked together in the same Celtic boat, you know what I mean? (Peter Heelan, San Francisco Ceili Band)

It was clear that it was in the areas of national politics and music performance that the distinction between 'Irish festival' and 'Celtic festival' was most overtly contested. The physical layout of the festival attested to widely divergent views held about the 'Celticness' of the musical component of the event. The different components of the festival, the 'Celtic Marketplace', the music stage, and food and drink areas were perhaps envisioned to serve different purposes. Because the festival is held in a large warehouse in the redeveloped dock district, use of space by festival organizers was at that time confined to the parameters of the building. The music stage and audience seating area occupied roughly the entire rear half of the festival space and were cordoned off by a black curtain spanning the width of the building. This area served as an arena for explicitly Irish expression: all musical acts for the two days of the festival were Irish acts, with Sunday giving performance space to Irish set dancing as well. Radio Telefís Eireann personality and civil rights commentator Eamonn McCann served as Master of Ceremonies, while a variety of Irish artists performed, including Irish folklorist and musician Mick Moloney, whose performances combined traditional Irish music and song with anecdotes of Irish history and folklore. If the Celtic Marketplace has been conceived of and marked as 'Celtic' out of practical need resulting in an imaginative promotion of a wider vision of expressive culture, then the musical space satisfied the goals of the festival as originally conceived by its progenitors: to showcase the best in contemporary *Irish* music. The two headlining bands, Sharon Shannon and

Altan, have large followings both in Ireland and in the United States, and billed as they were to close each evening's events they effectively shut down the Marketplace, with the festival essentially given over to its base of a local Irish and Irish-American community. Irish festivities even carried on after the close of the festival as performers, organizers and attendees gathered in local Irish pubs to continue music-making and visiting. The notion of 'Celtic' constructed in this particular festival setting was then bound by time as well as physical and metaphorical space.

Nationalist and other Irish service organizations such as the Gaelic Athletic League were placed along the periphery and the back end of the Celtic Marketplace, following perhaps the spatial trend of the festival to present the back region as Irish/Irish-American rather than pan-Celtic space. The selection of only Irish acts, including the headlining acts, along with the exhibition of nationalist and attendant ideologies, clearly indicate a narrower underlying cultural agenda than was actively promoted in the Marketplace area of the festival.

Celtic identity also conflates with political sentiment within the context of the festival and is an association with historical precedence. Nationalism in Ireland has historically promoted the idea of a Celtic past as the cultural foundation for an ideal nation-state (Hutchinson 1987). At this festival Irish Republican sentiments were clearly in evidence. Irish NORAID, an organization which provides funds to Republicans in Northern Ireland, the Irish Republican Socialist Committee, the Irish Freedom Movement, and the San Francisco H-Block Committee all had booths presenting themselves as public service organizations. All openly sympathize with the Republican cause, and their literature clearly supported the aims and actions of the Irish Republican Army. The NORAID booth sold t-shirts with IRA moulded into the shape of a soldier carrying a gun. Our respondents all claimed to be educating the public about the real situation of the Irish people, which is an argument that is actually consistent with the aims of festival organizers to present a more contemporary vision of Ireland.

Yet when asked, representatives of nationalist organizations saw themselves as being in sympathy with other Celtic causes and as part of a larger Celtic picture. Individuals viewed their participation in the festival as entirely consistent with the notion of a Celtic identity, not only as it evolved within the boundaries of this festival, but also within a wider historical framework. For instance, one respondent from the Irish Republican Socialist Committee conceived of Celtic not only in terms of shared language and culture, but also a shared history of oppression, noting the Scots, Welsh and Breton movements. Another respondent from NORAID placed the Irish movement in a larger context of Celtic national struggles, basing his educational strategies in terms of his assumptions about festival attendants' knowledge of and experiences with other Celtic causes. The strong presence of Irish nationalist groups presents an example of the tension involved in defining ethnic and pan-ethnic identity in the bounded space of the festival. Ultimately, Irish nationalism becomes a component of Celtic identity as it is constructed within this particular setting.

But how do we account for those participants without a identifiable Celtic affiliation? It is in this realm that we see the boundaries of Celtic identity as defined within this festival as being the most fluid. For instance, we spoke with a vendor selling hand-crafted silver jewellery that was not influenced by Celtic designs and asked her about why she was participating in the festival. The owner said that she felt that her product was entirely appropriate at a Celtic festival because of the quality and craftsmanship that went into her work, a quality that she felt she had in common with many of the other, more traditionally Celtic vendors. However, when we visited her booth in the second year of our research, she had prepared some jewellery with Celtic designs. On the other hand, a woman who sold hand-crafted contemporary children's clothes felt that although she was chosen by the organizers to exhibit because of the quality of her product, she felt that her booth was somehow inappropriate in a Celtic context, which made her somewhat uncomfortable. Values of quality and craftsmanship that had been identified as Celtic in some way, whether by organizers or participants, were not held to be applicable by all.

Other non-Celtic vendors seemed to define the space as 'festival' rather than 'Celtic'. The presence of a corporate massage booth and a children's ride marked the event as interactive and something outside the every day. In these areas there was no sense of incongruity, no sense of contest. Their function at the event seemed clear.

To conclude, 'Celtic' was defined in a festival setting which allowed for multi-vocalic expressions of identity: by cultural values associated with the importance of heritage, language and shared history forming the basis of nationhood, and by a particular aesthetic referencing an ideal past as well as a contemporary lifestyle. When asked to define what 'Celtic' meant to him, one of our respondents asked if he could give two definitions. He defined 'Celtic' first in terms of language that also united culture and mythology. But he also talked in terms of aesthetics: 'Celtic is a frame of mind for people ... it touches something in them that transcends ethnic identity and speaks to a broader sense of what it is to be a human being'. Further, Celtic festivals (and similar cultural events) are not 'a bunch of white people getting together to look into their Indo-European roots as much as it is people celebrating the richness of a culture and their ability to identify with that on their own level'. Celtic seems to be something people 'feel an affinity for' regardless of their own ethnic background. This points to the experience of 'affinity' as particularly important in examining cultural events and celebrations of the type explored in this chapter. While many of the expressions of Celtic we witnessed drew upon conceptions of the past, they simultaneously formed an important commentary on the modern condition and expressed hopes for a future reimagined in terms of the Celtic.

Notes

1. Due to the fact that the Irish traditional dance music repetoire is fairly fluid in diasporic communities with more people recognizing the distinctions within the category of Celtic music, and because much of the repertoire is shared with Scottish traditional musicians, this feature of the festival is changing somewhat, with the inclusion of more American, Scottish and Breton artists.

References

Ancient Circles. Catalogue. Laytonville CA, 1990.
Bowman, M. The Commodification of the Celt: New Age/Neo Pagan Consumerism. *Folklore in Use*, 2 (1), pp. 143–52. London, 1994.
Curtis, T. Introduction. In T. Curtis (ed.) *Wales: The Imagined Nation*, Mid Glamorgan, 1986.
Hutchinson, J. *The Dynamics of Cultural Nationalism: The Gaelic Revival and the Creation of the Irish Nation State*. London, 1987.
McManus and Sons. Jewellry Brochure Supplement. Berkeley, 1994.
Sommers, L.K. Inventing Latismo: The Creation of 'Hispanic' Panethnicity in the United States. *Journal of American Folklore*, 104 (411) pp. 32–51, 1991.

6

Re-inventing Celtic Australia

PHILIP PAYTON

'Diaspora studies' are back on the academic agenda with a vengeance. Until comparatively recently considered by many to be outdated, misleading, even dangerous, diaspora studies have not always enjoyed a good press. Back in 1979 Glanmor Williams warned of 'the besetting sin of the historiography of American emigration: excessive praise of the feats and merits of one particular nation or group' (1979, 233), while more recently Bob Reece has criticized the 'filial piety or nationalist and religious affirmation' (1991, 226) that has often characterized the writing of Irish emigrant history, an approach described by Patrick O'Farrell as a triumphalist 'me too' genre (Reece 1991, 226). As Reece concluded: 'We study the "contributions" of ethnic groups: Cornishmen, Welsh and Irish as well as the more recent arrivals [in Australia] such as Chinese, Germans, Italians, Greeks, Yugoslavs, and so on. One of the obvious hazards here is that extravagant claims will at times be made for the contribution of one group or another' (1991, 228–9).

However, while some work in this historiographical tradition (not least the current craze for family history) continues to perpetuate such filio-pietistic (even antiquarian and parochial) approaches, there is of late a new-found recognition that by looking afresh at diaspora studies important new insights into the dynamics of ethnic identity may be obtained. As Robin Cohen's *Global Diasporas* explains:

> Scholars of nationalism, international migration and ethnic relations need new conceptual maps and fresh case studies to understand

the growth of complex transnational identities. The old idea of 'diaspora' may provide this framework. Though often conceived in terms of a catastrophic dispersion, widening the notion of disapora to include trade, imperial, labour and cultural diasporas can provide a more nuanced understanding of the often positive relationships between migrants' homelands and their places of work and settlement. (1997, ii)

Indeed, such a widening helps us to locate 'complex transnational identities' within their host environments, setting the development of those identities against the background of socio-economic and cultural change in the countries where they have taken root. Especially complex is the transnational Celtic identity (or identities) and the manner in which it has developed in the new lands of the Celtic diaspora, principally in North America and the Antipodes. In the late eighteenth, nineteenth and (to some extent) twentieth centuries, these lands experienced extensive immigration from each of the Celtic countries. But while we may point to a widespread and often distinctive Irish, Scots, Welsh, Cornish, and (in the case of Canada) Breton impact in the new lands, it is not immediately clear to what extent this impact invites the collective label 'Celtic'. Moreover, the degree to which over time a common 'Celtic' consciousness may have developed amongst and between these constituent groups (both within the individual host countries and transnationally) is also a matter of debate—a debate that needs to take account of the socio-economic and cultural contexts in which such development has occurred.

By engaging in such debates we not only gain new insights into how the term 'Celtic' has been understood and deployed in the lands of the Celtic diaspora, but equally we may contribute to the more general discussion of how countries such as the United States of America and Australia have 're-invented' themselves as 'multicultural' societies. Today, for example, notwithstanding the passing of the Keating era and the short-lived emergence of the reactionary One Nation Party, Australian society is determinedly multicultural in its composition and outlook, leading to a contemporary reassessment of what it means to be 'Australian'. Although this multiculturalism is the result of new (post-1945) waves of southern European and (more recently) Asian immigrants, one ideological consequence has been the attempt to unpackage 'Celtic' from 'Anglo', to argue that those historians who have stressed the 'Anglo-Celtic homogeneity' of colonial Australia have been mistaken in their assessment of that society. O'Farrell, for example, has insisted that from its very beginning colonial Australian society was decidedly pluralistic, with inherent and deep-seated ideological contests, a society of individuals and groups of individuals with a multiplicity of backgrounds, cultures, habits, customs, prejudices, religions (1993, 10).

Such an approach has led to a steady stream of academic studies of the Welsh, Irish, Scots and Cornish in Australia (for example Reece 1990; O'Brien and Travers 1991; O'Farrell 1993; Lay 1998; Payton 1984, 1999), but it has also led to a new insistence (not least by Celtic activists themselves) that there has always been (and still is) an Australian historical experience that is definably 'Celtic', a Celtic ethnic identity that is distinct from 'British' and yet exhibits strands of commonality between Cornish, Irish, Scots, Welsh, and even Manx and Bretons. There is a tendency towards uncritical and exaggerated triumphalism in such assertions, a temptation to resort to a celebratory list of the Celtic 'great and good' ranging from 'Honest John' Verran (the Cornish first Labor Premier of South Australia) to Archbishop Mannix (of Melbourne Irish-Catholic fame) and culminating in Sir Robert Menzies, who, for all his disposition as a latter-day Australian imperialist, is claimed as a subtle distillation of all that is Cornish and Scots (AFCS Leaflet 1994). And yet, the very fact that such fulsome claims are made so routinely and with such conviction alerts us to the existence of a serious phenomenon that requires recognition and explanation: the contemporary attempt to define, re-define or even invent 'Celticity' as part of the late twentieth-century reassessment of what it is to be 'Australian'.

This chapter, therefore, seeks not only to explore the contention that there is an element of the Australian historical experience that might legitimately be defined as 'Celtic', but also enquires into the existence (or otherwise) in Australia of 'Celtic consciousness'—both in the past and today. This is, of course, not the first time that such questions have been posed. Peter Alexander, for example, has discussed 'the extent to which Australians descended from the various Celtic peoples ... have preserved a group consciousness of common ancestry and a sense of common history and culture' (1989, 11). But, while pointing to historical experiences in Australia that are recognisably Irish or Welsh or Scots or Cornish, tangible evidence of Celtic consciousness eluded him, except for his perception that 'In very recent times it ["Celticity"] has become a more conscious and apparent factor in the lives of the leaders of the various groups—that they are Celts of one origin and, to a remarkable degree, of one culture still' (1989, 14). However, such observations are paradoxical rather than explanatory, and pose more questions than they answer.

Part of the problem, of course, as this book attests, is that even in its indigenous, European context the term 'Celtic' defies easy definition and promotes conflict rather than consensus amongst academic and other observers. In the ancient world, the description 'Celtic' was given to a broad group of peoples who, to external observers (the Greeks, and later Romans), seemed to share common linguistic and cultural traits. The 'Celts' and 'Celtic culture' in Classical accounts were thus often other-defined rather than self-defining. Very much later, with the birth of modern scholarship in the eighteenth and nineteenth centuries, this process was perpetuated, with the term 'Celtic' being used as a convenient catch-all for a particular group of languages—including their modern derivatives in Ireland, Scotland, Wales, Cornwall, the Isle of Man and Brittany. By extension, speakers of Celtic languages became 'Celtic peoples' and their territories 'Celtic lands'. This, in turn, prompted the revivalist 'Celtic Twilight', the literary and romantic movement which busily re-invented notions of 'Celticity' and whose tenets still colour (often to a remarkable degree) our own perceptions of what it is to be 'Celtic'. Indeed, Malcolm Chapman has argued that our contemporary notions of Celticity remain 'other-defined', the result of an English 'romanticism [which] created the fringe Celtic minorities as figures of wish-fulfilment, of opposition to the prevailing philosophy of and actuality of industrialising England' (1992, 14).

Although much contemporary philological scholarship continues to apply a purely linguistic definition of 'Celtic', with some nationalists insisting upon a 'linguistic criterion' (Berresford Ellis 1993) for those claiming Celtic nationality (thus excluding Galicia from organizations such as the Celtic League), the term is used today by many academics as a convenient short-hand to describe the (in some respects) similar historical experiences of the Atlantic peripheries of Britain, Ireland, France and (occasionally) Spain. 'Historical experience' is the key here, for it is not restricted to questions of language (most 'Celts' today do not speak Celtic languages) but includes wider cultural considerations such as socio-economic conditions and political relationships within the state. Common experience of socio-economic and political oppression has on occasions prompted pan-Celtic sympathy and sentiment, although shared features of historical experience do not necessarily imply the existence of a common consciousness.

Certainly, in the nineteenth century there was little sense of a common

'Celtic identity' amongst the indigenous peoples of the Celtic countries. Indeed, what *was* noticeable were the divisions and differences between (and sometimes within) each of the Celtic lands. Conflict between Catholic and Protestant was a feature of both Irish and Scottish life, and wider religious contrasts included the prevalence of Nonconformity in Wales and Cornwall and the survival of Catholicism in rural Ireland and parts of the Highlands and Islands. There were similar contrasts between industrial and rural areas—between industrialized Ulster and the deeply rural character of the rest of Ireland, between the mining valleys and agricultural Wales, between the central industrial belt of Scotland and the Highlands and Islands. Such contrasts were also a function of 'modernity' versus 'backwardness', with, for example, English-speaking industrial Cornwall applauded as the epitome of modern technological advance, and the Gaelic-speaking peasant society of the west of Ireland (or Scottish Highlands) condemned as the worst example of unsustainable backwardness in the British Isles.

When 'Celtic identity' was articulated, the motivation was rarely pan-Celtic sentiment but suited the particular requirements of specific groups. Thus (to take an Australian extrapolation of the British experience) in the South Australian mining town of Burra Burra in the elections of 1851 the Cornish opposed the political ambitions of the Irish, describing themselves as the 'sons of ancient Britons' (*South Australian Register*, 4 July 1851), with the local Wesleyan preacher in 1859 assuring his Cornish congregation (again in defiance of Irish claims) that the Cornish were 'the real descendants of the Celts' (*South Australian Register*, 4 March 1859). Interestingly, such assertions not only confirmed the Cornish in their separate identity (albeit at the expense of the Irish) but, paradoxically, reinforced the claims of British imperialism. Whilst Irish notions of 'Celticity' could be dismissed as 'Fenianism' and 'Popery', the Cornish as 'ancient Britons' were in a sense elevated to the status of proto-Anglo-Saxons, rather like Boudicca and Caractacus, who in Victorian history books were presented as British (quasi-English) heroes in an attempt to co-opt Celtic history in the interests of the British Empire (Fraser 1988, 299).

In the United Kingdom, the re-definition in the nineteenth century of Scotland as a 'Celtic nation' was not only an attempt at nation-building, a bridging of the historic Highland–Lowland gap, but was also—in the midst of the dreadful Clearances—a mechanism of assimilation into the British state in which hitherto subversive symbolism such as bagpipes and tartan was depoliticized (or repoliticized, albeit in another direction) and invested with a new legitimacy. From the famous Edinburgh tour of George IV to the founding of Highland Regiments, Scottish 'Celticity' was also co-opted in the interests of British imperialism (Prebble 1988). By contrast, this was a far cry from the Irish nationalism that emerged after the Famine, where the Gaelic language, 'Gaelic sport' and other cultural attributes were invested with an exclusivity in which to be Celtic was not only to be Irish but also non-British and anti-British.

However, despite these conflicting notions of 'Celticity' and the wider contrasts and conflicts within the Celtic lands, there were aspects of the nineteenth-century experience in the United Kingdom which distinguished, often quite sharply, the (Celtic) periphery from the (English) core. Both rural and industrial regions of the Celtic periphery suffered from their relationship with the core or centre of the British state. In addition to the obvious 'obsolescent' agrarian societies of Ireland and the Highlands and Islands, ostensibly advanced economies such as that of Cornwall suffered from an industrialization that was over-specialized, imperfect and incomplete. In Cornwall's case, despite a brief period in the vanguard of industrial development, technological supremacy soon gave way to early de-industrialization as the Cornish economy was unable to diversify in response to rapid economic change.

Indeed, if one is to search for an icon of common Celtic experience in the nineteenth-century United Kingdom, then it must be the potato famine of the 1840s. It afflicted the Highlands and Islands as it afflicted Ireland and Cornwall, and one major consequence was the stimulus of mass emigration to overseas destinations, not least the Australias. Thus emigration became a central feature of all the Celtic lands (including Brittany, a peripheral appendage of the French state), with the partial exception of Wales where the continued dynamism of South Welsh industrial expansion absorbed the internal migration from rural areas. Not surprisingly, therefore, there were disproportionately large numbers of 'Celtic' immigrants in colonial Australia, which in turn led to an inevitable and discernible cultural impact. For example, the United Labor Party in South Australia was clearly 'Cornish', while its equivalent in neighbouring Victoria bore all the hallmarks of an Irish impact. Although the Nonconformist–Catholic tensions of these otherwise ideologically complementary groups made them mutually hostile on occasions (as in the Conscription issue during the Great War), their contributions could certainly not be described as English and—in this Australian context—perhaps invite the collective label 'Celtic'.

It is also the case that immigrants from the Celtic lands were often well-suited to colonial conditions. This was true to a degree of the Highlanders and Irish, used as they were to eking out a living in difficult conditions on the margins of the good earth with only minimal resources. But it was particularly true of the Cornish. They too were used to wresting a living from poor soils and wastral but they had much more to offer. They brought to Australia technical skills (and a matching reputation) that made them much sought after as miners, engineers and artisans. Often Methodist and always English-speaking, they were also tailor-made for a colonial society in which independence, individualism, self-improvement and the ability to 'get on' were important attributes. They posed no threats and suffered no impediments, unlike the Irish who were often perceived as 'subversives' or the Highlanders who were not always as well integrated into Australian society due to the 'disability' of being monoglot Gaelic speakers.

Wedded as they were to Nonconformist notions of thrift, social mobility and civil liberty, the Cornish were model colonists. As Bob Reece (1990) has noted, although the Irish struggled in Australian literature to establish their role as nation-builders, 'that no such claim needed to be made by the Welsh (or indeed the Cornish) in Australia reflects the fact of their assimilation into the majority Anglo-Scottish population'. Whilst remaining distinct, the very attributes of that distinctiveness made the Cornish (and Welsh) ideally suited to the socio-economic conditions of emerging Australian society.

In contrasting the contributions of the various Celtic groups in Australia, it is useful here to draw a comparative sketch of their relative impacts. The Bretons remain largely unchronicled, with the Manx only marginally more visible, but the Cornish, Scots, Irish and (to a lesser degree) Welsh are writ large upon Australian life (Jupp 1998). The contribution of the Cornish to the mining development of Australia is well-documented (Payton 1978; Colman 1985; Lay 1992), beginning with their enduring impact in the South Australian copper towns but also encompassing the silver-lead mines of Broken Hill, the goldfields of New South Wales, Victoria and Western Australia, and numerous other metalliferous rushes across the continent from Peak Downs in Queensland to Mount Bischoff in Tasmania. But the Cornish also became notable agriculturalists, especially in South Australia where they played an important role in expanding the farming frontier (Payton 1988), and they settled swiftly into commercial and public life. Given their statistical invisibility in official records, it is difficult to count the

Cornish but as many as 16,000 found their way to South Australia between 1836 and 1886, with perhaps as many settling in Victoria and others attracted elsewhere.

The Lowland Scots, more numerous than the Cornish, were English-speaking and largely Presbyterian in religion, also driven by the Protestant work ethic and the desire for self-improvement. They came from both the central industrial belt, at the forefront of British commercial expansion, and the go-ahead rural Lowlands, where 'improvement agriculture' had transformed both landscape and production methods. From town and country, the Lowland Scots came well-equipped to contribute to Australian development. In a sense, their emigration was a spin-off from dynamic change in urban and rural Lowland Scotland, and once in Australia the Lowlanders were able to benefit from their continuing links with specifically Scottish commercial and financial institutions. Although not exactly a state within a state, the existence and relative autonomy of Scottish institutions in Britain was a clear advantage to Scottish entrepreneurs in colonial Australia. Certainly, Scottish recruitment to Australian elites was impressive, statistically over-represented as they were in areas such as agriculture, business, politics and education, where their modernizing, egalitarian ethos won them prominence.

Not surprisingly, like the Cornish, relatively few Scots came to Australia as convicts, the overwhelming majority being free settlers who by 1860 accounted for 12.5 per cent of the population of Victoria and 6.2 per cent of that of New South Wales. During the Gold Rush of the 1850s some 90,000 of the total 600,000 Australian immigrants were from Scotland, while between 1860 and 1892 of the 114,023 assisted immigrants some 13,089 were Scots. In relative statistical terms, the Scots made a greater 'regional' contribution to the populating of Australia than any other part of Britain, except Cornwall (Jupp 1988, 781).

However, in amongst this sea of Lowlanders was a substantial minority of Highlanders and Islanders who, although indisputably Scots, possessed cultural and social attributes that made them in several respects a people apart. As Eric Richards has noted, the Highlanders and Islanders were 'an important component of the Celtic colouring of Australian civilisation' (1988, 765), and on occasions—as in the period 1837–42 and between 1850 and 1854—their immigration may have outnumbered that of their Lowland compatriots. Lachlan Macquarie, Governor of New South Wales from 1810 to 1821, was a notable early Island settler and he favoured fellow Highlanders. Similarly, other prominent early Highland colonists were Donald McCloed in Van Diemen's Land and John McArthur in New South Wales.

The first major influx of Highlanders and Islanders came rather later, however, as a result of the famine of 1836-7. Unlike Macquarie or McCloed, these were not men and women of substance but for the most part poor (and sometimes dispossessed) crofters, refugees from a failing peasant society. Despite pockets of Catholics, most of these Highlanders and Islanders were Presbyterian, which made them preferable to the Irish as immigrants. However, many were Gaelic-speaking (and not a few monoglot), which was viewed as a severe disadvantage, while despite their Protestant credentials many did not possess the entrepreneurial skills and modernizing energy of the Lowlanders. As Richards (1978) has commented, often Highlanders and Islanders were, in marked contrast to both Cornish and Lowlanders, 'mostly outcasts of a peasant society crumbling away on the very periphery of the British world', with devastation and confusion in Scotland followed tragically by destitution in Australia. However, being resourceful, hardy, and having an ability to endure hardship without murmur and to survive on the margins was in many ways the salvation for the Highlanders and Islanders in Australia.

The famines of 1836-7 and 1847-51 precipitated much Highland emigration to Australia, but so too did the Clearances (the forcible eviction of Highlanders and Islanders from their crofts), while some 'philanthropic' landowners (such as those who founded the Highland and Island Emigration Society in 1852) advocated emigration as means to self-improvement. But, like those who arrived in South Australia in the mid-1850s and found themselves reduced to breaking stones at the colonial government's depot at Dry Creek, north of Adelaide, their adjustment to Australian society was often traumatic. While many refused to be separated from friends or relatives by offers of employment, perpetuating the ties of kin and clan, in the longer term they rarely had the chance to recreate peasant or small-holder existence, Australian conditions not allowing the transplantation of Highland life. True, in the 1840s there were Gaelic-speaking churches around Port Phillip, while in 1857 the *Gaelic Messenger* newspaper was published in Hobart and circulated in several Australian colonies. Indeed, by 1879 regular Gaelic classes were being organized by the Highland Society of New South Wales, although by then the original peasant culture had already been largely replaced by an affected romanticized re-interpretation—not unlike that which had occurred in Scotland itself.

In contrast to both Cornish and Scots, the Irish featured strongly in the transportation of convicts, some 23 per cent (or 36,000 souls) of those being sent to Australia for criminal offences having originated in Ireland. However, these offences were 'political' in varying degrees, from anti-landlordism and sundry agrarian outrages to the Fenian rebels who were the very last convicts transported in 1868. As Robert Hughes (1987, 181) has observed, the Irish were viewed as ideologically and physically dangerous immigrants; they were in a sense a 'doubly colonized people'—first in Ireland itself, and then in Australia. Most were Catholic (except for the Ulster folk, who had much in common with the Scottish Lowlanders) and some were Gaelic speaking, and many came from what was seen—like the Highlands and Islands—as a failing peasant society. However, despite these unpromising credentials, Irish immigrants were easier to recruit than English or Scots, and Ireland was seen as an admirable source of marriageable (and trainable) women. And although the Irish did not always possess occupational skills, they met a continuing high demand for labouring workers, their tenacity fitting them for the rigours of Australian life.

Certainly, between 1840 and 1914 no fewer than 300,000 Irish people went to Australia. As early as 1871 some 25 per cent of those born overseas (i.e. 12.5 per cent of the Australian population) hailed from Ireland, and with the passage of the years very few Australian families escaped an Irish admixture. The Irish influence was especially noticeable in the eastern colonies of Victoria and New South Wales, not least in politics. Inevitably, some political groups devoted their energies to Irish rather than Australian causes, although the principal political effort was in support of the Australian Labor movement. Critics detected 'Fenian' and 'Popish' motives in Irish Labor politics, however, especially during the Great War when the anti-Conscriptionists were condemned as Republicans. Archbishop Dr Daniel Mannix perhaps personified the subtle relationship that grew up in Australia between Irish nationalism, Roman Catholicism, Labor politics and an emerging Australian consciousness.

Occupying a perhaps intermediary position between Cornish and Lowlanders on the one hand and Irish and Highlanders and Islanders on the other, were the Welsh. The Welsh language, like Gaelic, was viewed as an impediment in progressive English-speaking colonies, but, unlike the Irish or Highlanders, most Welsh immigrants came from an advanced industrial and Nonconformist society well-suited to the demands of Australian development. In this, and in their possession of sought-after skills such as mining and smelting, the Welsh were not unlike the Cornish as desirable immigrants. The 'disability' of language was soon swept aside, as Reece has noted, so that the Welsh and Cornish might compete side by side for a distinctive but welcome and successful place in Australian society. That said, the Welsh were never as numerous as the Cornish and 'Even in South Australia where they achieved one of their main concentrations they were vastly outnumbered by the Cornish' (Lucas 1987, 16). Nevertheless, there were Welsh language chapels at Llwchwr (Burra Burra) in the 1840s and at Wallaroo in the 1860s, with identifiable clusters of Welsh-folk in the 1850s Gold Rush in Victoria in places such as Ballarat evidenced by their Calvinistic Methodist and Baptist chapels. The coal mines of Newcastle in New South Wales also attracted more than a smattering of Welsh immigrants in the 1860s. By the turn of the century some 12,000 Welsh colonists had found a home in Australia.

If we may generalize from the above discussion, it is clear that Celtic immigrants in colonial Australia fell broadly into two categories. On the one hand there were the Cornish and Lowland Scots (together with the Ulster Protestants and Welsh), who were overwhelmingly English-speaking and Protestant in religion, came from modernizing societies and had a range of skills to offer Australian development. Separate identity, when it was articulated, was used to emphasize the distinctiveness and worth of their contributions—the Cornish, especially, were unashamedly elitist in trumpeting their own significance, carefully cultivating their 'Cousin Jack' myth. For the Cornish person or Lowland Scot, constructing as they were their status as superior colonists, to be seen as distinct from the average English settler was an advantage.

In sharp contrast, however, both the Irish and Highlanders and Islanders found their separate identities an impediment in colonial Australia. The Irish were seen as a threat, politically and physically, products of a 'backward' society hampered by the dead-hand of Roman Catholicism. Highlanders and Islanders, though often Protestant, suffered the disability of Gaelic-speech and were also, in the eyes of the dominant colonial elite (English and Lowland Scots), the products of a backward peasant society. The Irish, however, with their experience of political agitation at home and their sheer strength of numbers in Australia, were able to insist upon their place in Australian society, ensuring that their 'subversive' identity would nonetheless help to shape emerging notions of Australian nationality. The Highlanders and Islanders on the whole fared less well, often unable to adapt to Australian conditions and becoming swiftly invisible in the colonial melting-pot. Ironically, when in the later nineteenth century Highland and Caledonian societies were much in vogue in Australia, the cultural symbolism of a fast-disappearing Gaelic way of life was effectively hijacked by Lowland Scots in their attempts to deploy distinctiveness as a badge of status. The kilt, the tartan, even a smattering of recently learnt Gaelic, were symbols of success, not failure.

If many of these contrasts were reminiscent of the contrasts that existed within the British Isles, so notions of 'Celticity' were—as in the United Kingdom—articulated with differing motives. As noted already, the Irish and Cornish vied for the coveted title of 'true Celts', the former appealing to Celtic identity as a political weapon in opposing British imperialism, the latter asserting Celtic credentials as 'ancient Britons' to emphasize their superior Britishness. The Lowland Scots, for their part, adopted notions of 'Celtic Scotland' as a means of affecting Highland manners and enjoying the distinctiveness and status that this conferred. And yet, despite these contrasts and paradoxes, each of the Celtic groups exhibited, even articulated (albeit for differing motives), an identity and experience which was not English and which on occasions was self-described as 'Celtic'. Lack of common interest and the absence of a common consciousness had not prevented them from demonstrating their non-Englishness, nor had it prevented (conflicting) notions of Celticity from emerging.

Certainly, in developing their perspectives of colonial Australia, even those historians who have sought to emphasize homogeneity have admitted an experience that was 'Anglo-Celtic' rather than 'British', a recognition of both the strength of numbers of Celtic immigrants and their substantial contributions to the socio-economic, cultural and institutional growth of Australia. Even in the 1960s a distinctive 'Celtic' hue was observable in Australian public life; for example, in the emergence of the Democratic Labor Party, which, with its strong Irish-Catholic flavour, opposed what it saw as the Marxist infiltration of the Australian Labor Party. By then, however, Celtic Australia was already re-inventing itself in response to post-war change, a veneer of new-style Celticity superimposing itself upon the existing vestiges of Irishness, Welshness, Scottishness, Cornishness. Indeed, since the Second World War there has been a vigorous 're-invention' of Celtic Australia, firstly as part of the Australian search for 'roots' and historical identity, and more recently as part of the assertion of 'multiculturalism' and the celebration of ethnic diversity. This has involved not only a 're-awakening' of what it is (or might be) to be of Irish, Welsh, Scots or Cornish descent, but has also constructed a certain pan-Celtic consciousness.

This 're-invention' of Celticity in contemporary Australia is to some extent a mirror image of what has been happening in the Celtic lands of north-western Europe, where the emergence of Breton, Welsh, Scots, even Cornish cultural and political nationalism has re-emphasized the inherent ethnic and territorial diversity of the British and French states. This, too, has had a pan-Celtic component, so that developments in Europe and Australia have been both complementary and mutually reinforcing. As Reece (1990) observed, overt interest in Australia's Welsh inheritance is of comparatively recent origin, 'arising partly from the growth of cultural nationalism in Wales itself and from multicultural consciousness in Australia'. Indeed, as Reece concluded, perception of 'British or Anglo-Celtic stock is being replaced by its components, the Scots, Irish, Welsh, Cornish and even English: "we are all ethnics now"'. Or rather, as Brian Murphy explained, 'Based on ethnicity as a determinant of society, multiculturalism went beyond the [recent] immigrants as a component of the population and bore the message that all citizens stood to gain from ethnic infusion' (1993, 3–4).

Australians of Cornish descent, for example, were encouraged to admit their ethnic roots. In the 1986 Census the so-called 'ancestry question' indicated some 15,000 Australians who thought it relevant to declare their Cornish backgrounds. Charles Price, meanwhile, was encouraged to measure the extent of the Cornish-Australian community, and did so by investigating the incidence of distinctive Cornish surnames. His results suggested that in 1992 between 245,000 and 290,000 Australians were of significant Cornish descent (so-called 'ethnic strength'), while as many as 850,000 had some Cornish connection in their family trees. As Price concluded:

> It is clear that the Cornish people have made an appreciable contribution to the Australian population and that, in terms of ethnic strength, they rank among Australia's dozen largest ethnic groupings. In that list they are on much the same level as the Dutch and Chinese but a little more than the Welsh and Aborigines ... an active folk-conscious minority ... will push for greater recognition of the Cornish as an important Celtic ethnic group within Australia. (1992, 41)

Similar claims were made for the Welsh, Scots and Irish, a process that has led to heightened interest in the historical impact of the Celtic peoples in Australia, ranging from the widespread enthusiasm for family history to more specialised studies such as that of the transplantation of Cornish mining technology (Drew and Connel, 1993). But, more importantly, the emergence of 'Celtic consciousness' in contemporary Australia has involved not only this re-examination of Australia's Celtic past but also the borrowing of a new repertoire of symbolism invented by the Celtic revivalists of post-war Europe. Thus, to take one example, Cornish enthusiasts in Australia have adopted the Cornish flag, the Cornish kilt and tartan, and the Cornish language (even to the extent of importing the arguments as to the relative merits of the different versions of the revived language). And, unlike their nineteenth-century forebears, many Cornish-Australian enthusiasts are prepared to admit to a 'Celticity' which not only distances them from a British (English) identity but also claims common cause with the Irish. However, not all will do this, and one fascinating aspect of this process is the conflicting motives of contemporary Celtic enthusiasts, some genuinely embracing the ethos of multiculturalism but others (in a sort of 'if you can't beat 'em, join 'em' strategy) adopting the language of multicultural diversity as a means of re-asserting Anglo-Celtic hegemony. At the Annual BritFest in Sydney in November 1999, for example, participants were treated to Scottish pipe-band displays and rousing renditions of *God Save the Queen* and *Land of Hope and Glory* by the Cambrian Choir in traditional Welsh costume, while purchasing goodies such as 'Celtic Pride' carstickers or haggis-in-a-bap and Cornish cream teas (*Guardian*, 8 November 1999). The ambivalence that such display has created in the minds of Celtic activists is conveyed in the 'Editorial Note' in the 1989 volume of the *Australian Celtic Journal*:

> The Australian Ethos is massively founded on Celtic contribution in a polity based on English law and English language. The point is surely worth making in Australia's current confused discussion of multiculturalism that the Celtic contribution over two centuries makes nonsense of suggestions that the existence of more than one culture divides the nation.

As Alexander added:

> The substantial immigration programme which has been Australian policy since World War II has brought many non-English speaking communities to Australia. They have brought with them their own

languages, cultures, problems and needs. This has given them a group consciousness and has noticeably revived a sense of ethnic identity among the longer-established Celtic groups in Australia. Several Celtic groups have chosen to underline their ethnic identity by joining the Ethnic Communities Councils in some Australian States. (1989, 13)

Indeed, the re-invention of Celtic Australia has reached new heights, including not only the co-opting of revivalist symbolism (such as Cornish kilts) but the construction of new, specifically Australian Celtic symbols. Three important examples stand out. The most significant is the stone circle at Glen Innes in New South Wales. Adopting the stone circle as a symbol of pan-Celtic experience (itself an act of faith, given that such henges, although common in the Celtic lands, are in fact of distinctly pre-Celtic origin), the Glen Innes experiment reflects a remarkable self-confidence in that it is, in effect, re-inventing Australia's prehistoric past. Although to some observers this might appear a gratuitous insult to Australia's Aboriginal 'prehistory', it is probably in ideological terms no different from the activities of those super-confident settlers of the colonial era who recreated the architectural culture of medieval Europe in their construction of Gothic cathedrals in the Australian capitals. Of similar pan-Celtic significance is the Australian tartan, designed to appeal to Australians of whatever Celtic descent: 'The recently-created Australian tartan is a move ... to achieve a Celtic unison. Based on the colours of Central Australia and a variation on the sett of Lachlan Macquarie, this 'tartan for a Sunburnt Country' is intended to cater for those proud of being both Celtic and Australian. It is intended for all Celts' (Alexander 1989, 19). The third, and perhaps most intriguing, example of the current invention of Celtic symbolism is the construction of 'Map Kernow', the giant (7m tall) statue of a nineteenth-century Cornish miner at Kapunda in South Australia. Unveiled in June 1988 and costing over $A 100,000, Map Kernow is an interesting synthesis in that its name is drawn from the Cornish language: Map Kernow means Son of Cornwall. A neutral appreciation of South Australia's nineteenth-century history might have suggested an alternative name, 'Cousin Jack', the name by which emigrant Cornish miners knew themselves and were known by others the world over. Map Kernow, by contrast, would have been entirely unknown to the nineteenth-century Cornish, the Cornish language having disappeared long since as a general medium of communication. The choice of Map Kernow, then, indicates both a desire to use the Cornish language in contemporary Australia (part of the co-option of Celtic revivalist iconography) *and* a decision to avoid the 'obvious' designation, Cousin Jack. Cousin Jack, perhaps, was too redolent of nineteenth-century Cornish exclusivity, too reminiscent of an assertive ethnic identity (the 'myth of Cousin Jack') in which the Cornish alleged superiority over competing ethnic groups, notably the Irish (Payton 1999). Map Kernow, however, was conciliatory in tone, both pan-Celtic in sentiment (the deployment of a Celtic language) and multicultural in intention. As the explanatory leaflet produced by the District Council of Kapunda put it, at the unveiling of Map Kernow:

> The Cornish National Song 'Trelawny' was played ... [and] a Cornish Cream Tea was held ... Map Kernow, Cornish for 'Son of Cornwall', is a Monument to the early miners of Kapunda, Australia's first copper mining town. Map Kernow stands for all the people who are part of Kapunda's history—the Cornish, Irish, German and other nationalities. The Son of Cornwall is a reminder that Kapunda has a unique place in the history of South Australia. (District Council of Kapunda c. 1989)

Celtic Australia, then, as at Kapunda, is busily re-inventing itself in a manner consistent with the re-invention of 'Celticity' in contemporary north-western Europe but as part of (or in reaction to) the imperatives of Australian multiculturalism. This re-invention draws its resources from the new symbolism of European Celticity, the reservoir of Celtic historical experience in Australia, and a newly invented symbolism which is specifically Celtic-Australian. Its claim to authenticity relies to some extent on the inherent rationality of this process (it is, after all, an integral part of the multicultural re-invention of Australia) but is based more firmly on that diverse historical experience of Cornish, Scots, Irish and Welsh which was not only non-English but also on occasions self-defining as 'Celtic'. Today, perhaps, as sometimes enthusiastic, sometimes reluctant champions of multiculturalism, the descendants of Australia's nineteenth-century Celtic immigrants exhibit elements of common interest and common consciousness that eluded their forebears—the desire to preserve a certain vision of Australian history and destiny in which the Celts enjoy a central place.

References

Alexander P. The Survival of the Celts in Australia, *Australian Celtic Journal*, 2, pp. 11–20, 1989.
Australian Celtic Journal, 2, 1989.
Australian Federation of Cornish Associations. *AFCS Leaflet*. 1994.
Berresford Ellis, P. *The Celtic Dawn: A History of Pan Celticism*. London, 1993.
Chapman, M. *The Celts: The Construction of a Myth*. London, 1992.
Cohen, R. *Global Diasporas: An Introduction*. London, 1997.
Colman, A. Colonial Cornish: Cornish Immigrants in Victoria, 1865–1880. M.A., University of Melbourne, 1985.
District Council of Kapunda, *Map Kernow Leaflet*, c.1989.
Drew, C.J. and Connell, J.E. *Cornish Beam Engines in South Australian Mines*. Adelaide, 1993.
Fraser, A. *The Warrior Queens: Boadicea's Chariot*. London, 1988.
Hughes, R. *The Fatal Shore: A History of Transportation of Convicts to Australia 1787–1868*. London, 1987.
Jupp J. (ed.) *The Australian People: An Encyclopedia of the Nation, its People and their Origins*. Sydney, 1988.
Lay, P. One and All: The Cornish in Nineteenth-Century New South Wales. M.A., Australian National University, 1992.
Lay, P. *One and All: The Cornish in Nineteenth-Century New South Wales*. Qeanbeyan (NSW), 1998.
Lucas, D. *The Welsh, Irish, Scots and English in Australia: A Demographic Profile with Statistical Appendix*. Canberra, 1987.
Murphy, B. *The Other Australia: Experiences of Migration*. Cambridge, 1993.
O'Brien, J. and Travers, P. (eds) *The Irish Emigrant Experience in Australia*. Dublin, 1991.
O'Farrell, P. *The Irish in Australia*. Sydney, 1993.
Payton, P. The Cornish in South Australia: Their Influence and Experience from Immigration to Assimilation, 1836–1936. Ph.D., University of Adelaide, 1978.
Payton, P. *The Cornish Miner in Australia: Cousin Jack Down Under*. Redruth, 1984.
Payton, P. *The Cornish Farmer in Australia*. Redruth, 1988.
Payton, P. *The Cornish Overseas*. Fowey, 1999.
Prebble, J. *The King's Jaunt: George IV in Scotland, 1822*. London, 1988.
Price, C. The Cornish in Australia: An Invisible Minority with Distinctive Surnames. In A. McRobbie (ed.) *Arrivals, Departures, Achievements: Essays in Honour of James Jupp*. Canberra, 1992.
Reece, B. The Welsh in Australian Historical Writing. *Australian Studies*, 4, December 1990.
Reece, B. Writing About the Irish in Australia. In J. O'Brien and P. Travers

(eds) *The Irish Emigrant Experience in Australia*. Dublin, 1991.

Richards, E. The Highland Scots in South Australia. *Journal of the Historical Society of South Australia*, 4, 1978.

Richards, E. The Highland Scots. In J. Jupp (ed.) *The Australian People: An Encyclopedia of the Nation, its People and their Origins*. Sydney, 1988.

South Australian Register.

Williams, G. A Prospect of Paradise? Wales and the United States, 1776–1914. In G. Williams (ed.) *Religion, Language and Nationality in Wales*. Cardiff, 1979.

7

Creative Ethnicity
One Man's Invention of Celtic Identity

DEBORAH CURTIS

In her book *Ethnic Identity,* Anya Peterson Royce notes that while people make choices as individuals about their ethnicity, their choices must reference a particular ethnic group to have any meaning (1982, 6). Close relationships exist between individuals and social institutions such as ethnic groups. For this reason, it is difficult, if not impossible, to distinguish an individual's role in constructing his or her own ethnic identity from that of the broader culture and its ethnic symbols and stereotypes. What kinds of choices do individuals make regarding their ethnicity? How do these choices influence the 'invention' of an individual's ethnic identity? Further insight into the individual's role in constructing ethnic identity requires attention to the choices of particular individuals and the influence of their personal attributes. A project that describes and assesses the individual aspects of 'inventing' ethnicity must be ethnographic in methodology and a case study in approach. It must rely on a particular individual's self-reports and the researcher's knowledge of that individual's personality, life history and personal choices of ethnic display. The following is the report of the results of just such a project.

This chapter focuses on a particular person, my father, and his role in 'inventing' his ethnicity, the sense he has of being Scottish-American. His ethnic identity is neither wholly self-determined nor wholly culturally determined. I had assumed that it was formed from both the interplay of stereotypic Scottish ethnic symbols that exist in our culture, and his

CREATIVE ETHNICITY

individual characteristics and choices. An examination of his experience, however, suggested four ways in which individuals may affect the construction of ethnic identity. First, his experience shows that individuals may choose to emphasize certain aspects of their 'inherited' ethnicity over others. Second, individuals may supplement their heritage through the adoption of prevailing ethnic stereotypes or through the creation of esoteric 'ethnic' traditions. Third, an individual's construction of ethnic identity may influence others' ethnic identities, such as those of children. Finally, the adoption of an ethnic identity may be a means of individual expression and fulfilment. Examination of my father's personal experience increases our understanding of what Scottish-American means to an individual and reveals some of the highly complex processes at work when individuals 'invent' ethnicity, not least in 'new' societies such as North America where there is a rich repertoire of immigrant ethnicities from which to choose.

As this chapter's title suggests, concepts of 'ethnicity', 'ethnic identity', 'creative ethnicity' and 'invention' provide the theoretical context in which this case study exists. Some contemporary definitions of ethnicity emphasize the individual's role in the construction of ethnic identity. One of six working criteria for a definition of ethnic group and ethnicity in the United States (established in 1973 by the Social Science Research Council) proclaims that people view ethnic categories differently in different social settings. This, Royce notes, reflects the view that ethnicity is a strategy adopted by individuals to fit particular occasions (1982, 24–6). In other words, ethnicity is seen by some as a resource available for individual manipulation.

However, most researchers also define ethnicity in terms of 'groupness', emphasizing the primacy of group identification over that of the individual. Their definitions may admit individual affiliation, either real or imagined, within groups. Yet, the emphasis remains on identification with a group as almost a prerequisite for 'ethnicity'. For example, Wsevolod Isajiw states that in North America 'ethnicity' refers to 'an involuntary *group* of people who share the same culture or to descendants of such people who identify themselves and/or are identified by others as belonging to the same involuntary group' (1985, 16, my emphasis). The word 'involuntary' here is significant, for it plays a central role in most definitions of ethnicity. Almost all definitions explicitly include as a determining factor 'ancestral origin' or genealogical connections to members of the ethnic group. Even so, emphasis on the 'involuntary' aspect of ethnicity has lessened in recent years as researchers, like Royce, reconceptualize ethnicity as dynamic and subjective rather than static and essential. Ancestral origin, however, remains a powerful part of most conceptions (both academic and popular) of ethnicity.

Generally speaking, definitions of 'ethnic identity' also emphasize group affiliation. As noted above, individuals' choices about their ethnicity have little meaning unless they have a recognizable ethnic group as their referent (Royce 1982, 6). An individual's ethnic identity must be based on a connection, real or imagined, to some ethnic group. The experience of self-identity is, however, an individual experience and most contemporary conceptions of 'ethnic identity' also recognize that individuals play a major role in its construction. Francis E. Aboud (1981), for example, describes how individuals construct their ethnic identity from a combination of internal attributes (such as emotions, beliefs and values) and external attributes (such as appearance, social role and traditions). Thus an individual 'invents' a concept of his or her ethnicity by combining internal and external personal characteristics.

The term 'creative ethnicity' comes from the title of a book edited by Stephen Stern and John Allen Cicala (1991). The essays in their volume focus primarily on the continuity of ethnic folklore and traditions as performed by 'ethnics', a term Stern uses but does not define. Based on his discussion, I understand the term 'ethnics' to refer to minority groups in the United States of America whose ancestry is other than Anglo-white. The 'traditions' of these minority groups are considered to be dynamic, adapting to new settings, or are even new creations based on 'traditional' models. However, despite this emphasis on the dynamic and 'creative' aspects of identity, the book continues to suggest that ethnic traditions (and the ethnic identifications they signify) originate in ethnic communities or groups with ancestral, often Old World, continuities with a traditional past.

This use of 'creative identity' contrasts strongly with my own as used in this chapter. In contrast to the emphasis in Stern and Cicala on groups, non Anglo-whites and ancestral connection, this chapter considers an Anglo-white individual's role in the construction of his own ethnic identity. This is a construction where choices have only the vaguest connections to, and few continuities with, an identifiable ancestral past. Yet, as the perhaps ironic title of the chapter indicates, my contention here is that an individual's construction of ethnic identity, even if he/she is inventing it 'out of whole cloth', may be equally as creative and in some respects similar to the processes described in the book *Creative Ethnicity*.

The term 'invention' in the subtitle, and indeed throughout this chapter, alludes to post-modern perspectives regarding the 'constructedness' of experience. Werner Sollors notes in the introduction to his book *The Invention of Ethnicity* that 'invention' is 'an adequate description of a profound change in modes of perception', a change that has signalled a move from essentialist views of the world to a recognition of its 'cultural constructedness' (Sollors 1989, x). Following Sollors, this chapter takes the view that ethnicity and ethnic identity are as much 'constructed' within cultures *by* individuals as they are 'essential' elements of society.

In using the term 'invention', I also suggest similarities between constructions of ethnicity and the primarily institutionalized constructions of the past described by Eric Hobsbawm. His book *The Invention of Tradition*, co-edited with Terence Ranger, focuses on nationalistic inventions of history that Hobsbawm terms 'invented traditions'. In his introduction, Hobsbawm defines 'invented tradition' as 'a set of practices, normally governed by overtly or tacitly accepted rules and of a ritual and symbolic nature, which seek to inculcate certain values and norms of behaviour by repetition' (1983, 1). Such practices, says Hobsbawm, are normally meant to establish continuity with a historic past through 'constructed and formally instituted traditions and those [traditions] emerging in a less easily traceable manner within a brief and dateable period' (ibid.). The historical continuities that 'invented traditions' establish, however, are 'largely facetious'. For example, one essay in the collection by Hugh Trevor-Roper focuses on the 'invention' of 'ancient' kilt sets and Scottish Highland culture during the late eighteenth and early nineteenth centuries. As another example of an 'invented tradition', Hobsbawm refers to the forging of the Ossian text by James Macpherson in the eighteenth century.

Like 'invented traditions', constructions of ethnicity are often concerned with establishing a continuity with the past. In constructions of ethnicity, the focus is on an ancestral or cultural past rather than a historic past. Both invented traditions and constructed ethnicities establish links between the past and the present. Not surprisingly, interest in these two kinds of continuous constructed pasts often coincide. Nationalistic movements usually incorporate romantic 'invented' notions of both a historic past and an ancestral, ethnic past. Similarly, those conducting genealogical research are usually pleased when their ancestral past coincides with events from the historic past. For example, it is a matter of personal pride to many individuals in the United States if they can trace their family heritage to notable historic figures such as generals or famous early settlers. Studies of family folklore have revealed a number of family stories in which it is alleged that family ancestors knew famous outlaws of the American West. Many people proudly trace themselves genealogically to the *Mayflower* Puritans.

In addition, the ancestral continuities that inform constructions of ethnicity may also, like historical continuities of 'invented tradition', be largely 'facetious'. Hobsbawm notes that in some instances a historical continuity with the past may be established through a new creation based on old symbols, semi-fiction and forgery. A corresponding construction of ethnicity based on 'semi-fiction' might involve creative genealogy, based on a combination of oral history and documentary evidence. One researcher notes that ethnic groups are 'characterized by a sense of peoplehood: its members *believe that they have a common ancestry, whether in fact they do or do not*; they have memories of a shared past, and they have certain badges, physical or cultural or both, which enable them to identify one another and to exclude outsiders' (Burnet 1981,17, my emphasis). An individual might also assume a 'new' ethnicity, perhaps through adopting the symbols and stereotypes associated with an ethnicity other than his or her own. It is likely that some individuals would not necessarily feel an 'ancestral' justification for this shift but would deploy other modes of supposed affinity. Hobsbawm also notes that 'invented traditions' re-establish breaks in the historical continuities of genuinely old traditions. For example, Christmas regained its popularity as a holiday in the nineteenth century but incorporated and invented 'old' traditions such as carol singing. This re-establishment of pre-existing continuities is reminiscent of Isajiw's term 'ethnic rediscoverers', which refers to those people who 'develop a symbolic relation to the culture of their ancestors' (1985, 15). To use Stern's term, they are no longer 'ethnics' living an 'ethnic' lifestyle but connect to their ethnic culture through symbols and invented traditions.

The point of describing these strategies of constructing or 'inventing' ethnic identities and comparing them to 'invented traditions' is not to discredit them or to suggest they are somehow inauthentic. After all, recent conceptions of ethnicity as a dynamic and manipulatable category of experience suggest that one person's identity is neither more nor less 'constructed' than the next person's. On the contrary, as the following brief description and assessment of my father's Scottish self-identification shows, such constructions are valid and meaningful for the individuals who engage in them.

My father, Sherman Curtis, lives in a small town located in Western Maine in the eastern United States of America. Based on an informal interview I conducted with him in November of last year, the following picture of his developing Scottish identity, intertwined with his personal history, emerges.

Sherman heard many family stories as a child that referred to his ancestral background. In these stories, most family members were recognized as having a combination of Irish, English and Scottish roots. A few stories hint at other family connections to a Maine community of Native Americans and a possible Spaniard (his mother had once been told she looked Spanish). Sherman's ethnic identity is then, in part, a manipulation of this inherited oral tradition. He has, at different points in his life, adopted one, or a combination, of these ethnicities.

Sherman has most often identified with English or Celtic categories of ethnicity. At approximately age ten, during a Saint Patrick's Day party, his mother told him that he was partly Irish through an ancestor on his father's side. Sherman now recognizes this information to be erroneous because he has since learned that the said Irishman's name, MacCurdy, is more likely Scottish. At the time, however, he felt pride in 'being Irish'. Later, after graduating from high school, Sherman identified more closely with his English roots through his surname Curtis. His purchase of a small ceramic plaque depicting a Curtis coat of arms reflects this period of his ethnic identification. The plaque hung prominently in his living room for several years.

While still in his mid-twenties, Sherman began to redefine his ethnicity by focusing more attention and energy on his Scottish heritage. At this time, he was already married with one child and had a well-paid, blue-collar job in a paper manufacturing plant. He began to research his family genealogy and rediscovered that a number of family ancestors had Scottish names. I say 'rediscovered' because this information was not entirely new to him. He had known since childhood that his father's mother was born a Stuart and that his mother's maiden name was Grant, two recognizably Scottish names. For some reason, however, this information grew more important in my father's sense of who he was as he reached adulthood and began sifting through old family records.

Even as his genealogical research continued, an event occurred that even more greatly influenced the course of Sherman's developing Scottish identity. In 1971, Sherman read in a newspaper that a local man, originally from Prince Edward Island, Canada, would be offering classes to those interested in learning to play the bagpipes. My father remembers his own reaction to the article in this way (from transcript #1A):

> I looked at that [the picture of the man in the paper playing the pipes] and said I'm going to learn to play those things. And no, see, there was no desire growing up. I mean, things are starting to come together now. Bits and pieces of background, and all of a sudden, my mind or my spirit or whatever said, 'I'm going to learn to do this'.

That week, Sherman ordered a practice chanter and the next week he began taking lessons. He studied with this man for over two years and devoted an hour to practising nearly every day, a fact my mother corroborates. Within fifteen months he could play tunes on the pipes.

Sherman's interest in the pipes and growth as a piper were a major motivating factor in his desire to learn more about Scotland and his own Scottish ancestry. He purchased books on Scottish tartans and heraldry, and was given a series of 'coffee table' books on Scotland for birthdays and Christmas. His interest was encouraged by my mother, who says: 'I thought it was a good, you know, everyone needs a hobby'. This personal hobby quickly developed into a family way of life. My parents, my brother and myself took summer trips to see the Highland Games in Antigonish, Nova Scotia, and to Cape Breton, where Sherman twice enrolled in a two-week piping course at Saint Ann's Gaelic College, a summer folk school. For many years, we went to Scottish festivals whenever they were held within driving distance.

From 1980 to 1989, Sherman was an active member and leader of a local Shrine Pipe Band. In fact, he originally joined the Shriners and its associated men's group, the Society of Free and Independent Masons, because he learned they were organizing a bagpipe band. Sherman visited Scotland with other band members in 1984, an experience he still enjoys talking about. Many items from this trip are displayed in my parents' home, including a bottle of whisky, signed by Masonic Lodge members at a meeting Sherman attended in Scotland. Only during the last five years, due in part to the pressures of starting a new career, has he curtailed his band activities. Now he rarely plays the pipes.

Having summarized my father's experience, I offer some observations on how Sherman's personal choices influenced the 'invention' of his ethnicity. As noted earlier, Sherman's experience suggests four ways in which individuals may influence the construction of ethnic identity. First, Sherman emphasizes certain aspects of his ancestral heritage and plays down others in constructing his Scottish identity. For example, although many of his ancestors have Scottish surnames, many others are not recognizably Scottish. Yet my father tends to focus on those with an ancestral link to Scotland. In addition, the paternal line of Scottish descent in his family, the one he is most interested in, has been difficult to establish through genealogical research. This is because it hangs on the oral account of an unofficial adoption of a young MacCurdy boy by a man named Curtis. No records exist to verify this account or any lineage through MacCurdy. Despite this, Sherman strongly identifies with the name MacCurdy and has read accounts of the MacCurdy family and clan history. Other oral accounts, such as that of an ancestor with the German-sounding name of Fruen, are disregarded. Interestingly, oral accounts of Native American ancestors have been adopted by Sherman as a corollary to his Scottish ethnicity. He sees many connections between the temperaments and behaviours of 'Indians' and Scottish Highlanders. For example, he notes that the Picts, one of the 'original Celtic tribes of Scotland', were so named by Roman invaders because they painted their bodies. Sherman assumes that painted bodies are a trait of most Native American tribes, based on the many Western films he has seen. He also believes both Native Americans and Highlanders have close connections to the natural landscape and are great warriors. He chooses to affiliate himself with these ethnicities through his acceptance of the veracity of certain oral accounts.

Second, Sherman supplements the ethnicity and ethnic traditions he has inherited by adopting recognizably Scottish symbols and stereotypes for his own self-expression. Most of what forms Sherman's concept of Scottish culture comes from books, his experiences playing a Scottish instrument, and conversations with other people also interested in things Scottish. He tries to follow certain traditions closely, such as those associated with proper Highland dress. Sherman strongly believes that only ancestral linkage to a particular clan allows an individual to wear that clan's tartan. This means that he has consciously adopted a Stewart tartan under which the MacCurdy name is subsumed on tartan and clan charts. He also surrounds himself with images of Scotland and Scottish ethnicity that range from a small, framed print of the Duke of Wellington's charge of the Royal Scots Greys against Napoleon at Waterloo, to a T-shirt emblazoned with the phrase 'Up Yer Kilt' and the caricatured picture of a burly kilt-wearing Scot wielding a big knife.

Sherman also uses his knowledge of Scottish symbols and stereotypes to create new, esoteric beliefs and traditions. For example, based on his experiences in the Canadian Maritimes and Maine, Sherman has developed a belief that the Maine pronunciation of certain words is directly derived from the accents of Scottish immigrants. Sherman also identifies himself with certain personality traits that he believes to be distinctly Scottish. These traits include: a fierce temper; a tendency to bear grudges; a wild and 'free spirit'; and a tendency to be truthful, naive and in touch with nature. Again, there is an ancestral connection here as well through the figure of his red-haired, 'Scottish' grandmother, Rosilla Abigail Stuart, who is well remembered among family members for her violent temper and foul vocabulary.

Third, the ramifications of Sherman's 'invented' ethnicity go well beyond him as an individual. His thoughts about being Scottish have greatly influenced how his children, my younger brother and I, think about ourselves and our heritage. I have been unable to interview my brother about whether he identifies himself as Scottish now that he is an adult. I do know, however, that two years ago, much to my mother's dismay, my brother acquired a sizeable tattoo of the Scottish flag. As for myself, I immediately think 'Scottish' if someone asks me about my ethnic background, although, since my mother has some Irish roots, it is probably as much Irish as it is Scottish. I like plaid. I have tapes of pipe music. A piper played 'Amazing Grace' at my wedding. These seemingly superficial associations have deep roots in my earliest childhood memories.

Finally, Sherman's pursuit of things Scottish has been a means of personal expression and fulfilment for him in many ways. For example, playing the pipes is a display of ethnicity and 'connectedness' to a supposed ancestral past, but it is also a way to stand out and be original. Few other people in the area where he lives play the pipes. The nature of the instrument itself, and the traditional Scottish attire worn when playing it, also make the bagpiper difficult to ignore. The bagpipes' loud piercing sound rings through the entire neighbourhood when my father practices. Over the years, a number of neighbours' dogs have wandered to my parents' house and howled in accompaniment when my father is practising. Sherman has often been asked to give lessons, both privately and through local schools and colleges, or to play at events such as weddings, funerals, church services and private parties. My father enjoys the attention he receives as a piper and the somewhat unique status it affords him.

In addition, learning to play the pipes is an accomplishment in which Sherman takes some pride. Here, some biographical information provides a context for understanding the significance of this accomplishment. Sherman was a poor student in school and academic achievement was not a priority in his family. His brother left school after the eighth grade and Sherman quit after his second year in high school. He later returned to school after working for a year but often notes that he barely graduated. When Sherman talks about high school, he expresses regret about his poor performance. He also regrets that his father died when he was still a 'drop-out' and did not live to see him finish high school, join the Navy, get a good job and raise a family.

In the midst of these life experiences, regrets and memories, the accomplishment of learning to play the bagpipes stands out as a testament to Sherman's ability to persevere and succeed. When he first began to learn to play the bagpipes, he practised for an hour each day. Lacking a musical background, and still unable to read music on sight, every song Sherman plays must be painstakingly memorized, note by note, doubling by doubling. By learning to play the pipes, Sherman not only connects himself with his father's ancestors (and thus, his father), but also proves he can do something well when he chooses. In telling about learning to play the pipes, Sherman stresses that my mother doubted he had the patience for such a task. His mastery of the instrument answers her real or imagined criticism, the doubts of others (including those of his deceased father) and any lingering self-doubts Sherman might have about his own ability to learn or succeed in life.

Thus, Sherman's interest in his own ethnic background goes beyond a personal hobby or casual genealogical interest. It forms a significant part of his personal identity. And for a time, discovering more about this ethnicity, and the behaviours and traditions he now associates with it (including playing the pipes), assumed a central position in his life. I can remember, from an early age, how every day my mother packed a slim volume into my father's lunch basket. It was only recently, when I saw the book again, titled *Scottish Heraldry*, that I realized he must have been reading it during lunchbreaks for several years. Why the development of his Scottish identity became such an important part of his life in the early 1970s, or why he is less outwardly demonstrative about that ethnicity today, are questions that require further research.

In conclusion, the study of how individuals conceptualize and 'invent' their ethnicities reveals a great deal, not just about these individuals, but about the processes and effects of constructing ethnic identity. Although he now rarely plays the pipes, Sherman still views himself within the context of Scottish ethnicity that he has constructed. I believe he will continue to view himself and the world through that lens.

References

Aboud, F.E. Ethnic Self-Identity. In R.C. Gardner and R. Kalin (eds) *A Canadian Social Psychology of Ethnic Relations*. Toronto, 1981.

Hobsbawm, E. Introduction: Inventing Traditions. In E. Hobsbawm and T. Ranger (eds) *The Invention of Tradition*. Cambridge, 1983.

Isajiw, W.W. Definitions of Ethnicity. In R.M. Bienvenue and J.E. Goldstein (eds) *Ethnicity and Ethnic Relations in Canada*. Boston, 1985.

Royce, A.P. *Ethnic Identity*. Bloomington, 1982.

Sollors, W. Introduction: The Invention of Ethnicity. In W. Sollors (ed.) *The Invention of Ethnicity*. New York, 1989.

Stern, S. and Cicala, J.A. *Creative Ethnicity*. Logan UT, 1991.

PART THREE

CELTIC PRAXIS

Any research into a group of people, whether it is a study of past or present, will have an effect on the population, either affecting how others view them, or perhaps, more importantly, how they view themselves. Although Celtic Studies is not often at first inspection considered to be a field with great applied potential, in fact there is room for a broad scope of practical applications ranging from policy consulting to tourism, education and cultural and economic regeneration. Just as economic prosperity can lead to renewed cultural confidence, so cultural confidence can itself act as an economic regenerator, as the booming 'Celtic Tiger' economy of Ireland has shown in the 1990s.

The two areas addressed in this section are tourism and language planning. In Roy Pedersen's chapter the two topics are combined as he outlines strategies for strengthening the economic basis and possibilities for Gaelic while promoting the language as a unique 'selling point' for tourism in the Highlands and Islands of Scotland. Brian Stowell gives an honest account of language planning in Manx schools which could provide a template for anyone interested in language preservation issues. Moya Kneafsey compares attitudes to tourism in western Ireland and Brittany, exploring how host cultures both relate to and create tourist initiatives.

8

Provision of Manx Language Tuition in Schools in the Isle of Man

BRIAN STOWELL

Historical background

Manx, or Manx Gaelic, is the native language of the Isle of Man, a semi-autonomous island in the north Irish Sea. The Isle of Man, which has been a dependency of the British Crown since 1765, is not part of the United Kingdom, nor is it fully in the European Union.

Manx Gaelic is an offshoot of Old Irish, and naturally is closely related to modern Irish and Scottish Gaelic. Manx was the majority language of the Isle of Man until, say, the 1830s, although English was established in the island as the language of power and prestige centuries previously. Before 1765, most Manx had not needed to acquire much knowledge of English. However, following the acquisition of the island by the British Crown, the Manx economy went into decline, forcing Manx people to emigrate and hence leading to the spread of the English language in the island. An influx of monoglot English speakers from England and Scotland and the rise of tourism in the nineteenth century were further powerful factors which caused a rapid decline in Manx.

By the 1950s, only a handful of native speakers of Manx survived. The last native speaker of what can be called 'traditional Manx', Ned Maddrell, died in 1974. In most reference works, this is described as the 'death' of Manx. However, extensive tape recordings had been made of the last native speakers and the bulk of the language had been preserved in written form. In addition, there have always been those who have acquired fluency in Manx as a second language.

During the nineteenth century, most Manx people, generally as a result of huge social pressure from the spread of the new, prestigious English culture in the island, turned violently against their own language. Usually, they rejected the language but clung to other, lesser badges of identity. Over several generations, regret at the virtual loss of Manx grew, resulting in an increase in the numbers of those wanting to learn Manx.

Surprisingly for most people not familiar with the Isle of Man, Manx was never taught in schools in the island in a coherent programme until 1992. In the eighteenth century, the Anglican Bishop of the Isle of Man, Hildesley, had overseen an enlightened scheme whereby Manx children were educated through their own language in church schools. However, the scheme foundered after Hildesley's death. The nineteenth and early twentieth centuries saw a remarkable neglect of Manx. It would be no exaggeration to say that almost all Manx people viewed the language with contempt, or, at least, professed to do so. Calls from supporters of Manx for tuition in the language to be provided in schools on an organized basis were ignored. It was left to individual teachers, mainly in primary schools, to do what little they could to promote Manx Gaelic.

Recent developments

The early 1970s saw a particularly strong rise of interest in Manx. This interest can be considered within the framework of the general Celtic revival that was occurring in Europe during the late 1960s and 1970s. During this period there was a heightened interest in Celtic cultures and politics, which led to campaigns for devolution in Scotland and Wales as well as calls for cultural preservation and regeneration in each of the Celtic countries. As Celtic languages were perceived as significant (if not primary) markers of Celtic identity, certain educational strategies were initiated to attempt to halt their decline. Subsequently, language groups and individuals working for Manx were increasingly involved in informal discussions with Manx government officials and politicians concerning the provision of Manx tuition in schools. These discussions eventually led in 1991 to the creation of the government post of Manx Language Officer and funding for two full-time teachers of Manx.

A catalyst in this development had been the results of a Gallup quality of life survey in 1990. A total of 826 island residents was interviewed concerning a wide range of issues, including the Manx language. It was found that 36 per cent of respondents wanted to see Manx taught in schools as 'an alternative subject', a result which seemed to have some political impact.

More directly, the Department of Education of the Isle of Man government had prepared a paper explaining the need for urgent action to help arrest the further decline of the language. Following consideration of this paper by the Council of Minsters (the Manx 'Cabinet'), a government policy decision was made to make tuition in Manx available in the schools to those children whose parents opted for this. Manx would be taught on a voluntary, peripatetic basis, similar to the teaching of instrumental music. A Manx Language Officer would be appointed, funded initially by the Manx Heritage Foundation. In addition, there would be two seconded teachers of Manx who would work full-time with the Language Officer to prepare and deliver Manx courses for schoolchildren.

The job specification for the Manx Language Officer was very broad, the duties being outlined as follows:

1. to work with Department of Education advisory and teaching staff to devise and implement a Manx language programme of studies for schoolchildren;
2. to contribute to training of peripatetic teachers employed to deliver the programme;
3. to undertake and organize such research as is required by the programme;
4. to develop good professional relationships with all staff and other interested parties;
5. to promote positive attitudes to Manx in the community and stimulate interest further afield;
6. to serve the language-learning needs of existing speakers of Manx to ensure enhanced standards;
7. to undertake such research and tasks as would be needed to maintain and develop the quality of the language itself;
8. to provide a translation facility;
9. to contribute to strategies for the further use of the language;
10. to carry out other duties commensurate with the post and the level of responsibility.

Following competitive interviews, Brian Stowell was appointed as Manx Language Officer, taking up the position in January 1992. Stowell, a Manxman from Douglas, had been a physics lecturer at the then Liverpool Polytechnic (later Liverpool John Moores University). In the

1950s as a schoolboy, he had acquired fluent Manx by going round the island with Douglas Fargher and others, recording the Manx of native speakers. In common with most other Manx speakers, Stowell had no formal qualifications in Manx, but had worked on providing courses for learners. He also had a knowledge of Irish, which he had taught in adult classes in Liverpool.

The teachers appointed to work with Brian Stowell were Phil Kelly and Peggy Carswell, both primary school teachers. Phil Kelly had worked for many years promoting Manx, particularly in organizing and teaching non-official classes for adults at Kirk Michael, in the north-west of the island. Peggy Carswell had significant experience in teaching Manx to young children and in running a Manx-language mums and tots group.

In the first few months of 1992, the newly formed Manx Language Unit formulated an action plan, in close consultation with John Cain, the Department of Education adviser with particular responsibility for languages. It was very much the case that the Manx Language Unit was breaking new ground. Various courses of action were considered. For example, would it be advisable to offer Manx in just a few selected schools and concentrate on these schools? What would the criteria be for selecting such schools? Should Manx be offered in the primary schools (first level) and not in the secondary schools (second level)? Although the likely uptake of Manx was not known, such deliberations tended to be influenced by the model of instrumental music tuition, where small or very small numbers of pupils left compulsory lessons for optional instruction by peripatetic teachers.

It soon emerged that there would be severe problems in offering Manx tuition to very young pupils just starting their primary school careers. Some teachers of such children expressed strong views that either none of the children in their classes should take Manx, or the whole class should do so. In the latter case, this would have gone against the voluntary nature of the scheme and raised the spectre of 'compulsory Manx'. This factor led to the decision on the part of the Manx Language Unit to offer Manx tuition to pupils aged at least seven. Although there were decided educational advantages in starting language tuition at an earlier age, this was not possible.

There were other factors which, while perhaps less immediate, had to be borne in mind. The United Kingdom was introducing National Curricula in England, Wales, Scotland and Northern Ireland. As with most educational matters, the Isle of Man authorities decided to shadow English practice and adopt the English National Curriculum, even though this curriculum did not have the force of law behind it in the island (given its constitutional position outside the United Kingdom). Although the Isle of Man was to a large extent insulated from the intense controversies over the National Curriculum in England (where the curriculum quickly proved to be inoperable in its original form), nevertheless the new curriculum involved teachers in the Isle of Man in significant extra work, a large amount of which was widely regarded as pointless.

The common perception that the new curriculum was overly prescriptive (particularly in the secondary schools) and that there would be 'no room for extras' did not augur well for Manx. In addition, the Isle of Man had embarked on an ambitious programme of compulsory French for all primary school pupils aged seven and over. In 1992, this programme was in its initial stages of working towards four years of French tuition in the primary sector. While the French scheme was proving successful and was widely admired both on and off the island, it had aroused opposition from some teachers (including headteachers). This was another factor apparently militating against the introduction of Manx into the schools. It was likely that Manx would be seen by some teachers as yet another irritant which hindered their 'proper work'.

In the spring of 1992, the Manx Language Unit, with the approval of the Department of Education, decided to offer half an hour of Manx tuition per week to all pupils aged seven and over, including secondary schools. This was a decision to spread the available resources thinly and widely. Thirty minutes tuition per pupil per week would be just enough to teach useful language, while being short enough to facilitate the introduction of Manx into schools. Headteachers of the primary schools (there are about thirty in the island) and the five secondary schools were visited and arrangements negotiated for the best days and times for the half-hour teaching slots. It was still tacitly assumed that the instrumental music tuition model was completely valid for Manx language teaching (small numbers being taught on an optional basis by peripatetic teachers).

In May 1992, about 8,500 copies of a circular went out to parents and guardians offering Manx tuition to pupils who would be aged seven and over in September 1992. The circular said that 'Classes will last half an hour per week within normal school hours and will be taken by visiting specialist Manx teachers, similar to the way in which instrumental music is taught at present'.

The response from parents and guardians of primary school pupils was very much higher than might have been anticipated, with an overall figure of about 40 per cent opting for Manx tuition. The percentage figures for the secondary schools were much lower (average 6 per cent). Nevertheless, significantly large numbers (between 63 and 109) opted for Manx in each of the secondary schools.

In May/June 1992, a total of 1,949 of pupils registered as wishing to study Manx, 1,482 of these being in the primary schools and 467 in the secondary schools. These numbers could not be catered for by the two peripatetic teachers. Teaching in the schools had not been included in the Manx Language Officer's job specification, but the huge response to the offer of Manx tuition showed that he would be required to do some teaching. In fact, Brian Stowell welcomed this because it enabled him to keep in touch with the most important aspects of the work. He was assigned to take classes in secondary schools and (later) in one primary school.

For logistical reasons, Manx tuition was deferred for a total of 314 pupils in six of the larger primary schools. This rather arbitrary decision naturally caused resentment among some of the parents of these children. In September 1992, a total of 1,455 pupils started attending Manx classes: 1,141 in primary schools and 314 in secondary schools.

Before teaching started, the Manx Language Unit had considered concentrating virtually exclusively on the spoken language. However, it was decided to include reading and some writing from the start. At first, a three-year course was mooted. But, in fact, a two-year course called 'Bun Noa' ('New Base' or 'New Meaning'—a deliberate ambiguity) was later devised. In its written form, this consisted of six booklets, which were issued to pupils, one booklet (module) per term. In the school years 1992–3 and 1993–4, secondary as well as primary school pupils studied 'Bun Noa'.

The stated aims of the provision of Manx tuition were:

1. to provide tuition in Manx in schools for those pupils aged seven and over whose parents opt for this;
2. to foster a sense of identity and develop self-confidence;
3. to promote positive attitudes to Manx culture;
4. to promote positive attitudes to language learning.

With heavy emphasis on the spoken language and useful Manx, the course was designed to be as interesting and entertaining as possible. Where at all possible, teaching was through games, although the accommodation available in some schools militated against this. An audio-cassette was made professionally to back up the first year of the course, and computer software was developed to enable pupils to practice their pronunciation of Manx in their own time.

The aim of the 'Bun Noa' course was to enable pupils to understand straightforward aspects of the following main topics when they were heard them discussed in Manx and to talk about them in very simple terms in Manx:

1. greeting people, asking their names and where they live;
2. likes and dislikes;
3. questions about where things are and what people are doing;
4. counting and telling the time;
5. food, drink and shopping;
6. the environment and leisure;
7. health.

Manx classes were generally notable for the great enthusiasm and enjoyment of the pupils, particularly in the primary schools. This was in spite of some timetabling and accommodation problems and the discouraging attitude of a small number of teachers. Problems were evident from the start in one of the secondary schools where, initially, classes had been timetabled following the model laid down by the Department of Education. That is, Manx classes in normal lesson time, with pupils coming out of other classes to take Manx. Some teaching staff at this secondary school took issue with the headteacher over this, and the Manx classes were re-scheduled to take place mainly in the lunch period. This very clearly tended to get Manx off to a bad start in this school.

In two of the secondary schools, Manx was timetabled in assembly and/or tutorial periods. This was not the Education Department's model, but this arrangement worked well, given that Manx was not given a full place in the school curriculum.

It is useful to look at the numbers of pupils attending Manx classes at the beginning and end of the school year 1992–3, shown in Table 8.1. It can be seen that drop-out was low in the case of the primary school sector, where the scheme ran well with few problems. As expected, experience in the secondary schools was generally markedly different from that in the primary schools. Naturally, drop-out in the secondary school sector occurred mainly in those cases where there was thinly veiled hostility to, or (at best) lukewarm acceptance of, Manx tuition. But overall the scheme was regarded as a great success, confounding those largely tacit

Table 8.1

	No. attending September 1992	No. attending July 1993
Primary schools	1,141	1,027
Secondary schools	314	152
Totals	1,455	1,179

critics who thought it would collapse in a matter of weeks. At the end of the school year, pupils were issued with certificates which specified the parts (modules) of 'Bun Noa' they had completed.

Because the demand for Manx could not be catered for by the teachers allocated, the Manx Language Officer took the decision to operate a two-year cycle. In general, pupils could study Manx for two years and then 'make way' for those following them. This approach was largely dictated by the problems of providing Manx tuition in the larger primary schools. Timetabling difficulties meant that, normally, only two half-hour slots were available for Manx each week. In practical terms, it made sense to allocate one of these slots to pupils in one age group and the other slot to pupils in the next age group.

Operating a two-year cycle meant that, in general, it was policy not to recruit new pupils for the 1993–4 school year in either the primary or the secondary school sector. However, tuition in Manx had been deferred in the 1992–3 school year for considerable numbers of pupils in the larger primary schools. It was possible to offer Manx to some of these for the 1993–4 school year where groups of new pupils could be taught separately from those who had already studied Manx for the previous year. Numbers enrolled following this special recruitment exercise gave evidence that there had been no drop in enthusiasm for Manx between 1992 and 1993.

Shortly after the start of the 1993–4 school year, totals of 924 primary and 114 secondary school pupils were attending Manx classes, giving a grand total of 1,038 pupils. Most of these were proceeding to study the second year of the two-year 'Bun Noa' course, with some of the primary school pupils starting the first year. A special secondary school course called 'Bun-Choorse Gaelgagh' ('Basic Manx Course') was being developed for introduction in secondary schools in the following school year (1994–5). Table 8.2 summarizes the attendance figures for the 1993–4 school year.

Table 8.2

	No. attending November 1993	No. attending July 1994
Primary schools	924	852
Secondary schools	114	87
Totals	1,038	939

For the start of the second two-year cycle, circulars offering Manx tuition were distributed to parents and guardians in May 1994, giving the following numbers of pupils registered as wishing to study Manx in the school year 1994–5:

Primary schools:	813
Secondary schools:	139
Total:	952

The vast majority of the primary school pupils were new recruits. The recruitment figures for 1994–5 were very gratifying given the nature of the scheme (recruitment in primary schools for 1994–5 was often virtually confined to Years 3 and 4, whereas recruitment for 1992–3 was from Years 3, 4, 5 and 6).

There was increasing difficulty in adhering to a two-year cycle for all pupils. Such an exercise was becoming increasingly artificial in the smaller primary school where there were no great problems in arranging Manx classes made up of pupils of differing ages. Therefore, another Manx course was developed for those pupils who would be able to proceed to take more than two years of Manx. However, major recruitments would still be staged every other year.

For the 1995–6 school year, the numbers of pupils registered to study Manx were:

Primary schools:	791
Secondary schools:	129
Total:	920

It could therefore be concluded that:

1. There is solid demand for Manx tuition in schools in the Isle of Man.
2. The optional, peripatetic scheme has worked reasonably well in the primary schools and in those secondary schools where Manx has been timetabled in assembly or tutorial periods.
3. Whereas most school teachers have been supportive and sympathetic. a few have made clear their opposition to the teaching of Manx in schools.
4. The merits of Manx as an academic subject need to be made clear. This will be aided initially by the provision of a formal qualification in Manx for sixteen year olds.
5. The position of Manx in the school curriculum needs to made more secure.

More recent developments

In January 1996, the Department of Education presented a comprehensive report on the future of the Manx language to Tynwald (the Manx parliament). Many recommendations were made in this report, including a large increase in the number of teachers of Manx. This proposal came to a vote, which was very narrowly defeated. Although this was not a victory for Manx, it did show the much more favourable political attitude towards the language.

Formal approval was obtained to introduce a course in September 1997 leading to the award of the General Certificate in Manx, which will be equivalent to the British General Certificate of Secondary Education (GCSE), usually taken by sixteen year olds. Approaches had been made to examination boards in the United Kingdom with a view to introducing a GCSE in Manx, but the costs had been prohibitively high following the requirement for these examination boards to operate on a commercial basis. The Isle of Man Education Department had then decided to introduce its own, independent qualification in Manx.

In September 1996, Brian Stowell retired, and Phil Kelly took over as Manx Language Officer. In turn, Catreeney Craine was appointed as a peripatetic teacher of Manx, taking Phil Kelly's former post alongside Peggy Carswell. Continuity was thus maintained.

It was evident that the original job specification for the Manx Language Officer was unrealistically broad. In the report to Tynwald in January 1996, it had been proposed that the additional post of Manx Language Development Officer be created, in particular to aid the teaching of Manx in adult classes. This proposal was not taken up by government, but informal discussions were held in late 1996 and early 1997 concerning the feasibility of creating such a post.

9

The Gaelic Economy

ROY PEDERSEN

Each of the Celtic languages has experienced decline over the last millennium. The new millennium offers the prospect of renaissance and sustained growth if suitable policies, infrastructure and funding are put in place and appropriate language development techniques employed. This chapter considers the case of Scots Gaelic in the hope that it may give some inspiration to those in other Celtic language communities who seek the regeneration of their language and culture.

By 1981 the natural transmission of Gaelic from parent to child had almost reached the point of breakdown. It seemed only a matter of time before the language, and the rich store of values it embodies, would decline to the point at which extinction was inevitable. In the ensuing decade, although the number of Gaelic speakers continued to fall, a foundation was laid for the reversal of this prospect. This chapter describes the mechanisms by which this foundation is being built upon to achieve levels of growth which, if maintained, promise to yield substantial economic and social returns.

One of the most important aspects of the recent development of Gaelic has been the emergence of motivated and focused leadership. This leadership has been able, in a non-politically partisan way, to create a vision of a credible future for Gaelic and has encouraged the creation of a new support infrastructure made up of a mutually reinforcing network of agencies.

A key purpose of Gaelic development is to enable the language and culture within given communities to achieve a standing such that they can in due course sustain themselves and grow naturally within the normal social, economic, administrative, educational, financial and political regime of those communities. This language development process has been described as linguistic and cultural 'normalization'.

Each individual fluent speaker, learner or supporter is a source of energy with the potential to fuel the further development and sustenance of the Gaelic language and culture. When focused and co-ordinated, this energy can be harnessed to very powerful effect. One of the most productive techniques of the recent Gaelic revival has been to engineer the emergence of locations where professional people are employed to interact with others in the community through the medium of Gaelic. These 'local energy centres' are becoming the local foci for the rebuilding of Gaelic in Scotland.

The bones of an integrated strategy for the development of Scots Gaelic (Gàidhlig) were set out in May 1993 in the paper *The Dynamics of Gaelic Development* (Pedersen 1993). The rationale and priorities explored there were developed to form the mission, strategy and operational plan for Scotland's Gaelic development agency Comunn na Gàidhlig (CNAG).

Background

After centuries of decline, the 1980s marked the beginning of a new impetus towards the development of Gaelic. This was driven by an intense and successfully orchestrated effort by Scotland's Gaelic development agency Comunn na Gàidhlig, with government support, to create an infrastructure and the key practical measures essential for the Gaelic community's linguistic and cultural maintenance.

The key tasks of the 1990s have been to bring about a major shift in the age profile such that Gaelic will become increasingly the language of young people rather than the elderly, to develop new areas of Gaelic-based employment and thus generate economic activity, to strengthen cultural self-confidence within the Gaelic community, and to promote the value of Gaelic to government, public bodies and the Gaelic community itself. An effort will be made over the decade to hold the number of Gaelic speakers as close to the current 66,000 as possible. This is not likely to be achieved fully because of the rapidity with which the predominant older age group is disappearing through their own mortality.

The above key tasks have been adopted by CNAG to form its four strategic priorities of education, cultural development, economic development and promotion. These in turn are subdivided into twelve project categories, thus:

Education (Strategic Priority 1)
1. Pre and out of school provision
2. Gaelic-medium education
3. Adult learners of Gaelic
4. Further education

Economic Development (Strategic Priority 2)
5. Business creation
6. Investment by other agencies
7. Training

Culture (Strategic Priority 3)
8. Arts
9. Media
10. Heritage

Co-ordination (Strategic Priority 4)
11. Relationship with government
12. Promotion

By the beginning of the new millennium, it is expected that the language and culture will have been reoriented in such a way that sustained growth both in numbers of speakers and in related cultural and economic activity can ensue indefinitely thereafter.

By setting targets for development for each of these project categories, tentative estimates for numbers of Gaelic speakers in Scotland have been extrapolated, as shown in Table 9.1 (estimates in italic).

Table 9.1

	1971	1981	1991	2001	2011	2021
Total number	89,000	79,000	66,000	*60,000*	*65,000*	*79,000*
No. under age 25	18,000	17,000	14,000	*16,000*	*22,000*	*42,000*
% under age 25	22	22	20	*26*	*32*	*51*

The Development Process

The process by which the interrelated project categories drive forward Gaelic development is illustrated below.

Education
The creation of Gaelic-medium pre-school playgroups, mother and toddler groups and nursery schools has emerged as the fundamental element in the chain of measures for the regeneration of Gaelic. The number of groups in Scotland had grown from four, at the inception of the movement in 1983, to 150 by 1997. The principal effect of Gaelic pre-school provision is linguistic initiation of a new generation of Gaelic speakers, the confidence-raising effects on the associated parents and grandparents and the ensuing demand for Gaelic-medium schools.

The demand for Gaelic-medium schools derives from the linguistic initiation work of the playgroup movement on children and the confidence raising effect on parents. Gaelic-medium schools represent the next vital step in founding the new confident enterprising generation of Gaels. It is a fundamental characteristic of Gaelic-medium education that although Gaelic is the medium of instruction in early primary years, English is introduced in the later years such that pupils become totally fluent in both languages. The intellect-enhancing effect of bilingualism at an early age is widely recognized, not least in the greater ability of true bilinguals to learn a third or fourth language with relative ease.

From modest beginnings the parental demand for Gaelic-medium education has taken off with encouraging results (53 primary units and 1,700 children by 1995). As the key to linguistic reproduction, the rate of growth of Gaelic-medium education will determine the future pace of Gaelic development and the level of derived economic benefits. The single most serious constraint on rapid growth has been the current shortage of trained Gaelic-medium teachers.

Formal education alone is not sufficient for strong linguistic regeneration. Parental and peer encouragement are important supporting factors. The emergence of a new movement, characterized by 'Stradagan' which involves the participation of young people in a range of sports, arts and other enjoyable activities through the medium of Gaelic, provides further reinforcement. CNAG was successful in 1997 in attracting Lottery funding to aid the development of this sector.

For over a century university Celtic departments in Scotland have kept Gaelic scholarship alive. It is symptomatic of the past depressed status of

Gaelic, however, that the bulk of what was studied was orientated towards the past and undertaken through the medium of English. This is now changing and the three Scottish university Celtic departments are evolving new developmental roles and recognize the value of working more closely together and towards a more formal association. It is expected that the emphasis on language planning, promotion and training will grow to meet the demands of new Gaelic-based industries as well as the requirements for Gaelic-medium teaching.

From modest beginnings in the 1970s, the Gaelic-medium business college Sabhal Mòr Ostaig has evolved to become a versatile delivery service for Gaelic-driven development, not only through its educational, training and research functions, but as a generator of economic activity such as the establishment of 'Canan', a Gaelic-media support unit, and the creation of the associated 'Leirsinn' research company. In the longer term, the economic and social benefits already felt in Sleat and beyond will be enhanced by further ambitious developments already planned. In December 1997 Brian Wilson MP, the Scottish Office Minister with responsibility for Gaelic, announced the creation at the Sabhal Mòr of a new campus to cater for 250 full-time students taught through the medium of Gaelic.

A desire among adults to learn Gaelic has been stimulated in recent years by the development of Gaelic. This desire is likely to be boosted further by a number of factors. These include: parents of children attending Gaelic-medium education seeking to keep up with their children, the creation of new career opportunities where Gaelic is a requirement, the effects of Gaelic tourism, and the powerful stimulus of Gaelic television. It is significant that the recent Scottish television series *Speaking Our Language* has attracted a regular viewership in excess of 200,000 (who may be regarded as passive learners) and in its first three months elicited 15,000 enquiries about learning materials. This demonstrates that people are willing to commit themselves if effective language acquisition programmes can be provided.

It has to be said that until recently the success rate of adult learners in achieving fluency in Gaelic has been extremely low. This has been due largely to the use of old-fashioned and ineffective methods and support structures. For the first time, however in the 1960s in Scotland a one-year accredited immersion course was piloted and has since been replicated in various locations throughout the country.

The achievement of fluency itself by a significant number of learners in each ten-year inter-censal period will boost the demographic profile of the economically active Gaelic-speaking population and thereby the market for Gaelic goods and services. A strong demand is anticipated for Gaelic speaking graduates in Gaelic-medium teaching, broadcasting, business studies, development work, tourism and culture, Gaelic arts, and specialists in Gaelic language and literature.

Culture
Much of what distinguishes the Highlands today can be regarded as being based on or derived from Gaelic culture. Recently local historical societies in some communities have been working to conserve their Gaelic heritage for transmission to future generations. Nevertheless it is evident that the cultural assets of Gaeldom are still vastly under-valued and under utilized.

The Gaelic tradition has at least two millennia of outstanding achievement. In more recent centuries, Gaelic artistic contribution to European thought includes the key influence of James MacPherson's Ossian legends on the Romantic, and many ethnonationalist movements. The Gaelic element in British military prowess is also well recognized. Over the last century the annual National Mod has helped to maintain Gaelic music in the Scottish consciousness. Despite these achievements, much of Gaeldom's creative talent has remained suppressed.

The recent development of the Gaelic arts mainly under the 'National Gaelic Arts Project' has created a major new vehicle for focusing creative energy. Feisean (local non-competitive music festivals), Blasad den Iar (interpretative community-based tourist shows), Gaelic exhibitions, new literature, Celtic rock groups, dance, drama events etc. have melded tradition with contemporary forms capturing the collective imagination of Scotland's youth. The opportunities for further development are limited only by the availability of human and financial resources.

For reasons already stated, young people are the prime target for Gaelic development. It is nevertheless important to nurture the use of the language among Gaelic-speaking adults within families and communities. This requires support through a variety of community development techniques, one of which is the transmission of the rich store of traditional culture to the younger generation through historical societies, and through electronic means as proposed under the Dualchas project. It is most important, whatever the age group concerned, that artistic and heritage activity be carried out through the medium of Gaelic.

An extra 200 hours per year of government-funded Gaelic television programming started production during 1992 for the start of new transmissions in 1993, and the number of Gaelic speakers in television was increased to take account of this. A BBC Gaelic Radio service has been in existence for several decades but is also poised to evolve into a full-time national Gaelic service. As Gaelic literacy improves with the growth of both Gaelic-medium schools and adult learners, other media opportunities will emerge in journalism and publishing, particularly in connection with Gaelic periodicals.

On the evidence of experience in other countries, cultural expression is a fundamental driving force for linguistic revival. It is also an important driving force for economic development. The wealth and job creation potential of Gaelic cultural activity to the tourism and broadcasting industries are addressed below. Besides the domestic market, the new Gaelic television industry and the mounting of high-quality professional Gaelic touring shows can act as trade ambassadors for Gaelic Scotland.

Economic Development

One of the most important recent shifts in opinion is that the Gaelic language and culture is now seen as a powerful motor for economic development if harnessed in the right way. Development agencies are increasingly geared to exploit the economic opportunities which Gaelic offers. Educational and cultural development is fundamental to the regeneration of Gaelic but it is through the mainstream commercial application of Gaelic that prosperity and employment gains are likely to be most substantial. Ascribing a greater commercial worth to the language will undoubtedly raise its profile, stimulate demand for its use and justify increased education provision, particularly when wealth and jobs are created.

Obvious economic and employment opportunities are likely to emerge in the service sector as Gaelic is reoriented towards growth. Such opportunities are likely to include translation, printing, advertising/marketing, information processing, Gaelic-related computer software, restaurants, pubs and hotels with a Gaelic ambience, professional musicians and other entertainers. The manufacture of Gaelic signs, stationery and souvenirs and other Gaelic goods represents another area of opportunity. Further expansion may also be expected in book publishing, which has grown rapidly in recent years to meet the growing demand for children's books in particular. As it evolves and diversifies, the Mod itself could develop as a Gaelic trade fair. Fundamental to successful growth of Gaelic commerce will be quality coupled with mechanisms which maximize profit-retention within the Gaelic community.

In addition to the development of specifically Gaelic-based businesses, there will be increasing marketing advantage and scope for a wide spectrum of normal commercial operators to adopt a Gaelic face, be they in the retail, leisure, transport, distilling, brewing, food, land, cultural economy or other sectors. By thus reflecting Gaelic's growing status, such firms stand in time to gain market advantage, and in the process, other aspects of Gaelic development will be reinforced. It is likely that profit-making but non-profit-distributing community enterprises will feature in the range of business featuring Gaelic.

A detailed study carried out in 1993 identified almost 1,000 jobs which had been created as a result of the Gaelic renaissance (Sproull 1993, 22). Thus, for a relatively modest investment in national terms (about £13 million), Gaelic development represents a major opportunity for economic regeneration. Furthermore much of Gaelic-related activities will be a factor in retention of population in rural areas and the jobs created will frequently be of high income and status.

Gaelic Tourism

As the world tourism market becomes more sophisticated and competitive, the need to exploit Scotland's 'unique selling points' becomes imperative. 'Green tourism' and 'cultural tourism' are emerging as promising new opportunities to gain both market share and added value and are widely predicted as long-term growth sectors world-wide.

Analysis suggests that Gaelic tourism, if developed appropriately, will reinforce the existing tourism industry. It presents a major opportunity to create sustainable economic development which will employ an under-utilized resource (Gaelic) and enhance the development of Gaelic culture and society. A primary goal will be to optimize the economic and social benefits of tourism, resulting in a higher-quality product, more and better-quality jobs and increased income for local populations.

This new tourism product, which will reinforce the existing tourism industry, will be underpinned by Scotland's Gaelic resources and is expected to account for 2,000 Gaelic-based jobs over the next twenty years. A key feature is community involvement in, and control of, the industry by promotion of links between Gaelic and local businesses and co-operation with existing agencies. The new industry will be closely integrated with recent developments in Gaelic arts and broadcasting, and will be an important means of raising the profile of Gaelic Scotland nationally, within the European Union and world-wide.

The terms 'Celtic tourism' and 'Gaelic tourism' both have currency. Although there is some overlap between these concepts, they are different in character. The former may be regarded as tourism which promotes a wider and comparative interest in all things Celtic, ranging from the Iron-Age legacy of artefacts and the popular interest in standing stones (regardless of the fact that they are not technically 'Celtic') to the cultural distinctiveness of the various contemporary Celtic language communities. Specifically 'Gaelic' tourism, on the other hand, enables visitors and local people to interface actively with the modern Gaelic-speaking community in Scotland. Use of the Gaelic language and explanation of the culture would have a high profile, although interpretation would be provided in other languages for non-Gaelic speakers.

Gaelic tourism thus described will serve to support and enhance wider tourism objectives. It has the potential to extend the core season; broaden the range of visitors; provide reasons to visit areas of the Highlands and Islands outside of the four major hubs, bringing trade to fragile/remote areas and those with high unemployment; diversify local economies; and increase the distinctiveness of the areas tourism product. With its indoor/outdoor adaptability, Gaelic tourism will enhance all-weather facilities/attractions, and special interest holidays. It also addresses the additional priority of assisting communities to provide tourist attractions in remote and under-represented areas.

A further imperative is that within Gaeldom itself there is an expressed need for a new, more appropriate form of tourism industry, based in the Gaelic communities, under local control, and utilizing cultural resources and strengths already present.

The European Background

In the Europe of the 1990s and indeed into the next millennium tourism is destined to play an increasingly important role; it is presently regarded as the world's largest industry. As the market becomes more competitive and sophisticated, however, cultural tourism is gaining in importance. This offers particular opportunities to Europe's distinctive lesser used language regions. Recently there have been some attempts in local communities throughout Europe to capitalize on their minority linguistic heritage. Nevertheless in an age of improved communications, education and travel, it is evident throughout the Highlands and Islands that the cultural assets of Gaeldom are vastly under-utilized. Indeed the linguistic/cultural assets of all Celtic cultures (with the exception, perhaps, of Ireland) still remain largely untapped in terms of cultural tourism. In fact, regions throughout Europe from Portugal to Turkey could perhaps better promote and develop the ancient associations with named Celtic populations.

The Market
If the new Gaelic tourism sector is to have substance and credibility it must be rooted in and have the affirmation and respect of the Gaelic community itself. For this reason internal Gaelic tourism is a small but important legitimizing component of the Gaelic tourism market because it allows Gaels themselves to feel a sense of ownership of the product. Key dimensions are:

1. Children attending Gaelic-medium schools who seek Gaelic-medium interpretative facilities and events throughout the Highlands and Islands and elsewhere in Scotland.
2. Gaelic speakers of all ages on holiday requiring Gaelic-medium tours and services while out of their own community; this can include expatriates.

The volume market will mainly be visitors from the outside the Highlands and Islands made up of the following categories:

1. British Isles visitors with a variety of Gaelic/Celtic related interests/affinities, e.g. genealogy, music, 'culture collectors', archaeology, etc.
2. Minority language speakers in the European Union among whom there is a growing mutual interest.
3. American, Canadian, Australian etc. visitors of Gaelic descent or Scottish ancestry.
4. The rest of the mass market who have no specific Gaelic interest but who may be introduced *en passant* to Gaelic/Celtic tourism.

The market, therefore, ranges from small-scale but intense interest, through to the large-scale but superficial curiosity. The product should be devised to accommodate this range while endeavouring to educate and stimulate a greater intensity of interest at the 'superficial' end of the spectrum.

The Product

In the Scottish context, a Gaelic tourism facility should interpret, or provide an experience of, some aspect of the Gaelic dimension of Celtic culture or life. As an intrinsic part of its function, Gaelic/bilingual signage, written/audio-visual material, and staff should be provided. There is much yet to do but the following discussion may give some indication of scope.

If the market penetration and income generation are to be maximized, the product must above all be based on demonstrable quality. Switzerland and the Scandinavian countries offer models of positive tourism image and practice based on reputations for top-quality service, clean mountain, coast or lake environment, and a rich cultural and historical backdrop. The formula is to display modernity and efficiency founded on antiquity and tradition. The Gaelic community has the winning natural ingredients for a world-class product given effective organization, appropriate investment and rigorous control of quality, including cultural and linguistic integrity.

The main hardware element proposed for Gaelic tourism is a network of interpretative centres where the history/culture of Gaeldom is explained through the medium of Gaelic but with interpretation in English and other languages. Some of these centres, especially those at main tourist gateways, would have an orientation function to lead visitors into the network thereby to encourage multiple visits. For that reason there should be variety in style and content among these centres. Emphasis on locality/community would generally be desirable. Where appropriate, existing and proposed museums, with improved Gaelic content, should be an integral part of such a network.

The recent development of the Gaelic arts has created a major new vehicle for enhancing the appeal of Gaelic tourism. Gaelic exhibitions, events etc. all have potential, with good organization, for closer integration with the tourism product. The National Mod has long been an event with important off-season tourism benefits. As it evolves it may well have the potential to enhance these benefits further. The new Gaelic television industry and the mounting of high-quality professional Gaelic touring 'shows' can act as ambassadors for Gaelic Scotland.

Besides the passive experience of visiting interpretative centres and events, there is a growing demand especially among young people and learners for participatory activities carried out through the medium of Gaelic (e.g. arts such as drama and music, and sports such as sailing and hill-walking). In addition to this there is cultural tourism (e.g. attending

Gaelic performances, visiting Gaelic-speaking areas and communities, performance such as Blasad an Iar etc.) and educational tourism (e.g. language courses, historical lecture tours, visiting relevant Gaelic sites, genealogy and guided tours of the Gaelic movement in Scotland), providing accommodation in a Gaelic-speaking environment for tourists ranging from hotels and B&Bs and self-catering and identifying these clearly in the literature and marketing information. This could include thatched house restoration and other period buildings restoration.

Visual evidence of the existence of Gaelic is an important part of the process of affirming the distinctiveness of the Highlands and Islands to visitors (especially from the Continent) as well as to residents. A major, and relatively inexpensive aid to creating this 'Gaelic Face' to the product is the provision of Gaelic or bilingual signage and written information, including street signs, shop fronts, logos etc., especially in tourist hubs such as Inverness, Oban and Fort William. Initiatives to bring this about should be done in discussion with local authorities, chambers of commerce and possibly local common good funds. A body of information in Gaelic and from a Gaelic perspective should also be available to tourists in the form of booklets or brochures or videos. For tourists and local people an up-to-date Gaelic-medium/bilingual information sheet on current Gaelic events and facilities will be an important aid to visitor penetration of the Gaelic tourism network.

There is scope to extend greatly the range and quality of Gaelic souvenirs and products including gifts, bric-a-brac, stationery, cards, kitchenware, plaques etc. with Gaelic inscriptions, local Gaelic or bilingual pamphlets, guides and maps to areas of Gaelic interest. Where feasible, local manufacture by Gaelic speakers would be encouraged. Lists for tourists as to where such goods may be available throughout Scotland and beyond could be produced.

The provision of Gaelic accommodation/pubs/restaurants to create or to encourage a Gaelic ambience for the enjoyment of tourists and local people will not only enhance the Gaelic tourism experience but will further reinforce the development of Gaelic at community level. Guidance material needs to be created and delivered as to how to introduce good quality Gaelic traditional foods, music, customs, decor etc., employ Gaelic-speaking staff and use Gaelic/bilingual menus, signs etc.

A variety of specialized Gaelic package tours are possible as contributors to and customers of Gaelic tourism. Tours may be exclusively through Gaelic, for Gaelic speakers, learners, etc., or through English or such other languages as visitors may require. Gaelic tours would generally involve more than one aspect of Gaelic culture by combining, say, history, entertainment, food, interpretative centres and social experiences in Gaelic communities. Lecture tours or activity-related packages offer potential variants (see Gaelic Activity Tourism above). The key is to use the Gaelic dimension to enrich the tourist experience beyond what is now generally available in the Highlands.

A useful specialized market niche is inter-Celtic exchanges. These already take place to a limited extent but are capable of substantial expansion through reciprocal group package tours with Gaelic-speaking couriers, e.g. Scotland–Ireland and vice versa timed to link with feisean or other events.

The above components, which together form the Gaelic tourism product, require coherent and effective marketing as a distinct product within the overall Scottish and Highlands and Islands tourism market. Imaginatively designed campaigns and promotional material will be required. Such material, and associated on-the-ground facilities, could usefully give more prominence to the Gaelic 'G' symbol as a marketing device. In marketing Gaelic tourism, co-operation on cultural tourism projects with other lesser used language regions should be sought, together with European Union funding. Joint projects with Ireland, Wales, and Brittany may be particularly beneficial. In particular, joint marketing of 'Gaelic Scotland' with other Celtic countries should also be pursued.

The Potential Scale of Gaelic Tourism

As the concept of Gaelic tourism evolved it was necessary to develop a feel for the potential scale of the new industry. The official tourism industry statistics shown in Table 9.2 are revealing.

Table 9.2

Area (population)	£ Turnover	Employment	£/head
UK (55,000,000)	25,200,000,000	1,600,000	460
Scotland (5,000,000)	1,500,000,000	160,000	300
Highlands & Islands (360,000)	500,000,000	20,000	1,300

As a crude indicator, by drawing on the lowest of the above per capita ratios, the Gaelic community of 66,000 should be capable of generating a Gaelic tourism industry with an annual turnover of £20 million employing 2,000 people. Given proper development support and marketing there is no reason to believe that the Gaelic industry should perform less well than that of Scotland or the UK as a whole.

There are indeed a number of reasons to believe that the Gaelic tourism product, once fully in operation, has a number of competitive advantages:

1. It is associated with a beautiful, dramatic and clean landscape.
2. Traditional and contemporary Gaelic/Celtic arts (especially music), reinforced by Gaelic television, are vibrant, perceived to be distinct from 'homogenized' Western arts, and now excite international interest.
3. Interest in minority cultures and languages is growing rapidly particularly among the 40 million EU citizens who speak a 'lesser used language'.
4. Gaelic culture is increasingly of interest to continental Europeans interested in Celtic cultures in general.

The Gaelic tourism market and product is being developed in concert with existing organizations and initiatives as an enhancement of the existing Scottish tourism industry. A key priority is strengthening links between Gaelic tourism and other sectors. Besides the Highlands and Islands Enterprise network, Scottish institutional support has featured Tourist Boards, Scottish Natural Heritage, Historic Scotland, ScotRail etc. Links between these and specifically Gaelic organizations working in the fields of the Gaelic arts, broadcasting and the Gaelic learners industry have been forged to provide an infrastructural foundation for the creation of this new Gaelic tourism industry.

In this climate CNAG embarked on a pilot Gaelic tourism project named Fàilte (Welcome), which was made up of the following elements:

1. A 32-page full colour Gaelic tourism brochure in six versions: Gaelic, English, German, French, Spanish and Italian.
2. Origination and publishing of a new Gaelic phrase book in five versions: English, French and German, Spanish and Italian.
3. Devising and mounting training courses for tourism operators to introduce the Gaelic dimension to tourism.
4. Impact assessment study.

In parallel with the pilot study, CNAG also encourages the spread of bilingual signage, extension of the 'G' symbol scheme, and is aiding the design of a travelling exhibition to promote a wider understanding of the story of the Gaels.

The brochure itself, called 'Fàilte—Welcome to Scotland's Gaelic Renaissance', was launched in February 1995. It described the story of the Gaels in Scotland and lists key Gaelic sites, interpretative centres, events, courses, and 270 accommodation providers. The initial print run was 60,000 (subsequently 100,000), of which 25,000 were mailed directly to people who had expressed an interest in Gaelic. It has been widely acclaimed and it is interesting that at a time when many tourist facilities have been struggling to maintain patronage, the high-quality Gaelic facilities such as Aros in Skye and the Calanais Centre in Lewis have been attracting record numbers.

Conclusion

History and culture already provide strong and legitimate elements in developing the UK economy. All indications are that Gaelic has the potential to be an important new contributor to the Scottish economy, particularly in light of the creation of the new Scottish Parliament.

That Scots Gaelic is an economic motor is beyond dispute. The survival of Gaelic as a living language is not yet assured. But there is a growing sense that with good leadership, hard work and a measure of good luck Gaelic will make it. And we are not just thinking of maintenance of the status quo but of sustained growth as a well-founded feature of the next millennium. Let that be the prospect for all the Celtic languages!

References

Pedersen, R. *The Dynamics of Gaelic Development*. Iomairt na Gaidhealtacht. Inverness, 1993.
Sproull, A. *The Economics of Gaelic Language Development*. Glasgow, 1993.

10

Rural Tourism and Identity
Stories of Change and Resistance from the West of Ireland and Brittany

MOYA KNEAFSEY

The aim of this chapter is to explore the relationship between rural tourism and place identity in County Mayo, on the Atlantic seaboard of Ireland, and Finistère in western Brittany. The discussion is based on qualitative fieldwork carried out during the period 1994–5. Whilst the aim of research was not to focus specifically on aspects of Celtic identity, it is hoped that the material presented here may contribute to an improved understanding of processes of tourism-related change and resistance in regions which are often described as part of the 'Celtic periphery'.

The marketing strategies for County Mayo and Finistère make use of features which may be described as part of a populist perception of Celticity. These include aspects of cultural heritage such as traditional music, crafts, costumes, mythology and language, use of Celtic iconography such as crosses and knotwork, as well as aspects of the physical environment, such as wild rocky coastlines, rugged empty mountains and dramatic weather conditions. The general idea communicated by these images is that these places, and the people within them, are a world apart from urban industrial Europe and the socio-economic and environmental problems associated with it (Quinn 1994). The tourist product is portrayed in terms of an authentic experience, which involves contact with the people native to the area and an opportunity to learn about their culture and lifestyle.

Yet whilst there is visual evidence to support the argument that a Celtic identity is constructed through tourism representations of places such as County Mayo and Finistère, what is not clear is the extent to which this process has an impact on local place identities. To date, as Boissevain (1996) notes, little attention has been paid to the effect of tourism upon host communities in Europe. One response to this issue has been to argue that tourism has a negative impact on place identity through the commodification of culture, a process which is said to undermine the meaningfulness of cultural practices and lead to the homogenization of place identities (MacCannell 1992; Mason 1996). In the case of communities which are marketed as Celtic, the implication is that people will adopt particular facets of popularly perceived Celtic identity in order to attract tourists. The argument runs that this will result in inauthentic, staged cultural events. However, on the basis of fieldwork in two rural communities on the so-called Celtic periphery, I suggest that the relationship between tourism and place identity must be understood in more complex terms.

People do not necessarily appropriate tourist representations of themselves, nor do they necessarily commodify their own cultural identity. Rather, tourist expectations and attempts to promote tourism development are mediated through resilient local social relations. These social relations include the cultural practices, economic activities, kinship and friendship ties, political and administrative structures which are built up over time and contribute to the development of distinctive place identities. These relationships shape the kinds of tourism development which occur in different places. At the same time, the impacts of tourism cannot be separated off from the impacts of broader socio-economic processes which are currently affecting marginal rural communities in many parts of Europe.

In summary, therefore, the aim of this chapter is to present an analysis of the relationship between tourism and place identity in rural Finistère and Mayo which takes account of the ways in which tourism development is mediated through the social relations in and between places. More specifically, this involves a discussion of the processes of change and resistance which are involved in the commodification of culture and identity. Secondly, and perhaps indirectly, I hope that the issues raised will contribute to a conceptualization of Celticity as a fluid construct which may be appropriated over time by different groups for different reasons.

In order to meet these aims, evidence will be drawn from qualitative data collected in Foxford, a small town in north Mayo, and Commana, a commune in central Finistère. Ethnographic methods of participant observation and in-depth semi-structured interviews were used to gain an understanding of local attitudes to tourism development and cultural commodification (for a fuller discussion of the methodology employed please see Kneafsey 1998). However, before turning to the empirical data, it is first necessary to contextualize the research by briefly outlining a conceptual approach to the study of the relationship between tourism and place identity.

Understanding the Relationship between Tourism and Place Identity

It is generally agreed that tourism has an impact on place identity. What is not agreed is the extent and nature of that impact. Three broad arguments can be traced within the tourism literature. The first argument is that through commodification, tourism *constructs* place identities which are designed to meet tourist desires for particular characteristics such as authenticity or tradition. Through commodification, aspects of place such as the landscape, architecture, or the cultural practices of the people who live there, become a commodity which tourists pay to consume. As Hughes (1992, 39) notes, '[T]he commodification of places ... shifts the focus from simply "selling places" to the production of what will sell'. Similarly, Urry (1995, 163) suggests that through visual consumption, places which are visited 'come to be remade in part as objects for the tourist gaze. Their built and physical environments, their economies, their place-images are all substantially reconstructed.' Urry thus invests tourism with considerable power, arguing that in Europe at least, 'identity almost everywhere has to be produced partly out of the images constructed for tourists' (1995, 165).

The second argument is that tourism *preserves* place identities through the conservation of traditions and cultural practices which would otherwise have disappeared. Cohen (1988, 382), for instance, argues that tourism development often takes place when a culture is in decline, and that 'under such circumstances, the emergence of a tourist market frequently facilitates the preservation of a cultural tradition which would otherwise perish'. Arguing along similar lines, anthropologists Chapman (1987) and McDonald (1987) both suggest that aspects of Breton culture would no longer exist if it were not for tourism. As Chapman (1987, 67) states, 'the presence of the tourist conjures into existence, or maintains in existence, a traditionality that might otherwise have been completely forgotten'. Yet the very idea of cultural preservation is in itself something of a contradiction in terms, if we understand culture to be a constantly evolving expression of the daily practices, traditions and beliefs of a group of people. Preserving something in effect means keeping it the same, which could in fact be seen as the very death knell of a culture. Cultures survive through continual change and transformation. This is not to deny that tourism can have a positive impact on traditional cultural practices, but, as I hope to show, this impact is expressed in terms of change rather than preservation.

The third idea is that tourism in effect *destroys* unique place identities through incorporating hitherto remote and unique places into a global system of capitalist relations. Greenwood (1989, 179), for instance, argues that commodification 'in effect robs people of the very meanings by which they organise their lives'. MacCannell goes as far as to suggest that the commodification and consumption of places through tourism leads to the 'death' of cultures (1992). He argues that once a culture is commodified, it dies, and is transformed into a copy of global television culture. He sees tourism as part of the cannibalistic creature that is capitalism, a creature which has a 'voracious appetite' and which rapidly commodifies third world and underclass cultures and nature. Focusing particularly on ethnic and third world tourism, he argues that when an ethnic group begins to sell itself, or is sold as an ethnic attraction, group members begin to think of themselves not as people, but as 'representatives' of an authentic way of life; the group 'museumizes itself', becomes a thing. Continuing this line of thought, Byrne *et al.*, writing about Connemara, argue that in adapting to tourism, hosts conform to the expectations of visitors from more politically and economically powerful cultures. They suggest that in doing so, unique cultural identities are eroded: 'When indigenous inhabitants of places like the West of Ireland gradually abandon local criteria regulating forms of reasonable thought and feeling, they will have become much more similar to people everywhere else' (1993, 253).

Mason, in his study of Hawaii, is particularly outspoken on this point, highlighting the 'power' of tourism to create the 'myths of identity' in a society which has 'sold out' to the 'tourist dollar'. The result, he argues, is the 'prostitution' of 'what was once a unique culture' (1996, 121). He suggests that the Hawaiians, being placed in a position of subordination, quickly begin to lose their sense of self-respect and identity (1996, 131).

In this chapter, I propose that none of these three broad approaches is quite right, and that the relationship between tourism and place identity must be understood in more complex terms as one that is cast uniquely within the context of the social relations which intersect in particular places. The problem with analyses such as that proposed by Mason is that the people under discussion are portrayed as unfortunate victims of modernity whose own social relations and cultural identities seem to wither in the face of more powerful forces. Granted, Mason is referring to mass tourism, which will obviously have more powerful effects than the kind of tourism which operates in rural areas on the Celtic periphery, but as Ekholm-Friedman and Friedman (1995) demonstrate, more realistic and sensitive accounts can be developed. As they point out, Hawaiians have in varying degrees resisted the take-over of their islands within a context of vast economic expansion in the Pacific, the development of a large-scale plantation economy, and an era of US global hegemony. Tourism is just one aspect of the pressures facing the islanders, and furthermore, Ekholm-Friedman and Freidman note the re-emergence of Hawaiian self-identity which has been due partly to the efforts of the Hawaiian movement. Similarly, Boissevain, in his insightful report on tourism and the commercialization of culture in Malta (which has a population of 350,000 but received almost one million visitors in 1992), portrays a society in which rituals have not been destroyed, but have been imbued with new meaning (1996, 107). Black (1996) has also shown that the commodification of culture for tourists has not prevented the persistence and even expansion of another locally autonomous sphere of cultural autonomy in Malta.

Rather than investing tourism with enormous power to construct, preserve or destroy identities, such analyses pay attention to the social relations which already exist in places, as well as the other wider social processes which affect place identities. Through adopting such a perspective, we arrive at a more balanced conceptualization of the role of tourism as 'neither as crude nor spectacular as the critics of cultural commoditisation have suggested' (Boissevain 1996, 114). This interpretation can be applied equally to tourism in those areas which can be described as part of the 'Celtic fringe'. Therefore, I argue that whilst such areas may be marketed as Celtic in some way or another, this does not necessarily construct or preserve a Celtic self-identity amongst people who live in them. Further, it does not destroy an existing Celtic identity, partly because there is little evidence of one single sense of Celtic identity anyway. For instance, whilst some of the individuals I interviewed in Brittany expressed a sense of common Celtic identity with their Irish 'cousins', none of the people I talked to in Ireland seemed to feel a sense of shared identity with the inhabitants of Brittany. It is worth noting that Irish Celticity in general seems in any case to be expressed in terms of 'Gaeldom' rather than 'Celtdom'.

In summary, in order to understand the relationship between tourism and place identity, it is necessary to adopt an approach which, firstly, pays attention to the social relations which exist in and between places, and, secondly, takes account of the other social processes which affect place identities. Taking this approach illustrates the ways in which different individuals and groups of people combine to resist or promote the commodification of cultural identity. In Brittany and Ireland, this cultural identity may often be described as 'Celtic' by tourists, observers or academics, but is rarely described as such by participants themselves. The fact that the research was not focused on aspects of Celticity and that the term 'Celt' rarely arose is surely indicative of the idea that Celtic regions are often labelled as such by people and organizations beyond the region which is being so described. In the rest of the chapter, I present two different stories of two different places, stories which I hope will contribute to an understanding of some aspects of change and resistance in the Celtic periphery.

Introducing Commana: 'Gateway to the Monts d'Arrée'

The first story takes place in Commana, a small commune in central Finistère. Tourism strategies in Brittany have, over the last decade or so, begun to focus on developing inland tourism as a means to combat rural de-population and economic decline. Drawing on examples from Ireland, the 1986 Maybury report advocated the development of cultural tourism based around themes of 'la Bretagne mysterieuse' or 'Merlin the Enchanter', and suggested that the 'Celtic angle' and 'megalithic culture' should be further promoted. More recently, an article appeared in the 1994 newsletter of the Regional Tourism Committee entitled 'Our Celtic heritage—a new tourism': 'among the European nations, Brittany is one of the rare ones to have conserved some archaeological vestiges, but above all despite the Parisian *jacobinisme*, a language, a memory, and traditions, still alive today, which demonstrate incontestably Celtic origins'.

Historically, Brittany was by the nineteenth century established amongst literary and educated elites as a repository of moral, spiritual and Celtic values which were opposed to the rationality and modernism of the French Republic (Cachin 1989; McDonald 1989). By scholars and anthropologists, the Bretons were seen as examples of the last remaining Celts. As Trollope wrote in 1840, 'the inhabitants of this remote province, though certainly not the only remaining lineal descendants of the Celtic race, yet are by far the most perfectly preserved specimen of it'. Finistère in particular was regarded as the 'most Breton' part of the region, a theme which recurs in contemporary tourism representations such as the following brochure extract:

> The most typically Breton of all the departments, Finistère's name means 'Land's End' ... The further west you go, the more rugged the countryside becomes ... The people too, are prouder of their Breton heritage than elsewhere in the country. More of them speak the language, take part in traditional music and dance, and bring out their colourful Breton costumes for festivals and other special occasions. (*Enchanting Brittany*, 1994)

Commana, described as the 'gateway' to the 'mysterious' Monts d'Arrée, is located in the heart of Finistère, the heart of 'la Bretagne intense'. The Monts d'Arrée have long been a magnet to druids, artists and intellectuals, drawn by the legends and mythologies surrounding the strange rock formations and the empty marshlands of the Yuen. From the south, as seen from Roc'h Trevezel, one of the highest points of *les montagnes*, Commana is a small town perched on a hill-top at a height of 280 m, its tall church spire reaching heavenwards. The descent by road opens up views of gorse and heather-covered hillsides giving way to a patchwork of *bocage* and peaceful hamlets.

In the summer months a small tourist information point is opened, and volunteers staff exhibitions of sacred art at the church and run informal guides. Behind the church is the small and basic pre-fabricated *salle de fêtes*, adjacent to which is the *mairie* which proudly flies the French tricolor. In front of this there is another open parking space and an ancient Breton cross which stands unlabelled and almost hidden by bushes and trees. In the afternoons older people sometimes play Boules or *petanque* in this area, shouting across the dust to each other in a mixture of Breton and French. The houses are built of granite, with small windows to keep out the wind, and roofs of mountain slate.

After having looked at the church and visited the Café Breton, which houses an unusual collection of automated bone china puppets entitled 'La Basse Bretagne Autrefois' (Lower Brittany in Times Gone By), the visitor to Commana is directed by signs to the nearby prehistoric burial chamber, the Mougau-Bihan, known as l'Allée Couverte in French, but usually referred to by its Breton name, thereby maintaining a subtle association of things Breton with things ancient, prehistoric and mysterious. Bikes can be hired at the bar-tabac, and there are numerous walking routes in the mountains and around the nearby Lac du Drennec, a man-made reservoir which now boasts a water sports centre and beaches made with sand transported from the coast. There are also the nearby installations of the Parc Naturel Régional d'Armorique such as Les Moulins de Kerouat and Maison des Artisans, and a privately run interpretive centre, 'Art et Nature'. There are a number of *gîtes ruraux, chambres chez l'habitant*, a hostel which offers full board, and two self-catering walking hostels, one in the *bourg* and the other at the Mougau Bihan.

The current population of 1,117 inhabitants represents a figure that has fallen by about 50 per cent since the start of the century, with particularly rapid declines during the two world wars. The major cause of emigration of the native populace has been the decline in agricultural employment. There is no direct bus or train service to the village, and only a limited range of shops and services. The contemporary situation presents a stark contrast to the past. Within living memory, there was a whole range of industries and activities which gave the commune a high level of autonomy and economic vigour. The village was well known for its livestock fairs of cattle, pigs and horses, mentioned as early as 1786, and which in their heyday in 1906–8 attracted buyers from Bordeaux, the Midi and even Spain. Agriculture today is monocultural and intensive, requiring fewer people but a high level of capital investment. One of the principal activities of the area is poultry farming, which is characterized by long low sheds which dot the landscape.

Of course to the tourist on a first visit to Commana, none of this is readily apparent. The visitor makes assumptions about the place through reading signs and symbols which reinforce existing conceptions. Commana is part of the Parc Naturel Régional d'Armorique, an area which is marketed as 'an authentic region' (park brochure), a territory of tradition and natural beauty, where the Breton language and 'art de vivre' still exist. As McDonald points out (1987), the so-called 'intelligent tourist' looking for the 'real Brittany' will happily ignore aberrations such as poultry sheds and stereo-equipped tractors, or see them simply as distressingly invasive elements of modernity. For instance, on arrival, placards at the entrances to the *bourg* (centre) announce that this is a 'Commune de Patrimoine Rural', which means that it is part of an association of towns which share a common will to protect and enhance natural sites and architectural, historic and ethnological heritage. The small brochure produced by the municipal council focuses heavily on the church and its interior, and also contains photos of the Mougau-Bihan, the *écomusée*, the lake and the mountains. There are no people and no farm machines in any of the pictures. The name of the town is presented in both its Breton form (Kommanna) and in French (Commana). So already, the town is designated as rural, historic and authentic, and some reference is made to its Breton heritage. Commana as represented through these signs fits in perfectly with the public image of Brittany, and most especially Finistère, as a land of peaceful rurality, tradition and authenticity.

It soon became apparent that the lived experiences of people in Commana were very different from the ways in which their lifestyles and identities were portrayed in touristic representations. For instance, the appearance of the name of the town in Breton as well as French instantly raises a number of issues to do with the imposition of particular versions of identity on places and people. The existence of the name in Breton is an initiative of the department of Finistère, motivated partly by the desire to create a strong market image drawing on its reputation as the most 'traditional' and Breton part of Brittany. Although a survey found that 82.5 per cent of Finistériens were 'very or fairly positive' about the policy (Conseil Général 1992), I soon came across some ambivalence towards the imposition of a distinctly Breton identity. As this 63-year-old native of Commana well shows, Breton is still associated with hardship and prejudice:

> I speak Breton well—better than French.... I went to school here at Commana and I didn't speak a word of French. I only spoke Breton. So before starting to read and write it was necessary to learn French first. It took two or three years to learn French and after to start to read ... it was a handicap, it wasn't good.
>
> MK:—to not speak French?
>
> Yes ... it is good to learn it [Breton] for leisure, to pass the time if you want, but all the Breton schools—the children in the Breton schools, now I'm not for that. No, because they lose years of school. Whilst they're speaking Breton at school they don't learn French. It's not good.

He concluded that as he himself was a 'victim', he would not want to impose this 'handicap' on his own children or any others. He conceded that it is 'good to keep Breton', but that this must be done outside of school hours. He and his wife no longer participate in what could be termed 'typically Breton' activities such as the *festnoz*[1] or pardon, and he insisted that 'I spoke too much Breton, so I do not speak good French. There are certain words which I still have trouble finding because I am too used to Breton.' Despite this, he rejects the language because of its connotations of poverty and seems a little bemused at the strangers who wish to learn it. McDonald (1989) found a similar avoidance of too close an identification with Breton in her anthropology of the neighbouring commune of Plounéour-Menez. She noted, for instance, that for many people of an older generation, speaking Breton is something they will do only in certain circumstances, and rarely among strangers or in public.

This anecdote introduces the main theme of my story about Commana, which is the theme of resistance. I finished the fieldwork with a feeling that although small groups of energetic individuals were keen to promote tourism, in general, people in the commune were resistant to tourism, and resistant to the imposition of a particularly Breton or Celtic identity. As Boissevain (1996) shows, resistance to tourism can often take a passive form, being expressed through gossip, grumbling and non-participation in organized events. It was this kind of resistance which most typically appeared in Commana. A number of examples can be used to support this interpretation, the first of which concerns the Parc Naturel Régional d'Armorique.

I have chosen to discuss the park first because it is the most powerful producer of representations of the territory within which Commana is located. In its glossy brochures and posters, the communes within it are portrayed as repositories of tradition and authenticity. At its establishment in 1969, the park was strongly criticized by the UDB (Union Democratiques Bretonne) as being little more than an 'indian reserve' which would block the economic development of the communes within it and relegate the area to a tourist zone (see Barvel 1992). The park today comprises thirty-nine communes and is governed by a syndicat of twenty-seven elected delegates. The idea is that the maintenance of a strong sense of cultural identity through language classes, cultural activities, evening events and study tours, which are aimed primarily at the local population, will foster an atmosphere of vigour and entrepreneurship. The president of the park in 1992 argued that 'From "indian reserve" we have become a reserve of energy and authenticity' (*La Lettre du Parc*

1992). Yet evidence from Commana suggests that the extent to which the park is achieving its aims of reinforcing cultural integrity and maintaining traditional practices is limited.

For instance, the park runs an *écomusée* at the Moulins de Kerouat, situated a few kilometres outside the *bourg* of Commana. The aim of the *écomusée* is not only to preserve a valuable architectural heritage, but to present this as a living, working enterprise, and to encourage visitors and locals alike to experience it as such. The idea is to transmit *savoir faire* and to foster understanding and appreciation through participation. Typical activities, as advertised in the commune's summer bulletin, include learning how to make bread and crêpes the old way, learning traditional Breton games, watching craftsmen at work, going on nature walks and taking day courses in sketching and painting. In conversation with the director of the *écomusée*, it soon became apparent that the ideals of participation were not so easily obtainable. For instance, it was very difficult to get locals to attend events such as concerts and *festou-noz*[2] at the mill. McDonald (1987, 130) points out that the initial response to these *ecomusées* involved anger, disgust and hostility, with complaints that it was wrong to show visitors how poorly people lived in an 'all too recent past'. The director reported that although the museum is supposed to serve both visitors and locals, many locals visit only once. In her words, for them the museum is something '*figé*', fixed or frozen. Many of the older generation remember when people still lived on the site, as the last person only left in 1965. It could be that the mills have now passed into the realms of the museum, and in doing so have been placed behind some kind of barrier. What was once a living unit is now swathed in academia, interpreted, displaced from the real into the rarefied air of the exposition, the show case—objects for the modern gaze onto a world now gone. Perhaps, despite the intentions of the park to promote interaction between museums and population and to maintain a sense of a vibrant, living culture, there is no better indication that something is dead than to put it into a museum.

The park in general is perceived as a separate entity. The president of the Association pour la Defense des Monts d'Arrée complained that 'we are not partners', meaning that there was no real co-operation between the park and local associations. He described an incident where the park wanted to organize a *festnoz* but insisted on having it on a Friday when the usual night for such events is Saturday, and because of something 'as stupid as that', the event didn't happen. As another critic put it: 'they [i.e. park agents] have a theoretical will to serve and dynamize the local culture, but the problem is that they have lived ... not necessarily outside, but in any case, not implicated in the local cultural life'.

Enthusiasm for the park and its activities was hardly overwhelming. One *gîte* owner reckoned that 99 per cent of the holiday-makers who came did not even know of the existence of the Parc Naturel Régional d'Armorique. Other people thought it was failing to live up to its obligations to inhabitants. When I asked one bar-restaurant owner if she thought the park was an asset for Commana she replied

> what they have is all the publicity. With that, they do well, and we, we are in Commana, we are in the *écomusée* ... beneficiaries of the publicity of the *écomusée*, yes ... but after, for me, they do things that they shouldn't do. They run commercial enterprise—they have a bar for example at the café at the dam, so they create competition ... that's not right, it's not their role ... in the charter of the park, article number two or three I think, it says that they are there exactly to aid economic development

Other respondents were critical of the cost. One *gîte* owner argued that although tourists may spend money on their trips to the park, the authorities have to spend 'hundreds of millions of francs per year' to get the tourists in.

Besides these very pragmatic concerns, I did feel that there was a strong sense of resistance to any trend towards 'museumification' of the area. For instance, an attempt by the Morlaix Chamber of Commerce to construct a 'Museoparc de Légends' at the foot of Mont St Michel de Brasparts met with strong opposition from local groups and councillors. The museum, in the form of a dome-shaped building half-buried in the hillside, would interpret themes such as the ancient Gods, gates to other worlds and fairy stories through the use of hi-tech gadgetry including video, light and sound individual helmets. One of the key promoters of the project, a member of the tourism commission at Morlaix, told me with obvious disappointment how despite the fact that the plans had already secured funding from various sources, local people were opposed because, he supposed, they were afraid of being 'ridiculed'. However, slightly different versions were held by some of the individuals I spoke to. The director of the existing park *écomusée*, for instance, did not think it was anything to do with fear of ridicule, but more a case of there being too many museums already, and soon the whole region would be one—'we don't want a Eurodisney here'. Also, she pointed out that the legends of the area are still living, and it would be wrong to make a museum out of them. Another woman, proprietor of a café-restaurant at Commana, was strongly opposed to the idea, saying:

> you only have to go walking in the Yuen,[3] and that makes you scared, or makes you think of legends in the evening when the mist comes down—to put these things in a box, it's rubbish ... And if we say yes to that, what are they going to do after? They will put in a hotel ... a pizzeria, and then a 'quickburger' and I don't know what.

Although the museoparc was supposed to be a joint venture with local groups and communes, it seemed to be perceived very much as a project coming from the outside, from 'them' rather than 'us'. Indeed, a local newspaper reported that the people of the area felt excluded from the whole affair, and were irritated by the idea that this project was being granted to 'save' them from 'under-development', by these people with their money from 'the state' who didn't ask anyone's opinion. Further, there were fears that the twenty million franc project would weigh heavily on communes which already contribute to the upkeep of the existing museums in the park, and it was compared to other projects such as the Port Museum at Douarnenez which were seen to be examples of heavy expenditure for limited returns.

Although the museum was supposed to open in 1993, at the time of this research (1994) the project had ground to a halt and there was little sign of any effort to re-ignite it. What the case does serve to highlight is a definite reticence about the proliferation of museums and their subsequent impact on both environment and identity, as well as a scepticism about their economic viability. MacCannell's notion of groups 'museumizing' themselves does not fit here. Even though aspects of ethnicity are used to market the area, people do not necessarily want to fall into the role of ethnic actors in a staged version of their own authenticity. There is a high awareness of the moral, financial and environmental implications of such a course of action, and of the possibility of damaging the existing product through intense commodification.

Therefore, it seemed that a bedrock of resistance to 'museumification' existed in Commana. However, it is important to make a distinction between the different reasons for resistance. In some cases, such as the example of the locally born, native Breton speaker who wished to be disassociated from a language which for him symbolized poverty and ridicule, resistance could be interpreted as a reaction to the imposition of an identity which he has spent a lifetime trying to rid himself of. It has to be understood that Breton identity in the past was often something to be ashamed of rather than proud of. For instance, one mother recognized that she had not so far introduced her children to Breton or Celtic stories, but explained that it was because 'it's difficult to get rid of this conditioning'—meaning the attitudes which she was taught as a child whereby Breton culture was considered inferior and 'backwards' in relation to French culture.

In other cases, resistance stemmed from an appreciation of local identity and a desire to protect this from over-commodification. This kind of resistance was often expressed amongst people who had come from beyond the locale, and who therefore had a different perspective on place identity. These people tended to have an interest in learning Breton, even though they were not native speakers, as well as a high awareness of the natural environment and the local cultural heritage. This brings us to the central idea of this chapter, which is that the relationship between tourism and place identity must be understood in terms of the social relations in and between places. Within Commana, one set of social relations existed primarily amongst the farming community, who tended to be the Breton speakers, heavily represented on the municipal council, firmly wedded to farming as a way of life, unwilling to see their cultural identity as a commodity, and uncomfortable with the idea of speaking Breton amongst strangers, or participating in events such as *festnoz* which are perceived as traditional and authentic. In general, this group was resistant to tourism, especially on economic grounds. Another set of social relations existed amongst people whom I describe loosely as 'incomers', even though some of them had lived in Commana for many years. Tourist-related enterprises were run overwhelmingly by such people, many of whom had family links with the area through grandparents. A typical example would be a couple who were born in the area, had lived and worked in Paris for thirty years and returned to the family homestead and converted it into a *gîte*. People such as this expressed an interest in learning to speak Breton and were drawn to the area because it offered 'tranquillity', 'good quality of life' and something 'true' and 'authentic'. Overlaying the bedrock of resistance to certain kinds of tourist development, therefore, are uneven layers of revival and change. The incomers I have described tended to support events such as the *festnoz*, which at the time of research seemed to be enjoying enormous popularity throughout the region, and especially in urban centres. As one tourism official explained:

> Fifteen years ago there were hardly any dance groups ... now we see dancers, musicians, new groups forming ... the inhabitants themselves are rediscovering the tradition ... the tourists participate in the *festnoz* with inhabitants, but it is not only put on to amuse the tourists or make money ... we need to find out where we come from.

The people who attend *festou-noz* nowadays are often language enthusiasts, teachers, public-sector employees, members of dance groups, Celtic circles, students or visitors, with the archetypal Breton rural-dweller being in a minority, and very few coiffes or clogs in sight! The contemporary *festnoz* is quite different from those held to mark the end of collective work efforts such as the harvest in the previous century. In those days, it was attended by people from a relatively small geographical area, and the number of dances would have been limited. However, at a modern-day *festnoz*, you could quite as easily dance a Kost ar C'hoat from *les montagnes* as a Suite de Loudéac from central French-speaking Brittany (Shepherd 1989). Similarly, at a contemporary *festnoz*, people will have travelled by car from much greater distances to attend, paid an entry fee and learned the dances at evening classes. Thus it could be argued that the tradition continues, but it does so through a different set of people in a modified form.

In summary, the story in Commana is one of resistance to tourism, overlain with elements of revival of particular cultural practices amongst different groups of people. The relationship between tourism and place identity is defined by the social relationships already in place. Thus, the existence of a certain 'mentalité' which in the past denigrated the use of Breton continues to influence Breton speakers' attitudes to their own language, particularly amongst the older generations. This in turn is caught up in a set of historical relationships whereby Brittany was seen as an impoverished region of France, a place of ignorance and superstition. It is also intertwined with a desire not to be associated with rebellious movements for autonomy which in the late 1960s and 1970s demanded an end to Brittany's perceived status as 'internal colony' (Reece 1979). Some of the older respondents in particular were very critical of this movement, which in their eyes gave the region a bad reputation and was based on a ridiculous claim for autonomy. All these aspects work against the adoption of traditional, Breton or Celtic identity as represented by tourism images. Yet other processes work to renew these aspects of identity. These processes include tourism, which generates interest in cultures which are seen to be different and authentic.

Perhaps more significant, however, is the movement of new kinds of people to rural areas such as Commana, for it is these people who commodify features of place identity, and who participate in activities such as language classes and *festou-noz*. Therefore tourism must be seen as only one of the social processes affecting place identity in this part of the Celtic periphery.

Turning to another part of the Celtic periphery, we find a different story being enacted. In Foxford, County Mayo, tourism is still just one part of broad social processes similar to those affecting Commana, and tourism is still mediated through existing social relations. However, because these relations are different from those in Commana, a different response to tourism emerges, a response where change and renewal seem to outweigh resistance. I turn now to Foxford to try to explain why.

Introducing Foxford, Town of the Moy Valley

I described a situation of resistance and entrenchment in Commana, where even people involved in tourism displayed reticence about its further development because of socio-cultural, environmental, political and economic concerns. Foxford, however, is a place where the people involved in tourism and local development are much more 'up-beat' in their attitudes towards it. They are still wary of the dangers of over-reliance on tourism and there are still groups such as the farmers who resist through non-participation and ignorance of tourism-related matters, but this does not prevent a much more enthusiastic approach. This more positive outlook generally takes the form of optimism about the economic potential of tourism, and, amongst the local development community in particular, optimism about the ability of tourism to encourage a re-valuation of local human, natural and cultural resources.

As in Finistère, recent policy documents have outlined the need to promote tourism as a means of rural development in County Mayo (County Tourism Development Plan 1995). Plans advocate the close involvement of local communities and focus on the development of activity holidays such as golf, fishing, walking, sailing and geneology, as well as more specialized pursuits such as ecology tours, English language schools, shooting and crafts. The first significant attempt to promote the county tourist attractions was launched in 1989 under the banner 'Mayo 5,000'. The aim was to create a 'brand image' for the county using the idea of 5,000 years of farming as a central theme. The slogan 'Mayo Naturally' was created, and a marketing company of the same name set up to promote the county. The promotional material for the project emphasized aspects such as the 'skills of generations', 'new materials and ancient ways', the land, the skies, magic and tradition. Just as Finistère is marketed as the heartland of Brittany, so Mayo is described as 'more Irish than Ireland'. Whilst specific references to Celticity are not common, the publicity for Mayo draws on the historically constructed notion of the west of Ireland as the symbolic core of Ireland itself. As Nash (1993) notes, the west of Ireland was constructed both in opposition to Englishness and also within Ireland as a site of 'true Irishness', a last bastion of racial and cultural purity. Nash shows that the landscape of the west was contrasted with the landscape of England, which by the end of the First World War was epitomized by cricket greens, church spires and connotations of stability and continuity. The west of Ireland landscape was one of 'elemental bareness, vigour and vitality' (Nash 1993, 91), and as Gibbons shows (1996), was also associated with lawlessness, sensuality, physicality and violence. For Anglo-Irish writers such as Yeats and Synge, the west offered a 'refuge' from the 'suffocating moral atmosphere of an Ireland dominated by the emergent bourgeoisie, both Catholic and Protestant' (Gibbons 1996, 24). Meanwhile nationalists such as Pearce propagated a puritanical image of the west as a harsh, inhospitable environment inhabited by resilient and courageous peasants who were close to God and nature.

Foxford is located in north Mayo on the road between Ballina and Castlebar, not far from the shores of Lough Conn. To the west, rising steeply from the lake, stands the lump of a mountain known as Nephin, behind which range the lonely hills of Nephin Beg. To the east are the smaller, more populated rocky Ox Mountains. Foxford is thus surrounded by hills, mountains, lakes and rivers. The most important of these is the River Moy, which runs through the town and is renowned for its annual rod catches of up to 11,000 wild Atlantic salmon. The land is mainly rough open grazing for cattle and sheep, and in the autumn the lanes are thick with wild fruits, blackberries, rowan and sloughs. There are sheltered dells where small cottages hide, and old orchards are hidden amongst the trees. Some houses have chickens and geese scratching around the yard. Generally the land and climate here are not as bleak as in the vast expanse of bogland which stretches away to the west around the Nephin Beg, incorporating a small Gaeltacht on the northern coast around Belmullet. Compared to Commana, there are more shops and a greater variety of services. There is a general air of bustle which is added to by the traffic passing through from Ballina, Castlebar and Swinford.

Foxford attracts many anglers due to its location on the banks of the River Moy. The vast majority of visitors who are not anglers are either deposited at, or herded towards a visitor centre based at an old woollen mill. The mill centre also houses the Tourist Information Office, a café, art gallery and craft centre.

The current population of 987 represents a figure that has increased from about 700 in 1841 but decreased from a high of around 1,000 in 1986. Unlike Commana, Foxford has managed to sustain gradual population growth since the turn of the century, which may be partly explained by the drift from rural to urban districts. The surrounding area is characterized by high emigration, the population of Mayo falling by 3.9 per cent in the period from 1986–91 to just 110,696 (Department of Foreign Affairs 1995). Agriculture and related industries employ the largest proportion of the workforce, but this belies the decline in farming. Despite the relative vibrancy of the town compared to others in the area, and to Commana in Brittany, there is still a shortage of jobs for youngsters, a worry which was expressed repeatedly in interviews. One shop-keeper in his mid-thirties told me that he was the only one of his school year to have stayed in the area.

At the start of this story I suggested that in Foxford there is more evidence of change rather than resistance to change. In a way, the movement for change can be interpreted as a different form of resistance—a refusal to be defeated, to go the same way as many other small towns in the west of Ireland which have seen their populations decimated and efforts to promote development torn apart by internal wrangling. It is also a refusal to be abandoned by Dublin, a refusal to be consigned to oblivion despite poor infrastructure, inadequate educational and health facilities, and an agriculture dependent on grants and subsidies. In the case of Foxford change in itself may be a form of resistance.

In keeping with the main theme of this chapter, I argue that in relation to tourism, change is encouraged by the social relations existing in and between places. For example, Foxford is a source of emigrants. The result of this is that many visitors are either returning 'exiles' home from Dublin, Europe or America, or at least have roots in the area (O'Muire-Smith 1996, 33). Many of these visitors stay in relatives' homes, and may help with jobs such as collecting turf or hay ready for the winter (although in many cases hay has now been replaced by silage). They also join in local leisure activities, socializing in the pubs and bars. Although the return of emigrants does not encourage the commodification of culture, or the commercialization of services, it has in some senses created a global sense of place, producing a fluid interchange between the locality and its global outposts, weakening the boundaries between host and guest. The interchange may be fraught with personal tensions, and as Ní Laoire (1997), shows the return home can provoke complex and ambiguous emotions amongst the individuals involved, but it does I think dissolve some of the barriers between hosts, visitors, strangers, friends and tourists. It is a set of social relations which promotes a more easy acceptance of the very concept of tourism as an economic activity. There is already a historical precedent of hosting visitors and adapting to the arrival and departure of people which does not seem to have been so strongly established in Commana. In addition to this, many of the non-emigrant visitors are anglers, many of whom return to fish the River Moy year after year, building up relationships with local people. One woman captured the way in which tourists are generally perceived when she described them as being like 'the swallows' who return each summer.

Another set of relationships also facilitates a more easy acceptance of tourism and promotes change within the locality. This revolves around the woollen mill, which represents the driving force behind cultural commodification. For over one hundred years, the Providence Woollen Mills have been a focal point of Foxford's economic, social and cultural life. They were founded by an English-born nun, Sister Agnes Morrogh-Bernard, who arrived in 1891 with a mission to help the poor and needy of the district. Today the mills are the focus of a visitor centre which in 1995 received about 60,000 visitors. The tour uses audio-visual devices, including full-scale human models, to trace the history of the mills and create an impression of social, economic and cultural conditions in nineteenth-century Foxford. The tour ends with a promotional video of the Woollen mill's present-day products, after which visitors have the option of going on the industrial tour, where the actual processes of production can be seen first-hand. Visitors are then guided into the restaurant/café and the well-stocked gift shop. The visitor centre exists because of the need to sell products from the woollen mill. As the managing director put it: 'the only way that you could think of a retail operation here, because it's off the beaten track, was to create a visitor attraction'.

The mill had gone into receivership in 1987, which is when the current manager stepped in with the idea of setting up a company limited by guarantee which has on its board representatives of the Industrial Development Agency, Bord Failte, North Connacht Farmers, and the local business community. Over six months £1 million was raised from the European Structural Funds and private donations, and the mill reopened in 1992, exactly a hundred years after it was first founded. The whole reason for having the visitor centre is that it creates a market for the shop, where the real money is made. So although tourism is not the main earner, it is essential for the success of the retail trade. As the manager put it:

> Everything comes in circles, be it anything you look at, and when Mother Arsenius set up the mills in 1892, the wool industry was a huge industry, a massive industry all over Western Europe, and the tourist industry was only in its infancy. Now its a little bit in reverse, so you play your strengths. You use the retail operation to help develop the manufacturing.

An important point to understand is that the mill also houses the Integrated Resource Development (IRD) company which acts as a facilitator for local entrepreneurship. This means that the mill is central not only to the commodification of place for tourism, but to other development ideas for the town. Many of the projects which start up in the area have some connection with the IRD and hence with the mill. Thus, for instance, members of the Admiral Brown Society have been working with the IRD to raise money for a new heritage centre based on the extraordinary life of William Brown, a Foxford-born man who emigrated at the age of nine to become the founder of the first national navy in Argentina. Another example is the IRD's proposal to set up a walking club co-ordinated from the mill. Schemes such as these indicate new attitudes towards history and the natural environment as resources. They suggest that new imaginary geographies are emerging which posit the area as a leisure space, a place where the environment is clean and where heritage and history are available for ready consumption.

Yet the success of the visitor centre in terms of attracting visitors and raising the profile of Foxford has also raised questions about ownership and participation in the creation of a tourist product. Although local contributions and support have been praised, one commentator thought that 'they'd have far more people involved in it if they hadn't been so narrow ... an awful lot of people feel left out'. Contrary to the image of public participation, it appears that 'a lot of people felt they were never part of it, and should never be part of it, and that it was only for a few'. The feeling of exclusion is also carried through into a feeling that businesses in the town are not getting as much out of the mill financially as they should be doing. As one publican put it:

> Tourism would be very important, we all want them coming you know. But as far as I can see, at the mill they're just in and out. A lot of them come on coach trips and they're organized, and they'll go straightaway then to Ceide Fields and the Peat Bog[4] trail and different things ... So very rarely do they walk down the town or come in.
>
> MK: So you wouldn't get that many coming into the bar?
>
> No, no. One in probably 10,000, and that would only be a man who'd come in for a pint while his wife was going round a tour on the mill!

Similarly, the owner of a small store at the opposite end of the town complained that visitors 'don't come up the town', so she hardly benefits from their presence. At the beginning it wasn't too bad because locals came to see the mill and would then 'knock around town' for a bit, but now that it's only 'real tourists' they just don't bother. Further, she complained that out of season 'you could close the town'.

What comes through these comments is a sense that there are inhabitants who feel excluded, and that the ownership of the centre, which presents 'their' heritage to the outside world, lies not only with a small group in the town, but also perhaps with 'the tourists'. A further cause of conflict is the fact that the mill, part-funded by state agencies, is in direct competition with private enterprise. As one bar-owner put it:

> I have a very very strong feeling with regard to private enterprise and creating real jobs, jobs that the actual enterprise itself is paying for. And I am doing that here, whereas there is an awful lot of government money going into the interpretive centre where there are very few 'real' jobs—what I call real jobs —where they're no longer being paid by FAS[5] ... I created six jobs this year—and I could have created more if I had got more people [i.e. tourists].

She continued: 'you take the restaurant upstairs [i.e. at the mill]—that's direct competition with here and they're all FAS staff, everybody there is FAS and they're grappling to get everybody in'.

Despite these conflicts, the mill at least presents a version of place identity which is not completely alien to the local inhabitants. The mill does not try to suggest that contemporary people are in some way traditional or authentic, but emphasizes the skill of the modern workforce and the high quality of the woollen products. The visitor is presented with a story of the past which is used to suggest that the modern-day Foxford is a place of energy and dynamism in the face of adversity. Further, the individuals who first proposed the visitor centre and launched the campaign to raise funds were able to use a common sense of conflict between the embattled inhabitants of the west of Ireland generally and the policy-makers in Dublin. Even though many of the key players in the establishment of the centre came from outside Foxford (e.g. the textiles designer from Latvia, the manager born in another part of Ireland, the county architect, consultants from Trinity College Dublin and a private design company), they had, as the manager put it, 'a good feeling for the place', and they allied themselves with the community against the planners and officials from the capital. As the manager said:

> The important thing is that we didn't allow them to impose their ideas on us. We knew what we wanted.... And from their point of view it was quite painful because they couldn't understand why, what they would describe as 'rednecks down the country' was dictating to them how they should design.

Here, he is allying 'us rednecks' against 'them' in Dublin and later in the interview he enthused about the massive local support that they received:

> Oh it was, to look back on it, it was the same sort of reaction we got that Mother Arsenius got when she set up the place. It was weird, you know. Everybody came on board, everybody saw what we were doing was right and good, and couldn't have been more supportive ... you look back on it and it's a fairy tale! (Laughs).

The story of the woollen mills can be interpreted as one of change and renewal. From being in a state of receivership in 1987, the mills have been transformed from a manufacturing enterprise to one which combines manufacture and cultural commodification. 'Outsiders' or 'incomers' have been key actors in the process of change, but this in itself can be seen as an aspect of continuity in Foxford's history. It was a nun from England who first set up the mill, just as a whole set of outsiders and incomers had, in a broader sense, contributed to the construction of Foxford as a place throughout Ireland's long history of invasion and colonization. In particular, outsiders have been involved in the commodification of place identity because of their heavy involvement in tourism-related enterprises. An English couple, for instance, have created a traditional open farm which contains livestock and trees native to Ireland and runs educational activities for local school children. They came to Ireland to escape the 'rat race' and have imported their own notions of what a traditional farm should look like. As the owner said: 'It's obviously to everyone a genuine working farm with a family living on it ... it's very typical, very traditional west of Ireland farm. It's got all the beautiful old stone walls, the hills, the view, the stream running down through it.'

She also told of how the locals initially regarded the project as a 'big joke' and would come up with questions like 'when are the ostriches getting here?'. It does seem ironic that it should be a family of incomers who are re-instating traditional buildings and practices, whilst local families prefer to build themselves ranch-style houses and leave the old homes to disintegrate, spending the rest of their years as cow sheds or hay stores. Yet it is an irony which is seen repeated in many parts of rural Ireland and in Brittany too, and which is bound up with conflicting ideas of place and identity.

In summary, the story of Foxford seems to be one of changes which are directly linked to tourism, but are also linked to broader social processes such as counter-urbanization, emigration and changes in agriculture. As in Commana, the relationship between tourism and identity can be analysed in terms of the social relations which exist in and between places. In Foxford the social relationships appear to encourage tourism development. These relationships include the existence of the mill, which brings together a number of dynamic individuals, many of whom are incomers. This is in contrast to the commune administration of Commana, where the older generations and farming community were heavily represented and presided over by a mayor who was noticeably unenthusiastic about tourism. Other relationships which are important in Foxford are those with particular state agencies which have helped to fund the mill, and the historically layered relationships laid down through years of emigration and, more recently, counter-urbanization. This is not to say that aspects of the tourism place myth are simply incorporated into local identities. For instance, although there are many accomplished musicians throughout north Mayo, the town does not boast 'nightly music sessions' as is proclaimed in one brochure. The landlady of one pub, whose children play instruments and who loves the music herself, said it was 'very difficult now to get traditional music' because the townspeople 'aren't interested' and (as the daughter said) 'don't appreciate it'. The publicans lose out, and tourists who come expecting music and song leave disappointed, as is shown by the letters in the local newspapers from visitors whose preconceptions have been dented. The myth of traditional music in every pub is shattered, but if people are not interested in the music they will not play or listen, even if it is good for tourism. As in Commana, people do not appear to be responding to pressures to stage their own culture purely for the tourists. At the same time, there does not seem to be the same dissonance between representations and realities as in Commana. For instance, as Foxford is not located in the Gaeltacht, it is not portrayed as an Irish-speaking traditional area in quite the same way that Commana is represented as a Breton-language heartland. Further, within the current context of a national revival of interest in the Irish language and an international fascination with all things Irish, it seems probable that proclaiming an Irish-speaking identity is in any case not so problematic as proclaiming a Breton-speaking identity.

Conclusion: Tourism and the Complexity of the Celtic Experience

In the stories about Commana and Foxford I have tried to evoke a sense of place, and to communicate my own interpretation of what seems to be happening in each community in terms of the relationship between tourism and place identity. In the case of Commana, I suggested that there was a pervasive feeling of resistance to the idea of tourism and also, amongst some groups, to the imposition of a specifically Breton identity. In the case of Foxford I evoked a sense of change within the community, change which in itself could be interpreted as a form of resistance. There was also a greater openness towards tourism. In each case I tried to illustrate the idea that tourism is mediated through the existing social relations within and between places, and that any changes to place identity must be understood within the context of broad social processes of which tourism is only one.

Although each place has a different and specific story, some broad similarities emerge which may allow for an understanding of the complexity of identities in Celtic peripheries. The first similarity is that there is little evidence to suggest that inhabitants attempt to perform staged versions of their own cultural identity in order to appeal to tourist expectations. People in general are not 'becoming' Celtic just to satisfy tourists. Although it may be that tourism is contributing to a re-evaluation of some aspects of identity, this is not to say that traditions come to be staged simply for tourists, and therefore lose meaning in some way. On the contrary, communities or societies are capable of utilizing culture in different ways. In both Brittany and north Mayo, for instance, there are two expressions of tradition going on. One is very public, commodified by state-sponsored bodies and aimed at tourists, and the other is small-scale, locally organized and locally publicized through networks which remain largely inaccessible to the visitor. The former version in Brittany consists of 'folkloric' festivals which are held in larger towns such as Quimper and Lorient to appeal to summer visitors. Here you are more likely to see Breton dancers in traditional costume, women in coiffes and colourful parades of pipers. The dancers in costume will often be members of the Cercle Celtique, a popular organization established in Paris in 1917, which has done much to promote Breton dance in many urban centres (Mac Ruari 1995, 14–15). Meanwhile in Mayo, an equivalent is the recently revived Ballina Salmon Festival, where the streets are filled with traditional musicians, set dancers, old-fashioned poteen stills, and events such as curragh-racing on the river, demonstrations of bread-making and fishing competitions.

A further point about the whole question of the staging of tradition is that, as Chapman suggests in reference to Brittany, the people who are supposed to act as the 'guardians of tradition' very often do not regard this as their role at all. The native speakers, older people of a predominantly agricultural background, are the ones who are least likely to be involved in tourism. In his ethnography of the fishing village of Plouhinec, he notes that the inhabitants who seem to the tourist to be the key-holders to an archaic traditional life do not necessarily see themselves in that light: 'They are the first to admit that they have lost all their traditions, and show no particular regret for this loss ... [I]n general, they see themselves as a group, if not individually as a people that do not much believe in God, do not dance, [and] do not sing' (1987, 211).

In Foxford, too, people in general do not see themselves as being particularly 'traditional', even though they too are living in an area which is supposed to be a repository of tradition—the west of Ireland. However, it is important to note that it is increasingly difficult to talk about 'people in general' given the arrival over time of new inhabitants who were not born in the area, or the return of emigrants.

This brings us to the second similarity, which is that in both places incomers are often responsible for importing tourist place-myths through their involvement in the commodification of tradition and culture. As Paul Cloke (1994, 179) observes, 'traditional regional constructs of idyllic rural life are being reproduced, reinforced and re-presented both through the reflexive experiences of new in-migrant groups in the areas concerned and through the mechanisms by which regions are marketed as a commodity, particularly as tourist and leisure destinations'. In both case studies, the role of individuals who were originally from outside the immediate boundaries of the town was striking. Anthropologists have described these as 'culture brokers' (Nunez 1978), marginal people who for some reason have different experiences and attitudes from the majority of the population and are able to use these to capitalize on tourism development. It does seem to be the case that experience of life beyond the immediate locale is necessary for the objectification and commodification of culture, as are different sets of values. Nuala O' Faolain, reporting on tourism development on Gaelic-speaking islands off the west coast of Ireland, suggests that 'sometimes, preparing a community for visitors has to do with learning to value what was never considered valuable until seen through outsider's eyes' (*Irish Times Weekend* 9 April 1996).

The point about value is that it is given or allocated by people from 'outside'. As Chapman states, '[T]radition, archaism, authenticity and peripherality are defined and given value by the larger financial and moral system' (1987, 67). Some critics have suggested that the uneven relationship through which worth is allocated creates pressures on the inhabitants of the areas which are so valued. Brody (1972), for example, suggests that rural communities in the west of Ireland are *dependent* on tourists for reassurance. More recently, Fees (1996) has argued that it is the 'centre' which has authority to ascribe authenticity, and it is the 'periphery' which accepts the authority. In a similar vein McDonald, drawing on her research in Brittany, suggests that tourism puts pressure on locals to be 'proper Bretons' by speaking Breton and dancing at *festnoz*. She portrays the Bretons as constantly running to catch up with urban notions of Breton rurality, but speculates that once the population is 'wholly taken with the dances of the *festou-noz*, and struggling to speak Breton and only Breton all the time and to everyone, and living in dark, country stone houses heated by woodfires and furnished with solid, rustic oak, then the urban intellectuals will have focused their attention elsewhere, and the peasant will be one step behind again' (1987, 132).

Although urbanites and tourism do play an important role in defining rural identities in Brittany, McDonald's analysis perhaps implies that 'the Bretons' (who are in any case not a homogenous group) are cultural dupes, constantly performing and pandering to the needs of outsiders. Yet I think it would be more useful to think of Breton—and Irish—rural identities as being constructed through constant negotiation, rather than dictated by one source. It is the case that urban influence is fundamental in defining identity through tourism, but it is also the case that there is sometimes resistance to this influence, as with the example of the *écomusée*. It is also true, as mentioned earlier, that it is often ex-urbanites who are very much involved in tourism and cultural activities, but then is it not the case that it is *they* who are chasing their own image of Brittany rather than forcing locals to chase it? Many longer-term inhabitants such as farmers or retired people remain unconcerned with or by tourism, and unconcerned with issues of culture and identity.

In other words, rather than 'cultural alienation', there is a process of 'cultural transformation'—of change and revival—going on. Although cultural activities are now more commoditized (in that, for instance, you may buy dancing lessons), this does not mean that they are any less socially embedded or meaningful, but rather that they are being lived and experienced in different ways. These new ways of living culture have been influenced by tourism, but also by the increased prosperity, mobility and interaction between places and people. The fact that *festou-noz* take place all year round and not just in the tourist season is evidence that these events are not just put on for tourists. Boissevain notes a similar phenomenon in his discussion of the growing popularity of *festa* celebrations in Malta. He describes how such occasions are used by 'the modernized urban (mostly young and educated elite) to explore and take part in events that are part of their cultural heritage' (1996, 117). As Boissevain notes, the tourists, through their interest in traditional village events, have helped to make them 'more acceptable to the urbanized middle class elite who previously denigrated many parochial pageants' (1996, 115). As one observer from Mayo put it, tourism 'can help us to appreciate more what we have'.

In closing, I want to reflect briefly on what this analysis of the relationship between tourism and place identity in Brittany and Ireland can contribute to the understanding of contemporary Celticity. I hope that I have shown that through tourism, characteristics such as 'traditional', 'authentic' and 'Celtic' are often projected onto particular communities by people and institutions from beyond the immediate locale. This in itself is a continuation of a historical process which designated the Celtic regions as peripheral and 'other'. As Chapman argues, 'From Classical times to the present ... "Celts" were nothing more than "the others", the outsiders as viewed from a culturally dominant centre ... the only continuity of Celticity is a continuity of "otherness", a continuity retrospectively imposed from the centre on the periphery' (cited in Raftery 1993).

The notion of Celticity is a subjective one which may be appropriated by different groups and individuals in different ways and for different reasons. The term 'Celtic' remains vague and ill-defined, which in itself may help to explain why it is so popular as a tourist marketing device. It is a term which is suggestive of hedonism, freedom, creativity, music, spirituality and closeness to nature, and as such is an ideal device for appealing to particular types of tourist—especially those disillusioned with modern urban lifestyles. As Bowman notes (1994, 147) there is 'a lot of scope for the construction of a variety of models of what it is to be Celtic and what a Celtic lifestyle might be'. As she suggests, there are many people who may describe themselves as 'Cardiac Celts'—they feel in their hearts that they are Celts. There are others who can be described as 'free range Celts', who express their Celticity in fairly random and individual ways. It is a sense of identity which is easily communicated through language, art and design, and which is easily accessible to European, North American and Antipodean tourists who may wish to appropriate their own perception of what it means to be a Celt into their personal sense of identity. Yet it is also a sense of identity which is not necessarily adopted by the people who are portrayed as the 'real' Celts—those who speak Celtic languages and live in remote rural regions, and whose own lifestyles are often under threat from the economic pressures exerted in the global marketplace. Perhaps the conclusion, then, is that the story of Celticity, as has always been the case, remains one of conflict, change and resistance.

Notes

1. Lit. 'Night festival'—a traditional dance evening, in the past held to celebrate the end of communal work events such as the harvest.
2. Plural of *festnoz*
3. A broad tract of land sweeping down from the mountains to the dark waters of the Yuen Ellez, also known as 'the door to Hell', and the area where the museoparc would have been sited
4. Other tourist attractions in North Mayo.
5. Foras Aiseanna Saothair—Training and Employment Authority.

References

Abram, S. Reactions to Tourism: A View from the Deep Green Heart of France. In J. Boissevain (ed.) *Coping with Tourists: European Reactions to Mass Tourism.*

Oxford, 1996.

Barvel, B. *Un Espace Deshérité des Monts d'Arrée Face aux Enjeux Contemporains.* Commana, 1992.

Black, A. Negotiating the Tourist Gaze: The Example of Malta. In J. Boissevain (ed.) *Coping with Tourists: European Reactions to Mass Tourism.* Oxford, 1996.

Boissevain, J. Ritual, Tourism and Cultural Commoditization in Malta: Culture by the Pound? In T. Selwyn (ed.) *The Tourist Image: Myths and Myth-Making in Tourism.* London, 1996.

Bowman, M. The Commodification of the Celt: New Age/Neo-Pagan Consumerism. In T. Brewer (ed.) *The Marketing of Tradition: Perspectives on Folklore, Tourism and the Heritage Industry.* Chippenham, 1994.

Brody, H. *Inishkillane: Change and Decline in the West of Ireland.* London, 1972.

Byrne, A., Edmondson, R. and Fahy, K. Rural Tourism and Cultural Identity in the West of Ireland. In B. O'Connor and M. Cronin (eds) *Tourism in Ireland: A Critical Analysis.* Cork,1993.

Cachin, F. *Gauguin: the Quest for Paradise.* London, 1989.

Chapman, M. A Social Anthropological Study of a Breton Village, with Celtic Comparisons. Ph.D., Oxford University, 1987.

Cloke, P. (En)Culturing Political Economy: A Life in the Day of a Rural Geographer. In Cloke *et al. Writing the Rural: 5 Cultural Geographies.* London, 1994.

Cohen, E. Traditions in the Qualitative Sociology of Tourism. *Annals of Tourism Research,* 15, pp. 29–46, 1988.

Conseil Général du Finistère. *Perception d'Une Politique en Faveur de la Langue et de la Culture Bretonnes.* Rennes, 1992.

Department of Foreign Affairs (Ireland). *Facts about Ireland.* Dublin, 1996.

Ekholm-Friedman, K. & Friedman, J. Global Complexity and the Simplicity of Everyday Life. In D. Miller (ed.) *Modernity Through the Prism of the Local.* London, 1995.

Fees, C. Tourism and the Politics of Authenticity in a North Cotswolds Town. In T. Selwyn (ed.) *The Tourist Image: Myths and Myth-Making in Tourism.* Chichester, 1996.

Gibbons, L. *Transformations in Irish Culture.* Cork, 1996

Greenwood, D. Culture by the Pound: An Anthropological Perspective on Tourism as Cultural Commoditization. In V.L. Smith (ed.) *Hosts and Guests,* 2nd edn. Oxford, 1989.

Hughes, G. Tourism and the Geographical Imagination. *Leisure Studies,* 11, 31–42, 1992.

Kneafsey, M. Changing Roles and Constructing Identities: Ethnography in the Celtic Periphery. In A. Hughes, C. Morris and S. Seymour (eds) *Ethnography and Rural Research.* Cheltenham, 2000.

MacCannell, D. *Empty Meeting Grounds: The Tourist Papers.* London, 1992.

Mac Ruairi, T. How Breton Music Staged a Comeback. *Irish Music,*1 (1), pp.

14–15, 1995.

Mason, G. Manufactured Myths: Packaging the Exotic for Visitor Consumption in M. Robinson, N. Evans and P. Callaghan (eds) *Tourism and Culture Towards the 21st Century Conference Proceedings: 'Tourism and Culture: Image, Identity and Marketing'*. Centre for Travel and Tourism, Northumberland, 1996.

Maybury, B. *Une Région et son Avenir: les Problèmes et les Chances du Tourisme en Bretagne*. Paris, 1986.

McDonald, M. Tourism: Chasing Culture and Tradition in Brittany. In M. Bouquet and M. Winter (eds) *Who From Their Labours Rest? Conflict and Practice in Rural Tourism*. London, 1987.

McDonald, M. *We are not French!: Language, Culture and Identity in Brittany*. London, 1989.

Nash, C. The West of Ireland and Irish Identity. In B. O'Connor and M. Cronin (eds) *Tourism in Ireland: A Critical Analysis*. Cork, 1993.

Ní Laoire, C. Migration Power and Identity: Life Path Formations among Irish Rural Youth, Ph.D., Liverpool University, 1997.

Nunez T. Touristic Studies in Anthropological Perspective. In V. Smith (ed.) *Hosts and Guests*. Oxford, 1978.

O' Faolain, N. Island Hopping. *Irish Times Weekend*, 9 April 1996.

O-Muire-Smith Architects. *The Conservation of the Natural Heritage of North-West Mayo: A Study for the National Parks and Wildlife Service of Mayo County Council*. 1996.

Quinn, B. Images of Ireland in Europe. In U. Kockel (ed.) *Culture, Tourism and Development: The Case of Ireland*. Liverpool, 1994.

Raftery, B. A Cast of Actors on the Fringe. *Times (London) Higher Educational Supplement*, 17 January 1993.

Reece, J.E. Internal Colonialism: The Case of Brittany. *Ethnic and Racial Studies*, 2 (3) pp. 274–92, 1979.

Shepherd, D. *Breton Dance and Tune Book*. Northumberland, 1989.

Trollope, A. *A Summer in Brittany*, 2 vols. London, 1840.

Urry, J. *Consuming Places*. London, 1995.

Conclusion

New Directions in Celtic Studies
An Essay in Social Criticism

COLIN H. WILLIAMS

I am, naturally, both intrigued and delighted to have been asked to write a concluding essay for this volume. However, let me say at the outset that I am always suspicious of volumes with titles such as 'New Directions in' or 'Radical Paradigms in' such and such. The reason is that all too often such volumes end up being exercises in the vilification of the establishment and the high priests of current orthodoxy. Advocates of new directions engage in a little radical hectoring of the older generation's neglect of some vital core area and tend to generate a great deal of hoo-hah about the potential and promise of fresh perspectives.

Now this is a classic *modus operandi* of any discipline, although it may have different trajectories. In science, claims of revolutionary breakthroughs and startling inventions often have unanticipated consequences. Most scientific revolutions require decades, if not centuries, to see their full fruition, and even then it is the social impact of radical change on moral nihilism which is so often remembered.

Perhaps we can find other relevant analogies to shifts in Celtic Studies by examining developments in science during the twentieth century. Spielberg and Anderson (1995) remind us that all science consists of two parts: physics and butterfly chasing. This distinction emphasizes two aspects of scientific endeavour: the collection and classification of descriptive material and the understanding of the reasons for the various phenomena in terms of fundamental concepts. While the former activity is an essential and necessary service to science, it is breakthroughs in the latter which are always considered to be the real mark of progress. Understanding, the search for order and pattern, and unanticipated consequences, are what interest me in applying scientific analogies to the field of Celtic Studies.

Let me illustrate by taking physics and biology as examples. Physics is essentially concerned with seven themes which have structured its epistemology and occasioned a conceptual revolution or caused a new direction to be undertaken which affects the whole of the discipline. Spielberg and Anderson (1995) elucidate the history of physics by reference to the following seven propositions:

1. The earth is not the centre of the universe (Copernican astronomy).
2. The universe is a mechanism run by rules (Newtonian mechanics and causality).
3. Energy is what drives the physical universe (the concept of energy).
4. Entropy tells it where to go (entropy and probability).
5. The facts are relative but the law is absolute (relativity).
6. You cannot predict or know everything (quantum theory and the end of causality).
7. Fundamentally, things can never change (conservation principles and symmetry).

Physics, since 1955, has moved from quarks (the smallest known particles) to the apparent discovery of the faint echo of the Big Bang in the microwave background radiation that fills the universe. These were fundamental, revolutionary discoveries. But somehow, they led nowhere directly, even though individuals were mesmerized by their potential and the physics community was agog at such radical implications shaking the intellectual universe.

Biology offered a different potential according to a popular report in the *Sunday Times*, 4 October 1998 (40). When James Watson and Francis Crick deciphered the structure of the molecule of DNA in 1953, biology emerged as the young pretender. At last it had something to say. Certainly physics remained the foundation, but its history of matter suddenly seemed dry, distant, almost meaningless. DNA, in contrast, was the key to life; it offered a history, not of dry matter, but of the wet, organic stuff that made animals and ourselves; it told us how we all got here.

CONCLUSION

Structural preconditions determine the range of possibilities open to us but the historical narrative is the triggering factor which enables us to interpret which mutations and changes are most significant for our current condition. Peter Munz puts it thus:

> Our presence in the universe is a mystery which can be somewhat abated when we see ourselves and other people at the end of a long line of causes and effects. But the curious thing is that while we are quite certain that the past has taken place and that we stand at the end of it, the past does not lie out there or back there, for us to look at. If we want to know it and talk about it, it first has to be written and turned into a story. It has to be made ready for inspection. (1997, 852)

Is Celtic Studies Ready for Inspection?

Similarly, Celtic Studies has to be mapped, contextualized and laid out as if it were a real slice of time and space, not out there to be discovered as it were in a positivistic scientific way, but through the illusion of the narrative as if it were a representation of reality. This is not to agree with some post-modernist critics that such narratives and disciplines represent the author. On the contrary. For as Munz explains:

> A correct understanding of the role played by generalizations leads us, when we are dealing with explanatory narratives, to a criterion of truth. An explanatory narrative is true if the generalizations it employs correspond to the generalizations used by the people it is about. And when we are dealing with interpretative generalizations, it helps us towards a critical transcendence of parochial and self-serving explanations. (1997, 870)

What of Celtic Studies? Are we forging ahead with new discoveries or are we preoccupied with negating and re-constructing the assumed reality offered by previous generations of scholars? Do we, like physics, have seven pillars of wisdom that we can lay bare? Can we say that we focus so much of our attention on medieval literature or comparative linguistics because these core areas teach us fundamental things about Celticity and about the origins of human behaviour and Western thought? What are our paradigmatic revolutions and who is both proposing and using them in the conduct of their work?

In this essay I choose not to focus on the canonical core of Celtic Studies, even though this lies at the heart of the matter I want to address. To do so would be to rob this volume of its focus, freshness and urgency. But I do insist that there is a core to the field of study which needs to be critiqued and revisited periodically, so as to calibrate it *vis-à-vis* other configurations and frameworks of analysis in cognate disciplines.[1]

My concern is with epistemology and the relative paucity of reflective and critical self-awareness of the role of new initiatives within the field.[2] The themes which are woven throughout this critique are as follows:

1. The remit and boundary-definition of Celtic Studies.
2. The (re)-evolutionary thought and practice.
3. The linguistic turn.
4. Authentic versus syncretic definition of Celticism.
5. Indigenous gleanings versus exogenous adoptions.
6. Academic scholarship versus popular representation.
7. Temporal exegesis and tribal exophagy.[3]

The practice of social criticism is as old as society itself. It comprises elements such as the languages of criticism; the critic as hero or devil's advocate; critical pluralism; the motives of criticism; the arrow of criticism; and the target of consciousness.

These different facets of criticism necessarily involve us in the here and now, for the everyday world is a moral world, it does not depend upon some absolute truth being revealed to us. The social critic must be connected to the reality he or she wishes to represent. For 'unless we are in sight of the sun, like Plato's philosopher, we can make no judgement about life in the cave'. I agree wholeheartedly with Michael Walzer (1989, ix) when he avers that it does make a difference where the critic stands, inside the cave or out; and it makes a significant difference how he or she relates to the cave-dwellers. My professional training was in geography and politics, and so I bring a different perspective to the analysis of Celtic Studies than do most of my colleagues. However, my private passion has been the revitalization of the Celtic and other threatened language groups. I might therefore wish to claim that I stand, Janus like, at the mouth of the cave.

The Origin and Justification of New Directions

Over several years a group of Celtic Studies specialists have been discussing the need for a fresh appreciation of several issues which have normally lain outwith the canon of Celtic Studies scholarship. Some of their concerns are rehearsed in the editors' Introduction to the current volume, which describes a 'crisis' for Celtic Studies. Their analysis of the field encapsulates a justification, a frustration and an impasse which many within the discipline share (see Introduction). The editors argue that traditional Celticists define Celtic cultures on the basis of the possession of a Celtic language. Thus, the field of Celtic Studies, since its nineteenth-century inception, has been dominated by linguistics and the study of medieval literature, with archaeology and history providing a backdrop. From this central tenet they infer a bias which has had two major consequences. The first is that the field has not made a significant effort to address contemporary Celtic phenomena, such as new religions, politics, the Celtic diaspora and popular culture. In fact, they assert that many of the issues addressed by such subjects are dismissed by Celticists as not actually being 'Celtic' since they are modern, or they may not meet the 'linguistic criterion'.

The second bias is that Celtic territories without a significantly large body of medieval literature or a vibrant Celtic-speaking population, such as Cornwall, the Isle of Man and Galicia, have been marginalized or ignored. This has led to an abundance of research on Ireland and Wales, while other Celtic areas seem to fall by the wayside. The editors argue that this is one of the prime justifications for this current volume as all of its essays seek to redress this bias. In this concluding chapter I want to examine both the editors' claim and the contributors' response. I then suggest significant avenues for future research which could be informed by these new perspectives.

In 1997 the University of Exeter Press invited me to be one of the readers/referees for this current volume. In my detailed response to the editors' rationale and to the proposed chapters, I rehearsed several criticisms of their position and offered a few correctives and pointers for future. But the core of my disquiet may be summarized in one paragraph:

> I have no quarrel with the perspectives offered, except of course to add that for most people involved in a professional capacity in Celtic Studies, within the Irish, Welsh and Scottish contexts that are described as forming the core of the discipline, the rather antiquated, old-fashioned view which is presented here is a bit of a straw man. Clearly, there is a strong medieval and linguistic emphasis, such is the inheritance of the discipline and its academic division of labour.

However, many such people are actively engaged in preparing material or researching items which feed directly into the national curriculum at school level, or college and university level, or into the media through popular journals, or television and radio. In other words, the subject matter of much contemporary work is vital, alive and of direct relevance to contemporary social existence. It is largely the writing about Irish, Scottish and Welsh material in English, by non-native speakers, which reproduces this old stereotype, for that is precisely what such critics can access, argue against and thereby become specialists.

Therefore I adopt a rather more cautious approach to the oppositional elements contained in the volume. This is doubly important because often 'new approaches' have not in fact always delivered what they claim to. It is true that they have sometimes addressed issues which are not conventionally covered by Celtic Studies, but this is not the same as initiating new approaches or directions. In comparison with the canon of the discipline, several of the 'new perspectives' which have appeared previously in the general literature of the discipline may be characterized as being superficial, marginal, opportunistic, epiphenomenal and academically light-weight.

Perhaps the editors' introductory remarks in this volume tend to exaggerate the 'newness' of these insights and the nature of the 'closed prison' of conventional Celtic Studies. Many of these 'new' issues do get an airing in English-medium journals devoted to folklore, to museum studies, or to the social sciences, although admittedly only rarely within traditional Celtic Studies publications. Occasionally they also feature in Irish and Welsh-medium journals such as *Barn* and *Golwg*. What is undoubtedly true is that within the North American revival of interest in Celtic Studies (at a popular rather than academic level) there is a general tendency to focus on the 'newer' subject matter of Pagan mysticism, New Age values, the rediscovery of ecology, 'ethnic' music and art forms, rather than dwell on the linguistic-historical bent which the editors rightly say has been dominant within the formal study of the field.

What is really fresh about this volume in the current revivalist context is the focus on deconstructing the Celts, so much so that we are not entirely sure at times whether the resultant field of study is actually a cogent one. To both the novice and the trained eye the list of topics covered by the field of 'New Celtic Studies' might appear to be all periphery and no core. However, the volume challenges the complacency of so much that is assumed rather than spelled out explicitly in what constitutes the growing field of New Celtic Studies. It has presented the fresh work and voices of several younger scholars of Celtic society which either bring new perspectives to bear on conventional topics or add a dynamic Celtic element to main issues of social scientific/cultural studies thought and practice.

From my perspective the central tension which animates much of the volume is that between the lives and concerns of people who inhabit contemporary Celtic spaces and societies and their representation either by 'outsiders' or by professional Celtic scholars. This tension is particulary germane in the field of power politics, decision-making, economic development and identity re-formation. In this collection it is addressed explicitly in the chapters by Jones, Hale and Thornton, Pedersen and Kneafsey. In part it reflects the diffusion of wider currents of international scholarship into the field and in part it is a direct response to the malaise of Celticity as an operational concept.

The Malaise of Celticity

Celtic Studies is a wide-ranging and plural discipline with a core of linguistics, literary analysis, history and archaeology, and an outer, but not necessarily newer, skin comprised of many other disciplines which began to crystallize as distinct subjects at University level in the last quarter of the nineteenth century. A common claim I want to examine is that the impetus to change, to follow in new directions, comes essentially from the outer skin of free radicals, in contradistinction to the essentially conservative and traditional core perspectives. I want to challenge this conception on two grounds, first that it is too simplistic and secondly that it is unfair to the vital, internal debates which have characterized the core of the discipline.

What is interesting from my perspective as an outsider/insider caveman critic is the tension and challenge which the call for a new set of directions poses to Celtic Studies.[4] In the popular imagination the key practitioners who are responsible for the malaise of Celticity constitute the Court of the Sanhedrin or perhaps the Druidic Circle. In the far more prosaic academic imagination, they would be scholarly gate-keepers who authorize new programmes of study, bless new developments with their machinations at university committees and encourage or resist new initiatives as grant agency referees; in other words the business managers of Celtic Studies plc. Thus in the call for new directions I detect a certain frissance or tension between preservationist, and praxis, problem-solving scholarship.

However, it is important to stress that there is no inherent assumption that one cannot be a professional medieval scholar by profession and the most ardent, committed political mobilizer, rabble-rouser or disaffected anarchist in private life. Indeed so many of the greats within Celtic Studies writ large came to encapsulate in their very being the aspirations of many of their constituents that they too became mythologized, and at several turns used their position as gate-keepers, resource controllers and national, often establishment, figureheads to promote very practical programmes of social action in such diverse fields as mass literacy, bilingual education, Church politics, educational reform and local government initiatives.

The Challenge to Orthodoxy and the Canon of the Discipline

There are several key questions which emerge from this challenge to 'traditional' Celtic Studies and the call for new directions:

1. Is Celtic Studies a field of scholarly enquiry more akin to Development Studies and Area Studies (e.g. African or Canadian Studies) than to academic disciplines such as micro-biology, environmental science or history? If the field of Celtic Studies is analogous to Area Studies, are single-focus disciplines within it such as Welsh or Irish more akin to English or Italian? If they are do they thereby gain a respectability and focus which is perhaps lost within the vagaries of Celtic Studies?

2. Is Celtic Studies inherently more conservative than the norm for academic subjects—more interested in reconstructing the past than in representing the present or anticipating the future?

3. If it is, what are the field's hallmarks and how do these act as a filter of resolution for the integration of new directions and fresh perspectives? One obvious hallmark is a concern, nay a preoccupation, with maintaining standards from a mythical Golden Age of scholarship; of linguistic integrity if not necessarily purity; of maintaining an uneasy balance between the strict demands of language and the seductive attraction of literature; between the medieval and the modern; with an occasional outrider from the Ancients and the Greats being allowed to wander the passages of the Academy, tolerated much as a long overdue non-paying

hotel guest might be treated by the porters and chamber maids, part of the furniture, but no longer a core commerical attraction.

But the crunch issue which stretches the bounds of toleration is the tension between authenticity and communication, best articulated in the often hard choice as to whether to publish in one or more of the Celtic languages or to focus on communicating in one of the major international langauges, usually English, which binds all international and interdisciplinary scholarly enterprises together. Critics might argue that all disciplines have to communicate in the global language, and that Celtic Scholars have an additional advantage, compared with, for example, Iberian Studies, in that most authors have English as a co-equal language of expression. However, as the Celtic languages are weaker than Spanish or Portugese, there is a danger that significant Irish or Welsh scholarship will only be published in English rather than also in the original language. Whilst this is undoubtedly true, this power differential between English and the Celtic languages also causes peculiar difficulties which are not shared by most other area and thematic studies, in that the language of wider communication is also the historical language of conquest and subjugation. In this sense the dilemma of choosing a language within which to express onself is akin to many scholars engaged in post-colonial African and South Asian Studies, who also have to come to terms with the language of the oppressor.[5]

4. Is there a culture of expectation, of ambition within Celtic Studies, or are we relatively pleased at any level of interest being shown in our subject matter by students, colleagues, the media etc.?

5. What are the implications of such levels of ambition for the training programmes of Celtic Studies scholars? There may be a canon in terms of what constitutes the core of the discipline, but a related set of core skills and research training methods is far from being agreed. Might one of the 'new directions' sparked off by this volume and the related academic debate be a prioritizing of skills training, technique awareness and grounded competence, to say nothing of theoretical sophistication, as part of our core committment to raising standards within Celtic Studies scholarship?

Most of Celtic Studies scholarship, by definition, is very detailed case-study material, involving a review and interpretation of secondary literature with little explicit methodological advances or theory construction being emphasized as core functions of the discipline. There are updates on aspects of Celtic languages in *The Year's Work in Modern Languages*, but could an annual 'Progress in Celtic Studies' be encouraged, perhaps by *Studia Celtica*, who would commission a bi-annual field report on sequential aspects of linguistics, medieval and modern literature, archaeology, history, religion and public policy? For younger scholars a more self-conscious professionalization of the subject area would perhaps ensue.

6. Is Celtic Studies growing or in a steady state or are key elements such as historical linguistics and comparative linguistics atrophying?

7. Does Celtic Studies, in whole or in part, generate its own inner spontaneous changes or does it necessarily borrow its great ideas and grand traditions, and if so from whom and from where?

8. What is the nature of these new directions and where do they lead in terms of theory construction, context, methodological developments, insight into human nature and social organization? Perhaps the most critical issue is the contribution of these new directions in terms of the applicability and relevance of their findings for scholarship and praxis in the contemporary world.

9. How are these changes related to academic fashion, e.g. post-modernism, the rhetorical turn, social relevance and public policy?

10. Do the changes emanate from largely marginalized sectors, which are unable or unwilling to make in-roads into the central domains of the discipline? Like 'Perfidious Albion', do they therefore seek to engage in niche marketing of their own as a prelude to new empire construction, perhaps even to a popular form of Celtic Studies without the Celts?

11. Which are the sponsoring agencies of change, i.e. the roots of fresh initiatives? How do fresh ideas diffuse throughout the Celtic Studies information system? Is it primarily through influential individuals, academic networks, research centres, disaffected centralists, Trojan Horse usurpers e.g. from Anglo-Saxon Studies, Culture Studies, Critical Theory, the Social Sciences writ large?

12. Where are the centres of vitality in 'New Celtic Studies' offering substance to these new directions? Is it the Institute of Cornish Studies

at the University of Exeter, are they North American departments? What of Germany or Wales, Scotland and Ireland? How do 'new' and 'conventional' interpretations interrelate in major research centre projects such as those hosted by the Centre for Advanced Welsh and Celtic Studies at the University of Wales, Aberystwyth? Are the main currents of new thought outside academic life altogether, derived from individuals and agencies deeply involved in social change and identity re-configuration, and reflected in mass entertainment such as the songs of Catatonia, Runrig and the Rankin Family or the performances of Riverdance? What is the interrelationship between these different academic, media and popular socio-cultural networks?

13. How do these changes mirror or relate in any meaningful and sustained way to structural changes in society? In socio-cultural terms the challenge of new directions may be seen as a response to the erosion of Celtic languages, the awakened interest in varying conception of ecology and New Age spirituality, changes in organized religion, the role of the media and of information technology. In political terms they are best viewed as a renegotiation of the role of Celtic territories within the new international order as a response to political changes such as the growth of nationalism and ethnic-regionalism, the development of new international networks such as the European Bureau for Lesser Used Languages, the European Union, the Committee of the Regions, and closer to home such developments as devolution to Scotland and Wales, the Northern Irish Agreement and Transition Programme, the Irish-British Council (of the Isles) and the current Irish government's commitment to a new Language Act and possible appointment of an Ombudsman for Language Equality.

In economic terms they are a response to changes in structural development, regional planning policies and employment prospects. Development dependency and fresh impetus in the global–local nexus characterize internal divisions within Celtic economies, as witnessed by core–periphery differentials in Scotland, Ireland and Wales, and to a lesser extent Brittany. Cornwall, for example, has the highest unemployment rate of any 'English' county, a marginal economic position and high rates of seasonal and part-time labour fuelling relative discontent and a reappraisal of its position within the UK economic and political space. How is this structural dependency related to a revitalization of interest in Cornish identity and institution-building and with what sort of impact in renegotiating Cornwall's relationship with the UK and Europe?

In identity re-evaluation and representation a new fascination with the Celts is in fashion. Witness the upsurge in the popularity of Celtic names among British children, witness the international success of the music of Altan and Mary Black, the new computer-generated production of the Arthurian legends and the Mabinogion tales. Even radical Celtic nineteenth-century advocates of the rights of the workers to honest wages and decent conditions of work and housing are being repackaged as Deep Ecologists and Proto-Feminists in an attempt to update them and recast them in a new light, which says as much about our current preoccupation with authenticity and historicism as it does about their particular context.

14. Is this concern with new directions and the revitalization of Celticity the latest spurt or manifestation in the internationalization of an already plural discipline?

15. How do indigenous Celticists regard such developments? Do they (we) see them as an opportunity for more integrated interdisciplinary work, or as a threat to the orthodox, a diminution of core focus and a spurious and epiphenomenal side-issue which has little lasting impact on the canon they espouse?

Several Barriers to the New Directions

A hostile critique might suggest that the new directions might be seen as:

1. Peddling illusions.
2. Fostering a preoccupation with the marginalized other, the noble outsider, and the historically disadvantaged.
3. Promoting a situation where exceptionalism rules, because it is claimed the small size of the discipline *vis-à-vis* many other fields of enquiry inhibits adequate innovation and experimentation and is crucially reflected in the difficulty of economies of scale in teaching, resourcing and publishing material.
4. Illegitimate and presumably socially irrelevant in comparison, for example, with mainstream economics or the Law.
5. Initiating a derivative rather than innovative trend, so that Celtic Studies appears to the outside specialist to be at least one generation removed from main currents of social thought and praxis.

6. Promoting a tendency to rely, perhaps too much, on formulaic research methods, which may be tried and tested methods for subject matter such as reproducing and reconstructing medieval texts, but offer little by way of fresh ideas in terms of interpretative analysis. Here we have a division of labour emerging between reconstructionist, revisionists and interpreters who derive some of their inspiration from cognate developments in oral narrative perspectives, critical theory, linguistic deconstruction and other paradigm shifts in the humanities and to a lesser extent the social and natural sciences.

New Directions: Illustrative Issues

I accept that new directions involve new developments, but new developments do not necessarily involve or require new directions. Let me illustrate the dynamism and range of innovative work already being done by reference to seven key areas of interest which are woven into this volume.

1. Rethinking the Celtic languages.
2. Lifestyles and folklore of Celtic identities.
3. Politics and development.
4. Economic regeneration.
5. Issues in tourism and popular representation.
6. Celtic narratives.
7. Celtic spirituality.

The Celtic Languages

One of the key elements of the new directions is the spur given to national identity by recent political developments. So many hopes are tied into the role of scholarship in the service of the state, the nation and the community. Celtic Studies has been criticized heavily in the post-1945 period for paying too little professional attention to the plight of the decline of Irish, Breton, Gaelic and Welsh, let alone Cornish. It is claimed that compared with the late 1960s and early 1970s, today's generation of practitioners seem not to be as radical or as challenging, although they may be very individualistic. Yet in hindsight the 1965–85 generation were far less radical than they now believe themselves to have been. Take heart young minds, there is much to be done and higher peaks to scale! However, despite the political activism of many of its leading figures, little sustained work has been undertaken in sociolinguistics, language planning and language policy. In the past few years there has been a fresh appreciation of the need to integrate purely linguistic considerations into a more holistic socio-economic context as represented in the work of Pádraig Ó Riagáin (1997) or Máiréad Nic Craith (1996).

So how can Celtic Studies serve its non-academic constituents? Language transmission in the home, school and mass media is the bread and butter issue of survival. Serving public policy directly, through bilingual education, professional development and training, the translation requirements of new post-devolutionary institutions, is a key function of contemporary practitioners within the field. The long-term struggle to wrest language rights from a hegemonic state has been realized in varying degrees of legislative equality, at least in Ireland and Wales and currently also within Northern Ireland. In addition to the well-established growth of bilingual education, we may now add a fairly substantial list of themes wherein the role of the Celtic languages is being reassesed and some degree of positive social engineering is being achieved. Space does not allow illustration of the themes, but their range is sufficient testimony to the scale of the revitalization process which is underway to institutionalize both Welsh and Irish in particular, but also Gaelic and to a much lesser extent Breton, and to normalize the role of these languages in selected contexts:

1. *Language planning and language policy:* a comprehensive and holistic set of perspectives is being developed on language in society, with a focus on education, the community, the local economy and the workplace.
2. The maturation of the *Welsh Language Board/Bord na Gaeilge/Comunn na Gaidhlig* as central agencies directing and resourcing key changes within the respective linguistic communities.
3. *'Mentrau Iaith' and community social development,* which seek to inject an element of local empowerment to the process of language revitalization and local language planning.
4. *Language and economy,* a clearer specification of the need to reduce the over-dependence of Celtic languages on a cultural justification and a corresponding increase in relating language use to the economic sphere and integrating the needs of linguistic communities within regional development planning policy.

5. *Language training and professional development*, to enable employees, consumers and providers of bilingual services to operate at a high level of professional competence within a bilingual context.
6. *Translation requirements of new institutions*: intensive training programmes and certification of professional competence of translators and interpreters within the devolved representative assemblies/parliaments and burgeoning commercial enterprises which have a bilingual remit.
7. *Interactive software and computer-aided learning resources/internet developments*, which enable the virtual environment of Celtic speech to progress and widen its range of effective networks, so that a new definition of community without propinquity is realized.
8. *Stress-free Language Teaching Methods e.g. Suggestopedia, Neural Language Programmes*, to supplement the conventional drill-based teaching methods so beloved of adult second-language teaching programmes.
9. *Mass media and popular entertainment in a digital telecommunications era*: e.g. the social, information and entertainment functions and impact of S4C Digidol and Telegael Teo in realizing a Celtic presence beyond the Celtic territories.

The most promising boost to a reinterpretation of the role of language in social development is the major interdisciplinary research project on the Social History of the Welsh Language, directed by Professor Geraint Jenkins (1997). It is much to be hoped that similar authoritative national surveys will be undertaken for the Gaelic and Irish languages.

Lifestyles and Folklore of Celtic Societies

The popular representation of things Celtic owes as much to Glastonbury, New Age thinking, Celtic mysticism, a segmented rural idyll of poets, shepherds and a hundred and one craft-fair markets, by which Tourist Boards have sold the image of the Celt. As we have seen above, both 'Commodities and Lifestyles' and 'Popular Representation' are an important part of the 'debate' on authenticity, on legitimizing who in fact can take part in and speak with authority on Celtic issues. The authors in this volume go some way to analysing how contemporary media and popular representation are contributing to the modernized self-image of citizens of Celtic lands and their diaspora relations.

Within the ambit of popular representation, film, record and television so dominate the perception of the 'Celtic' world for non-Celts that the chapters in this volume by Thornton, Jones and Minard offer a dynamic and arresting way to open up the discussion on who constitute the Celts today. However, we need to go beyond such insights and pay attention to the growing media industry in Ireland and Wales as both an economic asset and as a means of 'controlling' or balancing the hegemonic interpretation of social life in these lands. In other words, we need to analyse both media and popular representation as means of contributing to the modernized self-image of citizens. Only when we cease to accept that descriptions of things Celtic are somehow pre-modern, exceptional, unique and dismissable in the contemporary world will we learn to validate what we cherish for what it is—our shared culture, not the antithesis of English or French culture.

Too often Celtic identity is trapped within the open prison of traditional, folklore images.This is particularly critical in Brittany, for as Minard demonstrates, contemporary Breton nationalism is frustrated by the chains of antiquity and the weight of folkloric narratives. And yet to rest content with a traditional–modern continuum is to deny the continuing appeal of both folklore and forgery in the construction of modern national identities. The real question is whether this sort of convoluted and selected invention invalidates the contemporary concern with reappropriating elements of the past to reconstitute the present. Celtic identity is heavily nuanced by a self-conscious culture, often mobilized for political aims as illustrated below.

Situating Celtic Politics

The evolving framework of the European Union has given a boost to the rearticulation of Celtic–English and Celtic–French relationships. Conventional core–periphery theory and empirical testing of the structural relationships between the Celtic regions and the modern, bureaucratic territorial state have gone well beyond Hechter's 'Internal Colonial' (1975) paradigm, although virulent elements remain. Scholars such as Neil Evans (1989), K.O. Morgan (1995), Declan Kiberd (1997) and Tom Nairn (1997) have relished the challenge of validating or falsifying post-colonial propositions. Sadly, Cornwall has been only a footnote in such treatises. However, with the revitalization of Cornish Studies, best typified by the work of Philip Payton, there has been a more focused treatment of Cornish politics as a variant of the wider structural tension between British state-building and Celtic nation-formation. In Philip Payton's *The Making of Modern Cornwall* (1992), togther with his revised analysis of 'Paralysis and Revival' (1997b) and 'Cornwall in Context: The New Cornish Historiography' (1997a), there is a consistent attempt to take the Cornish experience seriously.

Revised Cornish historiography is but part of a wholesale reconceptualization of the main tenets of British history and geography. Challenging variants to both Tory and Whig interpretations of British state development and identity have been provided by J.G.A. Pocock (1975), Keith Robbins (1984), H.Kearney (1989), Linda Colley (1992) and David Cannadine (1995). Similar reconceptualization of the main tenets of British geography, which echo the pioneering work of Estyn Evans, also abound. Among the more provocative are Taylor on the break-up of England (1993), B.J. Graham and L.J. Proudfoot (1993) on Irish historical geography, and P. Gruffydd's contributions on Wales (1995).

Within this revised context of time and space we can situate the new constitutional arrangements for the UK, *viz.* the Scottish Parliament, the National Assembly for Wales and the Northern Irish Assembly. This is not the place for a detailed discussion of such arrangements but I would like to signal four elements which could have a long-lasting efffect on the quality of intra-Celtic relations over the coming decades.

The first is to expose the vacuous attempt at the de-politicization of the language issue in Wales and Northern Ireland. It has suited the elected leaders of left-of-centre political parties to suggest that formerly contentious issues, such as language rights and access to bilingual education, have been taken out of the political front line. It is claimed that language conflict is now better seen as having transformed into a language consensus in terms of administrative arrangements and the routinization of partial or full bilingualism within the local state apparatus. The contributions to John Osmond's handbook for the National Assembly for Wales (1998) and Mac Póilin's dissection of the Irish language in Northern Ireland (1997) give the lie to this sort of neutering of the language issue. More fundamentally, some political party leaders, such as Ian Paisley in Northern Ireland and Rod Richards, Conservative Party leader in Wales, have sought to reopen language wounds as a means of garnering the votes of citizens who are disaffected by recent reforms which give greater recognition to Irish and Welsh within a British context.

The politicization of language issues is a widely documented aspect of various group empowerment and contexts. Genuine concerns related to equality of opportunity and to the implementation of fundamental language rights deserve to be addressed independently, as legitimate concerns in themselves that impact on the rights of speakers. But ridicule and dismissal rather than credence and legitimacy are what can be expected if the current practice of politicizing language claims cannot be overcome. In other words community empowerment in Wales and Northern Ireland needs to be viewed in terms of languages rather than political communities at this stage, at the stage of implementation rather than negotiation (Nic Shuibhne 1999).

A second issue is the re-energized commitment of the Irish government to allow the Irish language to flourish within more fruitful soil than has hitherto been the case. The cutting edge of this new political determination is the attempt to introduce a new Irish Language Equality Bill during the next Dáil session. Championed by Eamon Ó Cuív, Minister for Arts, Heritage, Gaeltacht and the Islands, and supported by a cross-section of political factions, it should provide a new basis for language policy and planning. Notwithstanding some of the caveats which Comhdháil Náisiúnta na Gaeilge (1998) and others have entered, there is a real possibility that a revised Language Act could kick-start the rather halting language services currently available. Comhdháil Náisiúnta na Gaeilge's report is particularly good on the implications of appointing an Irish Language Ombudsman who would be responsible for the quality, level and suitability of services provided through Irish; the appropriateness of the organizational structures and arrangements of public sector bodies for delivering services to Irish speakers and Gaeltacht communities; and the implementation of the Language Act in general.

A final issue is the character and political clout of new political arrangements following British devolutionary measures and the Good Friday Agreement. Let me illustrate by reference to the potential impact of the Irish–British Council on Celtic identities. When the Good Friday Agreement was being negotiated, nationalists were pressing for strong North–South ministerial and other institutional connections, whereas the Unionist community was pressing for more East–West ones. From a linguistic and cultural identity perspective there is clearly potential for both axes. The Irish–British Council (IBC) has been established 'to promote the harmonious and mutual beneficial development of the totality of relations among the peoples of these islands'. In paragraph 5 of the section it is suggested that two of the suitable items for early discussion in the IBC could be cultural and education issues. It is envisaged that the Council will meet in different formats: 'at Summit level twice per year, in specific sectoral formats on a regular basis, with each side represented by the appropriate minister; in an appropriate format to consider cross-sectoral matters'. One of these sectors will be Celtic linguistic and cultural concerns and is likely to be informed in its deliberations by expert working groups.

It is worth noting that the Council will have representatives not only from the sovereign governments but from devolved institutions in Northern Ireland, Scotland and Wales as well as representatives of the Isle of Man and the Channel Islands. This should bring representatives of Celtic countries together in a formal structure for the first time in modern history. If, as is possible, representatves of Brittany are also included, it would constitute a unique forum for the exchange of views and experiences in north-west Europe. In addition to establishing 'best practice' in relation to culture and language rights, the Council could provide a real filip to the political identity of Celtic peoples. Irish critics have warned that so long as the Council does not seek executive powers or becomes the means of imposing legislative requirments on executives, it could be relatively useful. If it becomes a means for England, through the UK, to shape the Council of the Isles as the Council of the British Isles, then it will provoke nationalist reflexes because of the political realities that the two sovereign entities are equal only in theory. The three devolved entities are still within the jurisdiction of the UK and dependent upon it for variety of vital interests including finance.

Economic Regeneration

Celtic identity within the European context relates essentially to the position of peripheral identities within the European context, particularly the European Union. A realization that both economics and culture should be treated in tandem has led to a greater specification of the relationship between cultural reproduction and economic development, especially in the Gaeltacht where new European linkages are being forged (Ó Cuív 1998). Illustration of the range of new initiatives which influence the preconditions of prosperity in Celtic societies is given below.

1. The Irish Tiger and the Gaeltacht's Kittens.
2. The 'Intelligent Region' of South Wales.
3. New European linkages, e.g. Region 1 status, INTERREG, LEADER, NOW, HORIZON, RACE, TELEMATICS, YOUTHSTART, ADAPT.

4. HIDB/CNAG Gaelic Economic Regeneration.
5. UNESCO cultural and economic initiatives.
6. 'Business in Irish' Údarás na Gaeltachta Development Plan.
7. Oireachtas Grants, Section 22 of the Údarás na Gaeltachta Act of 1979, as amended by Section 2 of the Údarás na Gaeltachta Act, (Amendment) Act, 1993.
8. Regional planning and language policies.
9. European Regional Development Fund.
10. Operational Programme for Industrial Development 1994-9 (Gaeltacht Sub-programme).
11. European Social Fund training and employment grants, up to 75 per cent of eligible expenditure.
12. Strategic structural developments for marginal regions, e.g. COINS (service training), TELEPROMISE (multi-media public information network) and LAMBDA (distance education).
13. Cultural reproduction and economic development.
14. Holistic planning and policy.
15. 'Menter a Busnes' seeking to promote Welsh-medium entrepreneurship.

Issues in Tourism

The representation of self within a naturalistic context and an acute sense of place has dominated writing about Celtic identity and landscape. Such themes have a long pedigree within Celtic and English literature from the natural and supernatural world of medieval scribes to the Irish Revival of Yeats, Lady Gregory and O'Casey and the Romantics' redefinition of Celtic rawness typified in George Borrow's *Wild Wales* published in 1862. The self-conscious cultural construction of place is also a fairly well - established genre. In contemporary writings it is best represented in the collection of essays on Cornwall edited by Ella Westland (1997), especially Chris Thomas on the 'Geography of a Railway Landscape' and Bernard Deacon's 'Images of Cornwall between West Barbary and Delectable Duchy'.

It is regrettable that both literary accounts and official Tourist Board propaganda tend to emphasize the rural bias of tourism in Celtic lands. By so doing, of course, they are reproducing a primitive, pristine, sanitized image of who we are which so many current residents are quick to abandon. Localized power conflicts, wage differentials, housing stock supply, planning controversies, incomers' 'correct' place in society, with or without a linguistic cutting edge, are all integral elements of the construction of place which the promotion of tourism often exacerbates.

In South Wales a slightly modified pattern has emerged with sanitized industrial tourist attractions located at St Ffagans, the Big Pit and the Rhondda Heritage Park. All of these reproduce a rather clichéd view of industrial Welsh culture based upon miners, male voice choirs, brass bands and the struggle against poverty by countless thousands of valley residents in their terraced rows.

As a reaction to this, as well as many other facets of modern life, there has been a literary make-over of Celtic landscapes. Now we interpret tradition as a reopened future. A prime illustration of this is Declan Kiberd's incisive study *Inventing Ireland: The Literature of the Modern Nation* (1996), which questions the authenticity of much that is laid before the tourist gaze because of the simple twist of medium. His central message is that 'The Irish Renaissance had been essentially an exercise in translation, in carrying over aspects of Gaelic culture into English, a language often thought alien to that culture' (624). A parallel analysis has been undertaken by Bobi Jones (1998) when he explores the impact of Anglicization on Welsh literature in his chapter 'Y Lloegr sy'n Gwneud Cymru' (1998). In more general terms both Irish and Welsh-medium literature is suffused with the symbolic role of the Gaeltacht and Y Fro Gymraeg, as representing the true locale of consciousness and patterned behaviour. Irrespective of the political use to which these core concepts have been put, there has been an acute concern with preserving heartlands as a cultural resource base for identity, an identity which is constantly being challenged by tourist development.

It is only rather recently that there has been a conscious marketing of culture, as opposed to the natural beauty of place, to boost and diversify the local economic infrastructure. Small and medium-sized enterprises are now in vogue following a scaling down of economic plans best represented in Comunn na Gàidhlig's report on 'The Dynamics of Gaelic Development' (1993). In chapter 10 above Roy Pedersen provides a rich, detailed illustration of this trend in Gaelic tourism and economic development which is derived from his involvement within the Highlands and Islands Enterprise. Moya Kneafsey addresses the implications of similar trends in Ireland and Brittany. Her thesis that the relationship between tourism and place-identity contributes to the understanding of contempory Celticity is replete with considerations of the ambiguities of Celtic identity. Designation of Celtic regions as peripheral and 'other' owe much to power relations and to the manner in which official and popular narratives have developed appropriate roles for Celts in the global scheme of things.

Celtic Narratives

Unlike political and economic development issues, ascertaining obvious or significant new directions within Celtic narrative is more problematic and that for at least two reasons. One is that much of Celtic literary output is inherently conservative in its treatment of stock themes. The other reason is that it is hard to disentangle original elements from the borrowed adaptations taken from other literary sources within such literature. Nevertheless, four trends may be discerned.

The first is a rearticulation of past and present, time and space as a continuous narrative process. Thus, for example, Mike Dunstan's work in the china clay villages of Cornwall (1997) weaves a tapestry drawn from contemporary story-telling interspersed with local variants on modern legends which situate the community in both time and space. A second significant departure is the recent emphasis on orality and performance as organizing principles in informing medieval textual analysis. Sioned Davies's *Crefft y Cyfarwydd* (1995) is a classic revisionist study of the 'Mabinogion' legends which is infused with these newer perpestives derived from comparative literature, drama and anthropology.

To the emphasis on performance and orality, we may add a relatively new concern with theory. The journals *Taliesin* and *Tu Chwith* provide a ready outlet for fine writing in critical theory, although R.M. Jones (1998) considers them 'somewhat immature and charcteristically fickle'. He avers that evaluation as a basic element in criticism has been lost and that 'the onset of relativism and pluralism (together with the self-contradictory claim that these attitudes are universally true) may be a determining factor in this loss, apart from a prevailing emphasis on the simplistic and popular, or on phonological externals and the journalistic "relevant"' (289). However, as the journals establish themselves I have no doubt that they will constitute vital and engaging vehicles for critical debate. A more scholarly and robust engagement with critical theory may be found in Jerry Hunter's work on the contextualization of consciousness and interpretation. More recently he has concentrated on ethnicity, identity and nationalism. His collaborative essay with Richard Wyn Jones (1995) 'O'r Chwith: Pa Mor Feirniadol yw Beirniadaeth Ôl-Fodern?' is a searching account of current Welsh writing on critical theory.

CONCLUSION

While recognizing that the labourers in the Celtic vineyards are too few a fourth area ripe for development would be a set of powerful critiques of the role of historicism in Celtic narrative. A good start would be an evaluation of the relevance of Hayden White's historicism (1987), as encapsulated in key phrases such as 'the value of narrativity in the representation of reality' and 'the politics of historical interpretation'. Welsh and Gaelic literature would be enriched by transposition of the insights of, for example, White's study *The Content of the Form: Narrative Discourse and Historical Representation* (1989). The volume has already impacted on a diverse range of disciplines from comparative literature to human geography. A leading American geographer, Edward Soja, describes White's treatise as a 'wonderfully creative defence and reassertion of the power and scope of the historical imagination. In his calculated embrace of the contemporary post-structuralist discourse and such figurative individuals as Michael Foucalt and Frederick Jameson, as well as in his inspirational and flexible recomposition of Paul Ricouer's theory of narrativity, White has produced an astutely postmodernized text' (Soja 1993, 131).

As with many such syncretic tendencies in the modern world there is a sense of urgency to construct a third way which negates the oppositional dialogism of so much narrative analysis. Soja (1993) avers that

> White argues for the necessity to historicize via a deconstruction and reconstitution of the narrative form. In his retheorization of narrativity, White dissolves the dichotomy between 'realistic' and imaginary or 'fictional' narratives, between 'scientific' and 'poetic' historiography, seeking instead a recombinant third way of looking at history that 'returns to the narrative as one of its enabling presuppositions', a commitment to a 'whole cultural movement in the arts gathered under the name post-modernism'. The content of the narrative form is not merely discursive, White asserts, but involves epistemic and ontological choices, with significant political and ideological implications.

The full quote which situates this line of reasoning is critical so as to establish the relevance of this mode of thinking for the narrative form within Celtic Studies:

> Philosophers have sought to justify narrative as a mode of explanation different from, but not less important than, the nomo-

logical-deductive mode favoured in the physical sciences. Theologians and moralists have recognised the relation between a specifically narrativisitc view of reality and the social vitality of any ethical system. Anthropologists, sociologists, psychologists, and psychoanalysts have begun to re-examine the function of narrative representation in the preliminary description of their objects of study. And cultural critics, Marxists and non-Marxists alike, have commented on the death of the great 'master narratives' that formerly provided precognitive bases of belief in the higher civilizations and sustained even in the early phases of industrial society, utopic impulses to social transformation. And indeed, a whole cultural movement in the arts, generally gathered under the name postmodernism, is informed by a programmatic, if ironic, commitment to the return of the narrative as one of its enabling assumptions. (xi, quoted in Soja 1993, 135–6)

One obvious implication for Celtic narratives and politics alike is the favoured form of resistance and marginalization, the sublimation of the pure and the good to the external force of the foreign oppressor, rather than focusing on the potential for evil which dwells in each of us. I wonder, now that there is a semblance of self-rule in Celtic lands, whether we will see an increase in emphasis on those narratives which treat with themes of responsibility and autarchy, self-confidence, the ability to rule wisely and justly, the noble and the heroic as forerunners of the now contented, the rule of law and the creatorial, imaginative energy seen in the first flush of Irish parliamentary nationalism's concern with de-anglicization (c. 1912). Of course, the classic narrative which dealt with these themes in the period prior to the current century was the Bible, especially the Old Testament histories. A less central tradition was the treatment of British history prior to the Anglo-Saxon invasions, as illustrated in the work of Theophilus Evans.

Even contemporary treatments of Irish famine and emigration (Crawford 1997) offer more sympathetic and historically accurate accounts of the great haemorrhage of Irish life to the New World. This is particularly so in relation to the work of the estate offices and emigration officers (Duffy 1997). Of course, one should be wary of over-sanitized accounts of the horrors and dislocation of emigration, then as now, and the excellent collection on recent emigration experiences edited by Mac Laughlin (1977) is a useful balance to overly generous revisionist accounts of Irish suffering.

CONCLUSION

In describing Irish political life just prior to independence, Kiberd (1996, 151) argues that some Gaelic Leaguers

> projected an ideal self-image of the Gael as a descendant of ancient chieftains and kings. Irish Ireland countered the petty 'seoinín' or West Briton, who asserted his superiority by imitating English manners, with its own form of invented Celtic snobbery. Ireland became not-England, an apophatic construct which was as teasing to the mind as the notion of a horse as a wheel-less car. Anything English was *ipso facto* not for the Irish, as it might appear to weaken the claim to separate nationhood, but any valued cultural possessions of the English were shown to have their Gaelic equivalents. Thus was born what Seán de Fréine (1965) has acutely called an ingenuous device of national parallelism:
>
> | | |
> |---|---|
> | English language | Irish language |
> | English law | Brehon law |
> | Parliament | Dáil |
> | Prime Minister | Taoiseach |
> | Soccer | Gaelic football |
> | Hockey | Hurling |
> | Trousers | Kilt |
>
> It mattered little whether these devices had a secure basis in Irish history, for if they had not previously existed they could be invented.

This, of course, is an early variant on the pick and mix instant archaeology which we are currently reinventing in our own choice of titles for post-devolutionary politics in the *Cynulliad*, the National Assembly for Wales, with *Y Llywydd*, (the Presiding Officer), *Y Llyfr* (Hansard equivalent) and *Aelod o'r Cynulliad* (Member of the Assembly). Time sanctifies invention as the search for a past conformity becomes the basis for a new legitimacy.

All this, of course, is subject to periodic revision and internal debate. Consider the current Irish position. For two generations after independence there were some people who continued to wear psychological and emotional chains and who entertained ongoing doubts about the wisdom of having broken from mother England (Ó Riagáin 1999). The whole spectrum ran from the craven West British desire to do nothing which would upset 'our betters on the other Island' to the other extreme of those who wished to break any connection with England and not just the political connection as desired by Tone. Such sentiments were fuelled by the official British narratives on post-independence relations. Under British legislation, the 'Republic of Ireland Act, 1949' says that the proclamation of a Republic would not result in any change in the status of Irish people in the UK, which is both convenient and patronizing. But there is in Britain still an insistence on not referring to the independent Irish state by the name its people have given it in its Constitution, namely Ireland, rather than the Republic of Ireland (Mac Unfraidh 1999). For the current younger generation of Irish citizens, such official narratives have been replaced by a forward-looking, self-confident and pro-European outlook.

Celtic Spirituality

If all the other themes treated thus far were indicative of a new set of directions in things Celtic, then the current preoccupation with spirituality and its impact is a major magnet attracting new devotees and interest. This threefold overlapping of Celtic spirituality, Christianity and nature obviously draws on many earlier paradigms, the majority of which are clearly not exclusively Celtic in design or application. The difficulty of interpreting this relationship, from my perspective, is best summed up in Donald Meek's account of Celtic Christianity in these isles:

> My concern is with the *interpretation* of that story, and I would wish to argue that 'Celtic Christianity' is not necessarily the same entity as 'Christianity in the British Isles in the period, c. 400–1100 AD'. The modern mind, under certain circumstances, has a way of interpreting the past to accord with the needs of the present. My view, in a nutshell, is that Celtic Christianity, which is currently enjoying considerable vogue in Britain, and possibly in Ireland, is, to a large extent, such a reinterpretation. It is perhaps misleading to say that Celtic Christianity is a reinterpretation; it is, in fact, closer to being a re-creation, founded on a rediscovery of older texts, mediated through modern translations and capable of carrying different interpretations depending on the needs of the interpreters. These interpreters are almost invariably unfamiliar with any of the Celtic languages, especially in the forms of Early Irish and Early Welsh which are central to genuine scholarly analysis of the critical period (c. 400–1100 AD). (1996, 143–4)

CONCLUSION

Again we see that the linguistic turn is essential for academic analysis, but for popular representation obviously not. This popular representation sees in Celtic Christianity a highly eclectic and noble reaction to mainstream religious experience. Ian Bradley's *The Celtic Way* (1993) suggests that 'Celtic Christianity was unique in its spirituality, theology and structures. It was a gentle, mystical, affirmative and holistic faith, firmly biblical and strongly influenced by the Desert Fathers, while assimilating many Pagan beliefs and practices.' However, an alternative rendition of the same religious system might argue that it was also highly fragmented, idiosyncratic, immensely 'this' not 'other' worldly, given to warfare and monastic territorial aggrandizement, partial to 'join in the looting and mayhem fermented by the Viking invasions, and the larger *paruchiae* were always ready to boost their own power, using the device of the saint's Life, or Vita, as a major propaganda tool' (Meek 1996, 149).

Contemporary interpretations assert that Celtic Christianity is characterized by primitivism, simplicity and tolerance, precisely those features which have been lost within mainstream institutionalized Church life and practice. This Celtic Christianity is characterized by its exceptionalism, integrity, historical reaffirmation of the Early Church precepts and intimate behaviour, both in relation to God and to fellow believers.

The main currents of Celtic thought thus elevated to primacy are derived from a base of Celtic antiquity, an admixture of pietistic dissent, more akin to the English separatists, the Anabaptists, the Amish/Mennonite connection and Brethren, a layer of colourful but harmless iconoclastic symbolism, acceptable because it is in the form of a Celtic cross or a complex pattern, a smattering of post-hippy New Age ecology and a heavy dose of selective post-modernism. In direct contrast to the structured authoritarianism of the Catholic Church or the Established Churches in England and Scotland, the Celtic Church thus recovered is syncretic, low-key, individualistic, and in my opinion charismatically non-challenging. More sympathetically Ian Bradley puts it thus:

> The great upsurge of interest in Celtic Christianity in recent years can be compared to the re-evaluation of the religious belief of other peoples who have lived on the margins like the Australian Aborigines and the native Indians of North America. It reflects a realisation that what is primitive and simple can also be profound and highly original. It expresses also a deeply Christian view that it is among the voices of the most marginalised and oppressed that we may find the greatest wisdom.

> Celtic Christianity is a faith hammered out at the margins. The Celts lived on the margins of Britain, on the margins of Europe, and on the margins of Christendom. They lived close to nature, close to the elements, close to God, and close to homelessness, poverty and starvation. (1993, 30)

A broader concern with spirituality characterizes Marion Bowman's work (1993, 1994, 1995) which examines the meaning of religious imputation for Pagans, Druids, and Christians within a contemporary context as an experiential resource. In Chapter 4 of this volume she explicates the various expressions of Celtic spirituality in terms of a religious not a historical phenomenon. The essay avoids seeking to demonstrate the necessary search for universal truth, because eclectic pluralism rather than revelation has become the lynchpin of late twentieth-century spirituality. However, Bowman does signal a central new direction, in that contemporary Celtic spirituality is very much concerned with the experiential reality of the here and now for its practitioners. It is a user-centered system of beliefs and practices. Her evocative typologies of 'Cardiac Celt', 'conventional Celt,' 'authentic Celt' and 'spiritual Celt' hint at the range of diverse experiences subsumed under the Celtic umbrella, but ultimately come back to the question of ownership. Unlike literature and politics, which is grounded from within the experience of the Celtic nations, religion and spirituality seem to have been grafted on to the contemporary agenda by others who wish to 'share' 'appropriate' or 'invent' a Celtic legitimacy and historicity for their contemporary Pagan, New Age and Christian tendencies.

As a counter to such moves there has been a redefinition of the specifically divine element in Celtic Christianity. The best illustration is Donald Meek's extensive treatment of the claims of modern Celtic Christianity (1992, 1996, 1997), unpacking the superficial from the profound. Meek's fundamental criticism of Celtic Christianity, as already indicated, is that it is not genuinely Celtic, in the sense that it is rooted in what Celtic Christians believed in the period before 1200 AD. He claims that 'it is focused pre-eminently on the needs of the postmodern spiritual consumer of the late twentieth century' (Meek 1998, 8). In their attempt to construct a naive panacea which offers solutions to some of the ills of the Church and state, Celtic-influenced Christians have focused on four themes which may be illuminated by the teachings of Celtic texts. Being at one with the *environment*, the Celts, unlike us today, lived happily with nature. They practised a form of *women's ordination*, for as they had abbesses and female druids they were not devoted solely to 'male ministry'. They evoked a *sympathy towards secular culture*, and were tolerant of diversity and a pluralism of approaches to God and religion. In contrast the modern church is said to have distanced itself from the secular world and to have adopted an intolerant, exclusive attitude toward divine revelation. Finally in the realm of *politics*, the Celts are perceived to have been beaten under the yoke of imperial, hegemonic state absolutism. Advocates of Celtic Christianity believe that they are peace-makers and bridge-builders engaged in healing the wounds of past centuries. In fact, declares Meek, 'they are merely continuing the same process of cultural attrition, by taking "Celtic" material and burying it under the weight of their own interpretations' (1998, 5).

Clearly there is a correlation between these spiritual movements and other issues specifically environmentalism, ecology and nature. Mary Low's *Celtic Christianity and Nature* (1996) examines the interface between 'outdoor spirituality' and the institutionalized Christianity which replaced earlier Celtic forms. One of the most fascinating new directions is the rediscovery of faith in a sacramental universe.

Natural phenomena have been reassessed in both Celtic and Biblical literature. Recognizing that the universe has a rhythm of its own 'and is governed by visible and invisible energies on which we are ultimately dependent' is but another way of saying that physics and religion are intimately connected. For Low, 'here, at the junction of the practical and the mystical, it is easy to see why nature so easily generates signs of the Sacred, both in primal religions and in the world religions which build on them or develop out of them' (Low 1996, 189).

A second trend has been to re-work the relationship between land, language and spirituality which was the original inspiration of writers such as J.R.Jones and Waldo Williams (Lloyd-Jones 1997; Phillips 1995; Conran 1997) and has been given a fresh impetus by the excellent analysis of Jones (1998) and Llywelyn (1999).

The fundamental theme facing research into 'Celtic' spirituality is to ascertain which parts of the syncretic view are influenced by earlier currents of thought and for what contemporary eclectic purposes. In this, as in so much to do with the Celtic world, individual preference is legitimized by reference to a time-honoured inheritance of a Celtic tradition. Yet, time and time again the contributors to this volume have demonstrated that this practice is questionable.

Conclusion

This essay has offered a personal critique which seeks to address many of the issues of the volume, and also argues for the cogency of developing a self-conscious Celtic Studies perspective which is attuned to the twenty-first century. From my viewpoint such a discipline would be less preoccupied with the ancient and medieval and much more interested in the contemporary issues which animate Celtic societies. Currently there is a sense of excitement derived from developments such as the Northern Irish Agreement, the Scottish Parliament and the National Assembly of Wales, which appear to recast the relationship between the UK's constituent parts, not to mention the Irish–British Council, and the attendant opportunities for integrating a Celtic perspective both within these islands and also within the EU and the wider international system.

If the 'past is a foreign country' (Lowenthal 1985), then the creative anachronism of the contemporary Celtic landscape is a country yet to be fully discovered and mapped. My hope is that Hudson Bay-like discovery volumes such as this will not only point us in the new direction we need to travel, but also equip us to appreciate from whence we came, so that the destination offered by seductive travel couriers will feed the mind and satisfy the soul—else we will drift remorselessly back to the archives, the pub and the prosaic, the natural habitat of the Celtic Studies scholar.

Acknowledgments

I am grateful to Dr Wyn James and Professor D. Meek for their constructive criticism of this essay which was given as the Plenary Opening Address to the 'New Directions in Celtic Studies' Conference, organized by Amy Hale on behalf of the Institute of Cornish Studies, University of Exeter, Truro, Cornwall, November 1998.

Notes

1. To this end I am currently constructing a representative university curriculum for Celtic Studies (Welsh in Cardiff's case) for the time-snap shots 1900, 1930, 1960, 1985 and 2000.
2. Notes this list does not seek to reduce Old Core and New Directions into two oppositional conceptions of a differing set of realities, for to do so would be to obscure the complexity, interrelatedness and heterogeneity of both conceptions.
3. By exophagy I mean the custom among cannibals of eating only the flesh of

persons not of their own kin—thus the definition of who is a Celtic Studies 'insider' and who is an 'outsider' is critical for survival in this discipline.
4. I include both Celtic Studies as a field of enquiry, and the contribution and influence of several of its key practitioners in determining priorities within the discipline.
5. Kibard (1997) offers an insightful treatment of this issue in the Irish context. For selected African equivalents see Rubgumya (1990), Mazrui and Mazrui (1992) and for an international perspective see Williams (1996).

References

Anderson, B. *Imagined Communities*. London, 1983.
Bentley, M. (ed.) *Companion to Historiography*. London, 1997.
Bowman, M. Reinventing the Celts. *Religion*, 23, pp. 147–56, 1993.
Bowman, M. The Commodification of the Celt: New Age/Neo-Pagan Consumerism. *Folklore in Use*, 2 (1) pp. 143–52, 1994.
Bowman, M. The Noble Savage and the Global Village: Cultural Evolution in New Age and Neo-Pagan Thought. *Journal of Contemporary Religion*, 10 (2) pp. 139–49, 1995.
Bowman, M. Cardiac Celts: Images of the Celts in Contemporary British Paganism. In G. Harvey and C. Hardman (eds) *Paganism Today*. London, 1996.
Bowman, M. Contemporary Celtic Spirituality. In A. Hale and P. Payton (eds) *New Directions in Celtic Studies*. Exeter, 1999
Bradley, I. *The Celtic Way*. London,1993.
Cannadine, D. British History as a 'New Subject': Politics, Perspectives and Prospects. *Welsh History Review*, 17 (3) pp. 313–31, 1995.
Colley, L. *Britons*. London, 1992.
Comhdháil Náisúnta na Gaeilge, *Plécháipéis: Towards a Language Act*. Dublin, 1998.
Conran, T. *The Peacemakers: Waldo Williams*. Llandysul,1997.
Crawford, E.M. (ed.) *The Hungry Stream: Essays on Emigration and Famine*. Belfast, 1997.
Davies, S. *Crefft Y Cyfarwydd*. Caerdydd, 1995.
Dawkins, R. *River Out of Eden*. London, 1995.
Duffy, P.J. Emigrants and the Estate Office in the Mid-Nineteenth-Century: A Compassionate Relationship? In E.M. Crawford (ed.) *The Hungry Stream: Essays on Emigration and Famine*. Belfast, 1997.
Dunstan, M. Telling It As It Is: Storytelling in the China Clay Villages. In E. Westland *Cornwall:The Cultural Construction of Place*. Penzance, 1997.
Evans, N. (ed.) *National Identity in the British Isles*. Occasional Papers in Welsh Studies. No. 3, Coleg Harlech, 1989.
Fréine, Seán de. *The Great Silence*. Dublin, 1965.
Glacken, C. *Traces on the Rhodian Shore*. Berkeley, 1967.

Graham, B.J. and Proudfoot, L.J. (eds) *An Historical Geography of Ireland*. London, 1993.
Gruffydd, P. Remaking Wales: Nation-building and the Geographical Imagination, 1925–50. *Political Geography*. 14 (3) pp. 219–39, 1995.
Hunter, G. and Jones, R.W. O'r Chwith: Pa Mor Feirniadol yw Beirniadaeth Ôl-Fodern? *Taliesin*, 92, pp. 9–32, 1995.
Jenkins, G.H. (ed.) *Y Gymraeg yn ei Disgleirdeb-Yr Iaith Gymraeg cyn y Chwyldro Diwydiannol*. Cardiff,1997.
Jones, R.M. *Llenyddiaeth Gymraeg a Phrifysgol Cymru*. Cardiff, 1993.
Jones, R.M. *Ysbryd y Cwlwm:Delwedd y Genedl yn Ein Llenyddiaeth*. Cardiff, 1998.
Kearney, H. *A History of Four Nations*. Cambridge, 1989.
Kiberd, D. *Inventing Ireland: The Literature of the Modern Nation*. London, 1996.
Kiberd, D. Modern Ireland: Postcolonial or European? In S. Murray (ed.) *Not On Any Map*. Exeter, 1997.
Leersen, J. *Mere Irish and Fíor-Gael*. Cork, 1996.
Lloyd-Jones, E.R. *Yr Athro J.R. Jones*. Caernarfon, 1997.
Llywelyn, D. *Sacred Place, Chosen People*. Cardiff, 1999.
Low, M. *Celtic Christianity and Nature*. Edinburgh, 1996.
Lowerthal, D. *The Past is a Foreign Country*. Cambridge, 1995.
Mac Cárthaigh, D. (ed.) *I dTreo Deilbcháipéise d'Act Teanga Éireannach*. Dublin, 1998.
Mac Laughlin, J. (ed.) *Location and Dislocation in Contemporary Irish Society*. Cork, 1997.
Mac Póilin, A. (ed.) *The Irish Language in Northern Ireland*. Belfast, n.d.
Mac Unfraidh, A. Personal communication, 1999.
Mazrui, A.M. and Mazrui, A.A. Language in a Multicultural Context: The African Experience. *Language and Education*, 6, pp. 83–9, 1992.
Meek, D.E. Modern Celtic Christianity: The Contemporary 'Revival' and its Roots. *Scottish Bulletin of Evangelical Theology*, 10 (1) pp. 6–31, 1992.
Meek, D.E. Modern Celtic Christianity. In T. Brown (ed.) *Celticism*. Amsterdam, 1996.
Meek, D.E. Surveying the Saints: Reflections on Recent Writings on 'Celtic Christianity'. *Scottish Bulletin of Evangelical Theology*, 15, pp. 50–60, 1997.
Meek, D.E. Contemporary Celtic Christianity: Fact or Fiction? Paper delivered to the New Directions in Celtic Studies Conference, Institute of Cornish Studies, 1998.
Meek, D.E. Between Faith and Folklore: Twentieth-Century Interpretations and Images of Columbia. In T. Clancy and D. Browm (eds) *Spes Scotorum: Hope of Scots*. Edinburgh, 1999a.
Meek, D.E. God and Gaelic: The Highland Churches and Gaelic Cultural Identity. In G. McCoy and M. Scott (eds) *Aithne na nGael: Gaelic Identities*. Belfast,1999b.
Morgan, K.O. *Modern Wales: Politics Places and People*. Cardiff, 1995.

Munz, P. The Historical Narrative. In M. Bentley (ed.) *Companion to Historiography*. London, 1997.
Nairn, T. *Faces of Nationalism*. London, 1997.
Nic Craith, M. (ed.) *Watching One's Tongue: Aspects of Romance and Celtic Languages*. Liverpool, 1996.
Nic Shuibhne, N. Personal communication, 1999.
Ó Cuir, B. Gnó le Gaeilge: Business in Irish. *ÚdarEas na Gaeltachta*, Galway, 1998.
Ó'Riagáin, D. *Language Policy and Social Reproduction: Ireland 1893–1993*. Oxford, 1997.
Ó'Riagáin, D. Personal communication, 1999.
Osmond, J. (ed.) *The National Assembly Agenda*. Cardiff, 1998.
Payton, P. *The Making of Modern Cornwall*. Redruth, 1992.
Payton, P. Cornwall in Context: The New Cornish Historiography. In P. Payton (ed.) *Cornish Studies 5*. Exeter, 1997a.
Payton, P. Paralysis and Revival: The Reconstruction of Celtic-Catholic Cornwall 1890–1945. In E. Westland (ed.) *Cornwall: The Cultural Construction of Place*. Penzance, 1997b.
Phillips, D.Z. *J.R. Jons*. Cardiff, 1995.
Pocock, J.G.A. British History: A Plea for a New Subject. *Journal of Modern History*, 47, pp. 601–28, 1975.
Robbins, K. Core and Periphery in Modern British History. *Proceedings of the British Academy*, 70, pp. 275–97, 1984.
Rubagumya, C.M. (ed.) *Language in Education in Africa: A Tanzanian Perspective*. Clevedon, 1990.
Soja, E.W. Postmodern Geographies and the Critique of Historcism. In J. Paul Jones et al. (eds) *Postmodern Contentions: Epochs, Politics, Space*. New York, 1993.
Spielberg, N. and Anderson, B.D. *Seven Ideas that Shook the Universe*. New York, 1995.
Taylor, C. *The Malaise of Modernity*. Concord, 1991.
Taylor, P.J. The Break-up of England. *Political Geography*, 12 (2) pp. 136–89, 1993.
Tully, J. (ed.) *Philosophy in an Age of Pluralism*. Cambridge, 1994.
Waltzer, M. *The Company of Critics*. London, 1989.
Walzer, M. *Thick and Thin: Moral Arguments at Home and Abroad*. Notre Dame, 1994.
Waltzer, M. *On Toleration*. New Haven, 1997.
Westland, E. (ed.) *Cornwall: The Cultural Construction of Place*. Penzance, 1997.
White, H. *The Content of the Form: Narrative Discourse and Historical Representation*. Baltimore, 1987.
Williams, C.H. Ethnic Identity and Language Issues in Development. In D. Dwyer and D. Drakakis-Smith (eds) *Ethnicity and Development: Geographical Perspectives*. London, 1996.

Index

Académie Celtique 3
Adelaide 116
AE (George Russell) 77, 78
African 205
African Studies 11
African-American 9
Afro-Celt Sound System 26
Altan 208
American Studies 11
An Ankou 56, 63
Anderson, Benedict 62
Anglicanism 49, 82
Anglo-Celtic 109, 121
Anglo-Saxon 41, 42, 47, 49, 112, 220
Anglo-Saxon Studies 206
anthropology 52
archaeology 7, 203, 206
Archbishop Mannix 110, 117
Aros 166
Arthurian legends 41, 42, 56, 62, 208
Atlantis 81
Aubrey, John 33
Australia 4, 71, 76, 95, 108, 109, 110, 113, 114, 115, 116, 117, 118, 119, 120, 122, 123
authenticity 8, 69, 82, 86, 88, 123, 176, 179, 180, 192, 193, 217
Avalon 42
Avebury 34, 76, 86

bagpipes 131, 132, 134, 135
Barn 202
Bath 76, 82, 86
Beltane 79
Berengaria Order of Druids 79
Berresford Ellis, Peter 83, 111
bilingualism 155, 162, 163, 210, 211, 213
Black, Mary 208
Black, Ronald 2
Blake, William 76
Blavatsky, H.P. 77
Bord Failte 185
Bord na Gaeilge 210
Borlase, William 33
Boudicca 43, 44, 45, 112
Breton 55, 56, 70, 106, 107, 109, 110, 114, 120, 173, 181, 191
Breton identity 53, 180
Breton Renaissance 53
British Druid Order 80
Brittany 4, 8, 20, 53, 55, 56, 57, 59, 62, 98, 100, 101, 111, 139, 167, 171, 172, 174, 183, 184, 189, 191, 192, 193, 207, 212, 215
Brocéliande 57, 62
Brown, Terrence 9
Bun Noa 146, 147, 148
Burning Time 40
Burra Burra 112
Bush, Kate 27

Calanais Centre 166
Callanish 34
Cape Breton 132
Cardiac Celts 70, 85, 194, 224
Catatonia 207
Catholicism 49, 118, 116, 117, 119, 183, 223
Celtic Christianity x, 75, 81, 82, 85, 224, 225
Celtic Church 82
Celtic diaspora 95, 109, 108, 201
Celtic Film and Television Festival 10
Celtic Gaul 4
Celtic Heart 22
Celtic identity ix, 5, 9, 53, 105, 106, 109, 112, 126, 142, 167, 209, 212, 214
Celtic jewellery x, 17, 74, 101
Celtic languages 83, 84, 111, 95, 142, 152, 166, 194, 213, 214, 205, 207, 209, 210, 215;
  Breton 60, 174, 175, 176, 190, 209;
  Cornish 60, 209;
  Irish 1, 204, 209, 210, 211, 213;
  Manx 142, 146, 147, 150;
  Welsh 60, 83, 101, 117, 204, 205, 209, 210, 213, 219
Celtic music x, 17, 19, 20, 22, 23, 25, 27, 28
Celtic Odyssey 22, 24
Celtic revival 77, 142, 193
Celtic spirituality 18, 69, 70, 71, 75, 76, 83, 86, 88, 209, 222
Celtic Studies ix, 1, 2, 3, 4, 5, 8, 10, 11, 13, 70, 139, 197, 198, 199, 200, 201, 202, 203, 204, 205, 206, 208, 209, 210, 219, 226;
  focus on medieval language and literature in 1, 2, 4, 11, 199, 201, 206
Celtic Tiger 139, 215

Celtic tourism x, 2, 160
Celtic-American 9
Celtica 74
Celticism 9, 80, 200
Celticity 9, 10, 12, 18, 69, 70, 75, 83, 86, 87, 98, 110, 111, 112, 113, 119, 120, 121, 123, 168, 172, 183, 193, 194, 199, 203, 208
Centre for Advanced Welsh and Celtic Studies 207
Channel Islands 215
Chapman, Malcolm 5, 6, 7, 9, 10, 13, 17, 21, 84, 111, 169, 191, 192, 193
Chieftains 24
Christianity 46, 48, 49, 70, 71, 73, 222, 223
Clan Dalriada 72, 78, 79
Clannad 24, 27
Comhdháil Náisiúnta na Gaeilge 214
Commana 169, 172, 173, 174, 175, 176, 178, 180, 181, 182, 184, 185, 189, 190
commodification 169, 170, 171, 179, 180, 184, 186
Comunn na Gàidhlig 210, 153, 155, 165, 216, 217
Corentin 66
Cornish 10, 70, 98, 109, 110, 112, 113, 114, 115, 116, 117, 119, 120, 212, 213
Cornish cream teas 121
Cornish language 123
Cornish Studies 12
Cornwall x, 20, 36, 61, 62, 74, 100, 101, 111, 112, 113, 201, 207, 212, 218
Cotswold Order of Druids 79
Council of the Isles 215
County Mayo 167, 168, 182
Cousin Jack 118, 122, 123
cultural preservation 170
Cultural Studies 11
Cunliffe, Barry 7

Dahut 58, 59, 60, 64, 65, 66
Dáil 214, 221
Democratic Labor Party 119
devolution 142, 207, 210, 214, 215, 221
Dietler, Michael 3
Dorson, Richard 54
Douarnenez 58, 59, 60, 64, 65, 67
Dr Who 36
Druids x, 32, 33, 34, 36, 37, 43, 44, 45, 47, 48, 49, 70, 71, 75, 76, 77, 78, 79, 80, 81, 83, 87, 173, 224
Dublin 184, 188

Ecole Druidique des Gaules 75
écomusée 175, 177, 178, 193
eisteddfod 6, 98
elective affinity 6, 18, 70
England 6
English National Curriculum 144
ethnic identity 108, 110, 127, 128, 132
ethnicity 33, 70, 120, 126, 127, 129, 133, 134, 135, 179, 218
ethnonationalist 157
European Bureau for Lesser Used Languages 207
European Union 207, 215
Excalibur 40, 41

festival 21, 22, 97, 98, 103, 104, 106, 107, 132, 191
Festival Interceltique 98
festnoz 176, 177, 180, 181, 182, 192, 193
film 32
Finistère 167, 168, 169, 172, 173, 175, 182, 183
Fisher King 42
folklore 28, 53, 54, 55, 56, 77, 78, 128, 129, 202, 211, 212
folklorismus 54
Fox, Matthew 82

Foxford 169, 182, 183, 184, 185, 186, 188, 189, 190, 191
France 6
Frazer, James 52

Gaelic 24, 77, 79, 113, 114, 116, 119, 139, 152, 153, 154, 155, 156, 157, 158, 159, 162, 163, 166, 192, 209, 210, 211, 219
Gaelic Athletic League 105
Gaelic sport 113
Gaelic television 157, 158
Gaelic tourism 159, 160, 161, 162, 163, 165
Gaelic-medium education 155
Gaeltacht 190, 214, 215, 217
Galicia 10, 20, 70, 100, 101, 111, 201
Gardner, Gerald 35, 79
Germany 4
Gillies, William 2
Glastonbury 81, 82, 84, 86, 87, 211
Golden Bough, The 38
Golwg 202
Good Friday Agreement 214
gorsedd 6, 98
Gorseth x
Gradlon 60, 64, 65, 66
Gwénolé 59

Hawaii 170
heritage 154, 167
Highland Mysteryworld 74
Highland Society of New South Wales 116
Highlands and Islands 112, 113, 115, 116, 117, 118, 139, 157, 160, 163, 164
Highlands and Islands Enterprise 165, 217
hiraeth 31
Hobsbawm, Eric 129, 130
Home Rule 4

identity x, 10, 12, 21, 31, 63, 64, 95,
    101, 106, 118, 135, 167, 168, 169,
    170, 171, 172, 175, 176, 179, 181,
    182, 189, 190, 192, 193, 194, 203,
    207, 208, 215, 216, 217, 218
Imbolc 79
Indo-European 1, 2, 3, 11, 13, 76
Institute of Cornish Studies ix
Insular Order of Druids 79, 87
International Celtic Congress:
    Tenth 1; Eleventh 2
Internet 53, 58
invented tradition 6, 129, 130
Iona 82, 83, 86
Iona Community 82
Ireland 4, 8, 20, 62, 74, 75, 111, 139,
    167, 170, 172, 183, 188, 189, 191,
    193, 207, 210, 212
Irish 10, 70, 77, 98, 100, 103, 104,
    109, 110, 112, 114, 117, 118, 119,
    123, 171, 205, 220, 221
Irish Arts Foundation 99
Irish Freedom Movement 105
Irish language 190, 214
Irish Republican Army 105
Irish Republican Socialist
    Committee 105
Irish Studies 12
Irish uncial 57
Irish-American 99, 103, 105
Islanders 118
Isle of Man 8, 20, 100, 101, 111, 141,
    142, 145, 201, 215

Jackson, Kenneth 11
James, Simon 7
Japan 4, 99
Jos le Doaré 56, 57

Kaledon Naddair 81, 83, 88
Kay Sommers, Laurie 99
Keltic Designs 100
Kervarker 60

kilt 89, 100, 119, 121, 122, 129, 133,
    221
King Arthur 61
King Gradlon 56, 58

La Marie-Morgane 59
Lady Gregory 78, 216
Lammas 79
Landévennec 55
language planning 12, 210
le Doaré 58
Lebor Gabala 34, 36
Lévi-Strauss, Claude 54, 62
Lindisfarne 86
linguistic criterion 111, 201
linguistics 199, 203, 206;
    linguistic category 104
Lowender Peran 98
Loyal Arthurian Warband 87
Lughnasadh 79
Lyonesse 60

Mabinogion 208, 218
McArthur, John 116
McCloed, Donald 116
McDonald, Maryon 8
McKennitt, Loreena 27
Macleod, Fiona 77, 78
MacPherson, James 157
Macquarie, Lachlan 115, 116
Maddrel, Ned 141
Manx 70, 110, 114
Manx Heritage Foundation 143
Manx Language Officer 143, 146,
    148, 150
Manx Language Unit 144, 145, 146
Map Kernow 122, 123
Masons 132
Matthews, Caitlin 86, 87
Mayo 169, 183, 184, 189, 191
Mebyon Kernow x
Meek, Donald 9, 84, 85, 222, 224,
    226

Menzies, Robert, Sir 110
Merlin 41, 61, 62, 63, 172
Methodist 114, 118
Mod 19, 98, 157, 158, 162
Moser, Hans 54
multiculturalism 109, 121, 123
Murray, Margaret 40
mythology 28, 52, 78

Napoleon 3
Narada 22
National Assembly for Wales 213, 221, 226
National Curriculum 145
nationalism 2, 4, 7, 33, 62, 64, 83, 104, 105, 106, 108, 117, 120, 129, 212, 214, 215, 218, 220
Native American 71, 76, 131, 133
New Age 21, 22, 24, 26, 27, 37, 47, 70, 71, 73, 79, 202, 207, 211, 223, 224
New Age travellers 10
New Agers 102
New Historicism 11
New Zealand 71, 95
Noble Savage 74, 85, 86
Nonconformity 112, 113, 114, 117
NORAID 105
North America 4, 71, 75, 95, 109, 127
North American 202
Northern Ireland 2, 210, 213, 214, 215
Northern Irish Assembly 213
Northumbrians 70
Nova Scotia 132

Oatlands Celtic Festival 100
'Obby 'Oss 98
Ó'Maolalaigh, Roibeard 2
One Nation Party 109
Order of Bards Ovates and Druids 80

Pagan x, 28, 34, 35, 37, 40, 43, 45, 46, 47, 49, 60, 70, 71, 72, 75, 78, 79, 83, 102, 202, 223, 224
Paisley, Ian 213
Pan Celtic 12, 24, 74, 111, 122
Peterson Royce, Anya 126
 Royce 127
post-modernism 21
postcard 17, 53, 55, 56, 58, 62
potato famine 113
Presbyterian 115, 116
Protestant 183
Providence Woollen Mills 185

Radio Telefís Eireann 104
Rankin Family 207
Rhino Records 25
Richards, Rod 213
Riverdance 207
Roar 46, 49
Rollright Stones 34
Romanticism 7
Rowlands, Henry 33
Runrig 207

Sabhal Mòr Ostaig 156
Saint Ann's Gaelic College 132
Saint Corentin 58
Saint Gwénolé 58, 59, 65, 67
Samhain 79
San Francisco 99
Scotland 8, 20, 111, 142, 154, 155, 159, 162, 165, 207, 215
Scots 70, 106, 109, 110, 115, 117, 120
Scottish 98, 131
Scottish Highland games 98
Scottish identity 132
Scottish Parliament 166, 213, 226
Scottish Studies 12
Scottish-American 95, 126, 127
sean nós 9, 19
Secular Order of Druids 69, 80, 81

INDEX

Sherman, Curtis 130, 131, 132, 133, 134, 135
Shriners 132
Sims-Williams, Patrick 2, 3, 4, 7, 8, 9, 30, 32
South Asian Studies 205
St Malo 59, 63
St Piran's flags x
Stivell, Alan 24, 27
stone circle 122
Stonehenge 32, 33, 34, 35, 46, 75, 77, 81, 86
Stowell, Brian 143, 150
Stukeley, William 33, 76

tartan 90, 119, 122, 132, 133
television 32
Tintagel 41
Toland, John 32, 33, 37, 39, 45
Toulson, Shirley 82
tourism 12, 141, 156, 157, 167, 168, 169, 170, 171, 172, 176, 178, 180, 181, 182, 184, 186, 187, 189, 190, 191, 192, 193, 216
Tower Records 23, 24
transformationalism 11
Tristram, Hildegard 2, 5, 9, 10, 11
Tylor, Edward 52

Tynwald 150

U2 9
United Kingdom 7

Verran, 'Honest John' 110
Viking Queen 43, 45
Virgin Records 24
Wales 8, 61, 62, 74, 111, 112, 142, 207, 210, 212, 213, 214, 215
Welsh 1, 70, 77, 98, 100, 106, 109, 110, 114, 118, 120
Welsh Language Board 210
Welsh Studies 12
West Country 70
Wicca 34, 35, 71, 78, 79
Wicker Man, The 37, 40, 46
Wood, John 76, 77
world music 24, 25, 28

Xena, Warrior Princess 45, 46, 49

Y Fro Gymraeg 217
Yeats, W.B. 27, 77, 78, 183, 216
Ys 56, 57, 58, 59, 60, 61, 64, 65, 66